FENG SHUI

TO THE RESCUE

Rearrange Your Space, Shift Your Energy,
Transform Your Life!

CAROL M. OLMSTEAD, FSIA

Feng Shui Master Practitioner

Copyright © 2020 Carol M. Olmstead
Published by Feng Shui Multimedia

ISBN: 978-0-9815735-4-0
Library of Congress Control Number: 2019900326
Interior Layout by Bronwen Blaney

Feng Shui For Real Life® is a registered trademark.

All rights reserved. No part of this publication may be reproduced in any form whatsoever without written permission from the publisher, except for brief quotations embodied in literary articles or reviews.

This book serves as a reference and guide for the principles of Feng Shui, and as such, the author bears no responsibility for the results that an individual might experience. Results may vary based upon an individual's participation and intent.

CONTENTS

Woe Is Chi 1
   So Many Questions 1
   Real Feng Shui 3
   A Few Words about Clutter 5
   How to Use This Book 6

Chapter 1: Five Powerful Principles 9
   Power Principle 1: Chi 10
   Power Principle 2: The Five Elements 11
   Power Principle 3: The Bagua 12
   Power Principle 4: Yin and Yang 16
   Power Principle 5: Continuity and Connectedness 18

Chapter 2: Wealth, Harmony, and Love 21
   Wealth 23
      Activating the Wealth Area 23
      Improving Personal Finances 26
   Harmony 28
      Achieving Harmony 28
      Celebrating Holidays 28
   Love 34
      Attracting Love 34
      Enhancing Love 38

Chapter 3: Bedrooms, Beds, and Blissful Sleep 45
   Master Bedroom 47
      Look Above 47

  Look Under 49
  Look All Around 52
 Bedroom Mirrors 57
 Beds 60
 Children's Bedrooms 62
  Bedroom Colors 65

Chapter 4: Room by Room 69
 Attics 71
 Basements 72
 Bathrooms 73
 Dining Rooms 80
 Enclosed Porches 81
 Foyers and Entries 81
 Garages 82
 Home Offices 84
 Kitchens 90
 Laundry Rooms 93
 Living Rooms/Family Rooms 94

Chapter 5: Rearranging, Shifting, Transforming 97
 Apartments and Condos 99
 Aromas 103
 Beams and Sloped Ceilings 104
 Cemeteries and Graves 106
 Clearing Rituals and Remedies 107
 Colors 108
 Doors 109
 Dorms and Shared Spaces 115
 Family 116
 Fashion 118
 Food and Diet 119
 House Shapes and Styles 122

Landscaping 125
Location 128
Neighbors 130
Numbers and Symbols 132
Pets 133
Poison Arrows 137
Real Estate 137
Religion 141
Stairs 141
Trash 142
Travel 143
Trees 143
Windows and Skylights 144

Chapter 6: Objects of Desire From A-Z 147

Antiques and Previously-Owned Stuff 149
Art 151
Books and Book Shelves 155
Diplomas, Awards, and Citations 156
Cars and Commuting 157
Clocks and Watches 160
Décor 161
Dried Flowers 163
Fireplaces 164
Fountains and Fish Tanks 165
Gifts and Re-gifting 166
House Plants 171
Letters 173
Mirrors 174
Photos 178
Purses and Wallets 180
Vision Boards 183

Workout Equipment 183
Zen 184

Chapter 7: Trouble, Chaos, Clutter 187
Breakups 189
Broken Things 192
Clutter 194
Cobwebs and Bugs 201
Death and Bereavement 201
Divorce and Blended Families 204
Electronics 207
Financial Woes 208
Floods and Leaks 210
Health and Medical Issues 212
Military Deployment 215
Negative Chi 215

Chapter 8: Workplace, Career, Business 221
Workplace 223
Career 232
Business 237

Chapter 9: Questions for All Seasons 247
January: Resolve to Start with Good Feng Shui 249
February: Rev-Up Your Romance 250
March: Spring Clear Easy-to-Forget Places 251
April: Invite Feng Shui to Your Holiday Dinner 252
May: Eliminate Tax Filing Clutter 253
June: Bring Feng Shui to Your Wedding Party 255
July: Take Feng Shui on Vacation 257
August: Go Back to School with Feng Shui 258
September: Transition into Cooler Weather 259
October: Celebrate Halloween Colors 261

November: Give Thanks for Extra Space 262
December: Relocate the Christmas Tree 263

Conclusion 267
A Final Question and a Story..267
Pulling It All Together 269

About the Author 273

Acknowledgements 275

Index And Resources 277
Fast Five 269
Success Stories...269
Resources 269
Topics in Feng Shui..269

WOE IS CHI
SO MANY QUESTIONS

Soon after I launched my Feng Shui consulting practice and my *FengShuiForRealLife.com* website, I received an email from Cameron, an elementary school student who was writing a paper on Feng Shui. Since Cameron assured me that my expertise would help her "intellectual growth and understanding of the world," how could I resist answering her questions?

Here's what Cameron asked:

Q: What are the origins of Feng Shui?

A: Feng Shui originated in China. It's estimated this art of placement was created anywhere from 3,000 to 5,000 years ago.

Q: For what purpose was Feng Shui created?

A: Feng Shui initially helped farmers determine where to locate their farms so their crops would thrive, rather than just survive. As people moved into cities, Feng Shui began to adapt to new, more urban environments.

Q: What is a common misconception about Feng Shui?

A: Some people have the misconception that Feng Shui is a religion or a superstition. That's just not true. Rather, Feng Shui is a design system for arranging a home or workspace in balance and harmony with the natural world around us.

Q: Is Feng Shui still practiced regularly in Asia today?

A: Yes. One place where Feng Shui has been especially popular is Hong Kong, where major government buildings weren't built until a certified Feng Shui master approved the design. In China, after decades of official discouragement of the practice, Feng Shui is experiencing a remarkable renaissance.

Q: What is a common way in which chi is blocked?
A: Chi, or energy, can be blocked from entering a home by a large tree or telephone pole in line with the front door, or by anything else that obstructs the front door. Chi is also blocked when you're surrounded by too much "stuff," especially things you don't want, need, or no longer use.

Q: What is your favorite Feng Shui tip?
A: Clear the clutter and tidy up. Too much clutter keeps good things from flowing into your life. When you clear clutter, you make room for wealth, harmony, love, joy, and much more to find you.

Thus began my 20-year history of answering the basic, the predictable, and the unexpected questions about Feng Shui, the ancient art and science of arranging interior surroundings in balance and harmony with the natural world. But unlike Cameron's questions that were aimed at her intellectual growth, most of the questions I receive from all over the world come from people asking how Feng Shui can rescue them from unpleasant situations. Or, as one questioner described her home: "Woe is chi!"

Most questions center around our basic human desire to attract wealth, harmony, love, and happiness. Frequently, the inquiries start with phrases like *I read that...*, *I heard that you shouldn't...*, *My friend said...*, or *What does Feng Shui think about....* The clients, students, and readers who ask these questions come from different backgrounds and face different situations. The only commonality is their questions center around these top 10 concerns:

1. **Love** (finding it, losing it, finding it again)
2. **Wealth** (making it, keeping it)
3. **Family Harmony** (especially at holidays)
4. **Clutter** (everyone has it)
5. **Careers and Business** (finding jobs, attracting clients)
6. **Weight** (how to lose it—never how to gain it)

7. **Wallets** (especially red ones)
8. **Mirrors** (where to put them)
9. **Bedrooms, Beds, and Sleep** (or lack thereof)
10. **Real Estate** (finding or selling a home)

Including young Cameron's inquiries, I answer more than 400 questions in this book, organized into nine chapters. The categories, rooms, situations, and objects covered all came from the questions that readers like you sent to me. I'm an *if-it-ain't-broke-don't-fix-it* kind of Feng Shui practitioner. That means in addition to the Q&A, throughout this book, you'll find find special tips called "Fast 5" to help you avoid Feng Shui problems in the first place.

Real Feng Shui

I am often asked which school or approach to Feng Shui I practice, and sometimes, whether it's the "real" Feng Shui. My response is that there are now as many approaches to Feng Shui as there are to architecture or interior design. All are real. The approach that works for me is the one that allows me to help you live how you want to live in your home, work in your workplace, and run your business. That's why I call my approach "Feng Shui For Real Life." It's all about helping you rearrange your space, shift your energy, and transform your life.

I often start my workshops and lectures by explaining how we are all profoundly affected by our interior environment, and that Feng Shui gives us guidelines for rearranging that environment to help attract good things, especially wealth, harmony, and love. Feng Shui seeks to create environments that are in balance with our individual sense of harmony and serenity. It's the practice of understanding how the energy in your living spaces impacts and affects the quality of your life.

Based on a 5,000-year-old Chinese art and science, Feng Shui evolved as people saw how their surroundings determined whether they would just survive or thrive. In ancient China, people planned cities in concentric rectangles surrounded by walls that were flanked by lakes, hills, valleys, gardens, courtyards, and parks. As people moved from agrarian to urban societies they modified this Feng Shui planning to fit their environment, resulting in several major schools, or approaches, to Feng Shui. This gives the modern practitioner a range of techniques and tools to use during a home, workplace, business, garden, or real estate consultation.

The one constant in Feng Shui is change. According to Feng Shui principles, everything is constantly changing, everything is alive, and everything is interconnected. Modern applications, like the Feng Shui For Real Life approach, include diverse and varied perspectives. That lets Feng Shui evolve and adapt in response to the the changing culture where it is practiced.

As a design system, Feng Shui helps you harness and use this energy to your best advantage. This applies not only to how your interior space looks, but also how it feels. While the tools that each approach to Feng Shui uses to make changes can sometimes be quite different, they are not better or worse – just different.

There are nine basic tools of Feng Shui that I refer to throughout this book to help you fix or "cure" negative situations and achieve harmony:

1. Color
2. Sound
3. Lighting
4. Art
5. Living Things
6. Water
7. Wind-Sensitive Objects
8. Mirrors
9. Crystals

So, what is real Feng Shui? All perspectives of Feng Shui are valid and effective, and therefore, no one approach is better than another. I believe that any perspective that you understand, that makes you feels comfortable, and that makes a change for the better in your real life, is the real Feng Shui.

A Few Words about Clutter

I get questions about all kinds of clutter issues. Readers ask questions about holding on to broken things, or about jamming sentimental family items into their closets. Clients ask me about things like filling the garage with unfinished projects, or storing so many objects in the extra room that it's no longer usable for guests. Others want to know why keeping mementos from past relationships isn't such a good idea. All kinds of people want to know how to tidy-up. That's why I chose to include the most-often asked questions about clutter in their own section, as well as topic-specific questions in almost every other chapter.

Before you head straight to my answers to your clutter and tidying-up questions, I have a few questions for you:

Q: When you open a kitchen cabinet, do you get attacked by falling debris?

Q: Can you actually walk into your walk-in closet?

Q: Can you find the top of your desk?

In Feng Shui, clutter represents postponed decisions and the inability to move forward. Think about that for a while as you look around your home and workplace. Then, consider the Feng Shui fact that *you are what you see*. When you're surrounded by clutter, there's no room for all the good things in life to find you. Plus, clutter pulls down your positive chi and makes you feel worn out.

Where and why you have clutter says a lot about what's going on in your life. To improve positive energy flow and open up new possibilities for the future, first take a look at the reasons you have clutter, then take steps to reduce it. Often, clutter is merely an accumulation of stuff that you haven't had time to throw away. More often, it represents your inner *stuck-ness*.

One of my favorite tips for reducing clutter—I call it the "One Out/One In" technique—comes from my sister-in-law, Suzanne: *Never bring anything new into your home until you first get rid of something you already have stored in your closet.* Following this simple rule will help keep your storage spaces from accumulating stagnant energy.

My own Feng Shui mantra is just as simple: *Nothing good flows into your life until you make room for it.* Studies show that of all the things we keep, we only reuse one item in 20. That means most people pile rather than file, cluttering their spaces and filling their closets with things they never use.

How to Use This Book

This book is meant to be a companion to my previous book, the *Feng Shui Quick Guide For Home and Office: Secrets to Attracting Wealth, Harmony, and Love*, which explores the basics of contemporary Feng Shui in great detail. Each book stands alone, and together, they will give you a full experience of how to use Feng Shui to attract good things into your life.

I recommend you use this new book by reading it through from start to finish. Chapter 1, "Five Powerful Principles," is a summary of the basics of Feng Shui. If you have burning questions that just can't wait, read about the Power Principles first, and then skip to the section that addresses your topic. Certain frequently-asked topics, like mirrors, naturally fell into more than one category. It was the same for questions about wealth, harmony, and love. Similarly, you'll find questions about beams above your bed in the "Bedroom" chapter, as well as in the "Rearranging" chapter. That means if you want to read all the questions about a specific topic, you'll want to check the Contents to find them fast. Sometimes, you'll see more than one question before the answer. That happens when someone asked a slight variation of the question, and I wanted you to see the different situation the answer can cover.

Throughout this book, I've shared my clients' Success Stories. I love doing this, because their stories show how even simple Feng Shui changes can make a big difference in what you attract into your life. For those of you who asked for anonymity, I respected that and changed your name (and sometimes even your gender) to protect your privacy. I know you'll recognize your story. Thank you for letting me share it with the rest of the world.

I'm writing this from the East Coast of the US, and my tips for the seasons are based on those seasonal variations. I write from the perspective of American customs and habits. But, the good thing about contemporary Feng

Shui practice is that you can easily adjust my tips accordingly for your own location to make them match your needs.

The practical magic of Feng Shui happens quickly and in surprising ways. In light of that, it's fitting that the first story should be one of my own.

SUCCESS STORY

*Carol Makes Room for
New Clients to Find Her*

I caught a miserable cold and cancelled several days of appointments. My Feng Shui mantra has always been nothing new comes into your life until you make room for it, so I decided that being stuck inside was the perfect opportunity to clear my email inbox. I spent my time reviewing every email. I read all the newsletters that had been piling up, checked out the links in my Google Alerts, downloaded all the promised free ebooks and fact sheets (and actually read a few), and replied to requests for information. I cleared out all but five emails, then emptied the trash. Wow, did that feel good.

The next day, I headed out to meet with my Mastermind group. One lead I received was to an interior designer whom I had met at a networking event but didn't know beyond a handshake and a brief conversation. The following morning, I opened my email and there was a message from this designer, asking if I could give a Feng Shui presentation to the interior design class she taught at the local college. This was total Feng Shui synchronicity, because she had no idea that her name had come up at my meeting. I had simply made room in my inbox for the new opportunity to find me. I gave the presentation, and signed up two new clients from the class. Feng Shui works!

CHAPTER
1

FIVE POWERFUL PRINCIPLES

The words *Feng Shui* mean *wind and water*, and they represent the easy flow of positive energy that we each want to attract into our lives. To understand how to use Feng Shui to attract wealth, harmony, love, and happiness, it helps to understand the underlying five powerful principles:

1. **Chi** – the energy around you
2. **The Five Elements** – the colors, shapes, and textures
3. **The Bagua** – a mapping chart to decide where to place the Elements
4. **Yin and Yang** – the balance of opposites
5. **Continuity and Connectedness** – the link between what you see and what you attract

Once you have a basic understanding of the Feng Shui Power Principles, you can put what you have learned into everyday practice throughout the seasons of your life. The practical magic of Feng Shui is different for each of us. That means when you start making Feng Shui changes, the speed at which you see transformations can be unexpected. Sometimes a shift happens literally overnight, while other times if your behavior patterns are deeply ingrained, it can take weeks or even months for the effects of your Feng Shui improvements to appear.

CHAPTER 1: FIVE POWERFUL PRINCIPLES

Power Principle 1: Chi

Chi (pronounced *chee*) is the living energy that comes from nature. It's the constantly moving and changing force that makes you feel either good or bad in a location. Each person, object, and environment has chi. Chi is always in motion, swirling around people and around the objects that people place in their surroundings.

Outside in nature, everything flows and moves like wind and water. However, in our indoor-built environment, we are all too often surrounded by sharp angles and straight lines, or by objects placed in the locations that don't support what we want to attract. All this can block the positive flow of chi. In your home or workplace, the chi will flow in through the front door and head straight out the first window or door in its path. The goal of Feng Shui adjustments is to keep the chi flowing gently throughout your indoor environment, just like gentle wind and water.

Chi can be either positive or negative. Like Goldilocks, you instinctively know when the chi is not too strong, not too weak, but feels just right. That means it's often necessary to move objects or add new ones to bring about a change in the chi around you.

To better understand about positive chi, think about your favorite restaurant where you feel at home—a place that makes you want to linger over your meal. Visualize the layout, colors, fabrics, the decoration on the walls, and the aromas that made you feel happy and welcome. There might have been small tables arranged strategically to suggest intimacy, fresh-cut flowers and candles on the tables, and inspiring artwork on the walls that transported you to the countryside. All of this contributed to the positive chi that attracted you to the spot. By contrast, think about an indoor space where you have felt uncomfortable, like an office. Visualize the layout, colors, furniture, decoration on the walls, and aromas to get a sense of what aspects created its negative chi. For example, there may have been stark white walls, angular metal desks, harsh fluorescent overhead lighting, split pea soup-colored carpet, and generic or no artwork, making you feel alienated, unwelcome, and unhealthy. That's how it feels to be in a location that has an overabundance of negative chi. The goal of Feng Shui adjustments is to change negative chi into positive energy.

Power Principle 2: The Five Elements

The Five Elements is the Feng Shui term to describe the colors, shapes, and textures around you, and the energy they bring into your life. Each Element has a characteristic shape and colors and represents specific attributes. This is the way you use Feng Shui to color your world. The Five Elements are: **Fire, Earth, Metal, Water, Wood**. The goal of Five Element theory is to use the actual material of the Element in your indoor environment to bring its power into your life. For example, a roaring fireplace adds the Fire Element to a room, and a granite counter adds the Earth Element to your kitchen. When using the actual Element just isn't possible, you can use the colors or shape associated with it.

What do the names of the Five Elements conjure up in your mind? Most likely, it's the same thing as their attributes:

Fire is the Element that represents passion, emotion, and high energy. Actual Fire Element objects are hot and blazing, like burning candles or a roaring fireplace. The colors of Fire are also hot, like red, crimson, scarlet, orange, deep purple, and pink. The shape of the Fire Element is triangular, like a flame.

Earth is the Element that grounds you and makes you feel stable and balanced. Actual Earth Element objects are composed of substances made from the earth, such as the tile floor in your bathroom, clay pots on your patio, the granite countertops in your kitchen, and the soil in your living plants. The colors of the Earth Element are the colors of your world: brown like the soil, yellow from the sun, terracotta like clay. The shape of the Earth Element is square.

Metal is the Element that brings strength and clarity into your life. Actual Metal Element objects include wrought-iron furniture, bronze light fixtures, or metal headboards. All electronics and computers are considered the Metal Element, as are fluorescent lights. The colors of the Metal Element are the metallic colors like gold and silver, plus all the pastel and light colors like white, gray, and light colors. The shape of the Metal Element is round, like a metal coin.

Water is the Element that brings movement, flow, inspiration, and relaxation into your life. Actual Water Element objects are represented by an aquarium, a fish bowl, or a fountain, while symbolically, the Water Element is represented by glass and mirrors. The colors of the Water Element are deep blues and black, as if you were looking into deep water. The shape of the Water Element is anything that has a swirling or curving pattern, like a paisley throw pillow.

Wood is the Element that represents growth, expansion, and vitality in your life. Actual Wood Element objects are composed of natural wood, like wood furniture and hardwood floors, as well as plants and flowers. The colors of the Wood Element are green and teal, like tree leaves. The shape of the Wood Element is rectangular, like a straight tree trunk, or like a two-by-four of the resulting lumber.

Power Principle 3: The Bagua

Once you get familiar with the Feng Shui Elements, you can decide where to place them, in the form of furniture, objects, art, and color. The map used to place Elements is called a bagua (pronounced *bag-wha*), a word that means *8-sided* in Chinese. The traditional Feng Shui bagua is an octagon that contains eight areas plus a grounding center, for a total of nine areas (called *guas*), corresponding to critical aspects of daily life. Contemporary approaches to Feng Shui use a grid-shaped chart instead of an octagon.

The nine areas of the Feng Shui For Real Life bagua are:

Power/Wealth/Abundance

Fame/Future/Reputation

Love/Marriage/Relationships

Creativity/Children/Legacy

Compassion/Travel/Helpful People

Self/Career/Work

Knowledge/Harmony/Wisdom

Family/Health/Community

Well-Being/Balance

You can activate each area of the bagua by adding objects that match the colors, shapes, and meaning of each area.

The bagua is a fundamental tool of Feng Shui. No matter what shape house you live in or workplace space you occupy, the bagua chart is always oriented from the front door or main entrance, looking into the home or room to be mapped. Not surprisingly, most of the questions I get about the basics of Feng Shui center around how to use the bagua.

I've included a bagua map at the end of this section that shows the attributes of each area, and the colors and shapes needed to activate it. You can download a color version from the "Basics" tab on my website, *FengShuiForRealLife.com*. Choose either the vertical bagua or the horizontal bagua, depending on the shape of your house. The location of each gua is always the same, and the bagua is always oriented by standing at your front door, holding it in front of you, and drawing the floor plan of your home.

Yes, the bagua can be the most complex of the Power Principles to understand. I get so many questions about using the bagua that I've included a few of the more representative ones below. Also, I provided a detailed description of how to use the bagua to map your home or workplace in Chapter 6 of the *Feng Shui Quick Guide For Home and Office: Secrets For Attracting Wealth, Harmony, and Love*.

CHAPTER 1: FIVE POWERFUL PRINCIPLES

Q & A

THE BAGUA

Q: How do I use the Feng Shui bagua to place things in my house for good luck?

A: These simple steps will help you orient the bagua and use it to map the areas of your home, office, or business. Once you have divided your space into the nine areas of the bagua, you can decorate and accessorize these areas in order to activate the specific energy for each area:

Step 1: Orient the bagua by standing at your front door looking in to your home. Even if you usually enter your home through the garage or side door, orient the bagua from the true front door.

Step 2: Draw the floor plan of the first floor of your home, including all attached structures like the garage, side porch, and deck. Ultimately, you can draw the floor plan for each level of your home, including the basement and attic.

Step 3: Divide the floor plan into the nine equal areas. Then, determine where the rooms lie within the bagua. Once you know what each area of your home represents, you can add furniture, accessories, and colors to activate these areas.

Q: Does each room have a bagua map, or is it only for the shape of the whole house?

A: You use the bagua in each room in addition to the whole house. First, stand at the front door looking into the house holding the bagua in front of you to determine which rooms occupy specific bagua areas. For example, if your bathroom in the Love/Relationship area, you could be symbolically flushing your love down the toilet, and you'll need to make some adjustments. Next, stand at the door to each room and hold the bagua in front of you and map out that room. For example, if you were mapping the kitchen, are the knives stored in the Love/Relationship area of that room? If so, they could be cutting your relationships, so they need to be relocated.

Q: How does one determine where the wealth corner is in a condominium home? Also does this apply to every room in the home? Many thanks in advance!

A: No matter what kind of home you live it, you always find the Wealth/Prosperity area by standing at your front door, looking in, and holding the bagua in front of you. The Wealth area is the upper left corner. For a condo or apartment, stand at the front door of your unit, rather than the entrance to the building, and hold the bagua in front of you. First, use the bagua for the floor plan of your entire home to determine which rooms occupy each bagua area. Then, stand in the doorway of each room and hold the bagua in front of you to map each room. There is a detailed description of how to use the bagua in Chapter 6 of the *Feng Shui Quick Guide For Home and Office: Secrets For Attracting Wealth, Harmony, and Love.*

Q: How do I fix a missing bagua area in an apartment? I can't put a correction outside of my space because by my calculations, it's in the middle of my neighbor's living room.

A: The correction for a missing bagua area when you don't have control over the space is to hang an object on the wall adjacent to the missing area. This will symbolically move the wall and bring the missing bagua area back into your own space. Two kinds of objects will work to symbolically move walls: mirrors and art with an outdoor theme. When you hang a mirror on the wall, you no longer see the wall, but rather, you see what the mirror reflects. It's like seeing through the wall and therefore moving it symbolically outward. Be sure the mirror reflects a positive view. When you hang colorful images of things you see in nature, like trees, flowers, meadows, rivers, or mountains, you no longer see the wall but a representation of what you would see if you could look through the wall. As with a mirror, this symbolically moves the wall.

The BAGUA

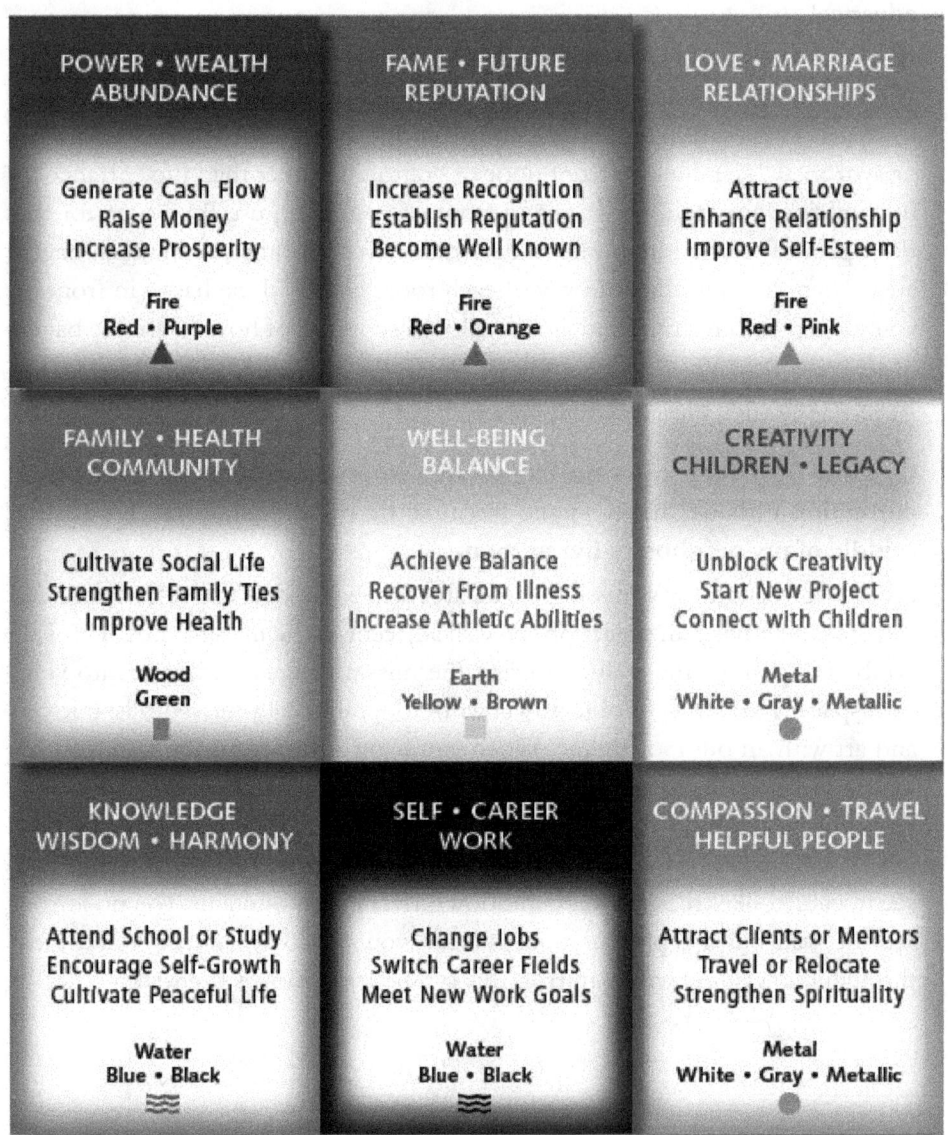

ORIENT WITH PRIMARY ENTRANCE ALONG THIS LINE

Power Principle 4: Yin and Yang

Feng Shui aims to achieve a balance of the opposing, but interconnected, characteristics in the world around you: yin, which is feminine, and yang, which is masculine. You've seen the symbol for yin and yang—a circle with a curved line in the middle that divides the black and white halves of the circle, with a spot of each opposite color on the opposite side. Yin qualities are female, soft, passive, nurturing, and dark, while the yang qualities are male, hard, active, aggressive, and bright. Yin and yang are the everyday opposites we see around us: soft and hard, cold and hot, dark and light.

In most cases, we balance yin and yang naturally and instinctively in our homes: we add soft seat cushions to hard wooden chairs, and we paint one wall a darker accent color to keep an all-white room from looking too bland. That's because when these two equal and opposite forces are in balance in our interior surroundings, we feel comfortable, secure, and at peace. Each aspect of our lives has yin and yang attributes we need to balance.

When we explain these two forces in terms of the Feng Shui Elements, yin is represented by the color black, which is the Water Element, and the passive energy of silence, darkness, and slow, relaxed movements. This is the predominant energy at night when you go to sleep, or when you need to relax and replenish your energies, so it's often appropriate for bedrooms. On the other hand, yang is represented by the color white, which is the Metal Element. It is the strong energy characterized by vibrant sounds and colors, bright lights, and upward moving energy. Yang colors and objects are used in public rooms in your home.

CHAPTER 1: FIVE POWERFUL PRINCIPLES

Power Principle 5: Continuity and Connectedness

This power principle is related to the concept of the Tao (pronounced *dow*) in classical Feng Shui. Tao means *the way or the path*. In contemporary Feng Shui, we modernize Tao to mean continuity and connectedness. Because every action has a reaction, we are influenced by everything around us, and in turn, we influence everything. Related to this is my Feng Shui mantra *you are what you see*. The colors, shapes, and images you use to decorate your surroundings will influence what you attract into your life. The more you surround yourself with symbols of what you want to attract, the more likely you're to achieve it.

For example, if you surround yourself with artwork that's bleak and expresses isolation, you'll attract experiences that make you feel isolated and lonely. If you hold on to furniture that's shabby and worn, your life will feel impoverished. If you allow your faucets to drip and your toilets to run, your wealth will drain away. However, if your artwork includes images that spark joy and prosperity, your life will be prosperous and happy. If your furniture is up to date, clean, and comfortable, you'll feel abundant. If your plumbing is working, you'll feel like your wealth isn't drying up.

You can reinforce connectedness by adding symbols of the natural world to your interior environment, such as flowers, plants, rocks, water, nature sounds, artwork of nature scenes, and aromas, textures, and colors. When you bring the natural world inside, you bring peace and harmony into your life.

In nature, nothing is perfect and everything is perfect.
Trees can be contorted, bent in weird ways, and they're still beautiful.
— Alice Walker

SUCCESS STORY

*Jackie Uses
the Power Principles*

I love when clients send their success stories, and I'm especially proud when they tell me how they use the Five Power Principles of Feng Shui. That means they have the skills to make adjustments to bring positive results to any situation. Jackie is a special client who's become a friend. She was the first person to buy my previous book! She asks questions, makes Feng Shui adjustments, and shares success stories that make me smile.

Here's what Jackie wrote:

❝ Some people won't believe that this story is due to using the Feng Shui power principles, but it is! My husband had a case coming up with his largest client, but found out it posed a conflict of interest with another large client. The second client was angry about the conflict. My husband was distraught. He couldn't sleep and thought he might have presented his carefully-wrought plea incorrectly. I read in your book about how the bagua area for future and recognition is activated by triangles, fire symbols, and the color red. So, I did a Feng Shui remedy: I put a red triangle (made by hand, with his name written on the back) and a candle in that bagua area of our house. Wouldn't you know, he called today and said that everything worked out—the second client isn't angry anymore and will let him work with the first client. This is a huge case, one that doesn't come along frequently. I am so relieved! Wanted to let you know, and thank you again for bringing the Feng Shui power principles into my life. ❞

CHAPTER 2

WEALTH, HARMONY, AND LOVE

Over the years, my clients, students, and readers have asked questions about all sorts of things depending on what's going on in their lives, and about what's happening in the world around them. No matter what issue people write or call about initially, ultimately, they end up asking about one or more of these "Big 3" topics: wealth, harmony, and love. In the more than 20 years I've been a practicing Feng Shui consultant, these primary topics have stayed constant.

Typical questions about wealth range from dealing with personal finances, locating and activating the Wealth area, and finding the right objects to display in this area to increase income. Wealth-related questions break down into distinct categories: how to make changes to activate the Wealth area, how to improve personal finances, and how to attract a new job, more business, or better clients.

Most of the questions I answer about harmony are about holidays and family events, especially in the spring around Easter and Passover, and then toward the end of the year, as the winter holiday season approaches and people have to deal with Thanksgiving, Hanukkah, and Christmas. Questioners want to know how to keep their family dinners harmonious. They want to know what gifts to give—and not give—according to Feng Shui principles. They want to create harmony when dealing with family crises and situations. I frequently advise them to create a home sanctuary, which is a space where you can relax and let the worries of the day dissolve.

I get the most questions about love. These inquiries range from attracting love, to retaining love they already have, to moving on after breakups. I hear

CHAPTER TWO: WEALTH, HARMONY, AND LOVE

from a lot of single women who don't want to remain that way, and single men who wonder what they're doing wrong. I do remind my single clients to be careful what you wish for, because in a romantic partnership, when sharing the same space, you'll have to make Feng Shui compromises when choosing and rearranging your combine stuff.

I get so many questions about that dreaded February holiday, Valentine's Day, that I've often thought I should start a matching service to connect my clients who are looking for love. Instead, I'm offering an assortment of easy Feng Shui changes, large and small, that can have a big impact on your love life and on your relationships.

Home is where you feel at home
and you are treated well.
— Dalai Lama

Q & A

WEALTH

Activating the Wealth Area

Q: What is the one best Feng Shui symbol to display to bring in more money and prosperity?
A: There's no one object that symbolizes wealth to everyone. Instead, display objects and art in your Wealth area that *you* think represent prosperity. Think about what you value most in your life, and that will give you ideas for symbols of wealth, abundance, and prosperity. For example, if wealth means being able to take fabulous vacations, display photographs from your favorite trips or images of new places you want to visit. If the concept of abundance means something more emotional for you, choose images based on your core values.

Q: I really need to make more money. I've been following your blog, and I've done a lot of the things you suggested in what I think is the wealth corner of my apartment. Is there anything else I can do?
A: Which room occupies the Wealth/Prosperity area in your apartment? You'll have the most success when you make adjustments to your Wealth area that closely relate to the function of the room. Here are some options for adjustments in various rooms:

Kitchen: Food is associated with wealth, so display a bowl of oranges or apples on the counter to symbolize prosperity, and keep the kitchen scrupulously clean.

Bathroom: Keep the toilet lid down and the door to the room closed so you're not symbolically "flushing your wealth" down the toilet.

Garage: Clear the clutter so you can actually park cars in there. Store only those items you use frequently.

Living or Family Room: Display your valuable objects such as collections of expensive things, fine art, crystal, etc. Add healthy plants in beautiful pots to symbolize flourishing wealth.

Dining Room: Food and guests are associated with wealth, so hang a mirror that reflects your dining room table, and you'll symbolically double your wealth.

Bedroom: Hang artwork that depicts water, such as rivers and streams, flowing into your room.

Porch or Deck: Choose high-quality outdoor furniture, and try to use this space all year, even if it's only to go out to clean the area.

Q: The Wealth area of our home is in the bathroom that my teenage son uses, and no matter how hard I try, that room always looks like a tornado just ripped through. Is there anything that will help keep our wealth, at least until he leaves for college?

A: The first thing you can do to ground the wealth energy in the bathroom is to add the Earth Element, either in the color you paint the room (brown, yellow) or in the accessories (square shapes and earthy materials). Next, add a plant to represent the Wood Element to grow your wealth and abundance. You can try growing lucky bamboo because it doesn't need much work and your teen probably won't kill it. Finally, keep the toilet lid down and the bathroom door closed to keep the positive chi from symbolically going down the toilet. Yes, I know it is one more thing for you to do since your son will probably forget, but it's worth the effort. Hang artwork in the room with an image that represents wealth to you. You might want to hang a poster of the college he is hoping to attend to attract the wealth to send him there, and to send his bathroom mess with him!

Fast 5

Attract and Keep Wealth

Trying to earn more? Having trouble holding on to money?
Try these 5 Feng Shui tips for mastering your money:

1. **Front Door**. The front door is the mouth of chi where all wealth enters your home. That means if your door is dirty or faded, your ability to attract wealth into your home will be diminished. Dust and clean your door frequently, and repaint or replace if it looks worn or old.

2. **Knobs and Door Handles**. If your door handles and knobs are loose, you can't get a grip on your money and finances. Tighten knobs and handles and replace broken ones to symbolically strengthen your financial future.

3. **Dead Plants.** Dead plants represent dead energy, so replace them with healthy living plants to symbolically grow your wealth. Avoid Bonsai or other miniature plants since they represent stunted growth. If your plants always die, display high-quality silk versions instead.

4. **Gaps.** If you have places around the house where energy can escape—like cracks in your walls, broken shingles on your roof, or gaps in your fence—these represent wealth leaving your home. Money spent on making these kinds of repairs will be returned many times over.

5. **Drips and Leaks.** Water is associated with wealth in Feng Shui, which means leaking water symbolizes losing your wealth. When you stop the leak, you stop the drain on your finances.

CHAPTER TWO: WEALTH, HARMONY, AND LOVE

Improving Personal Finances

Q: Where is the best place to store financial records, such as paid-off debts, debts currently owed, taxes, and other important financial papers that you just can't get rid of? I lost my job, so the wealth isn't pouring in, but the debts sure are. I would like to make sure I'm not encouraging it. Can I store them in the attic?

A: In Feng Shui, we say "you are what you see." That means when you're looking at evidence of your debt, it can have a negative effect on the energy around you, and it could attract more negative energy. It's the same when you keep paperwork related to debt visible in the room where you conduct your job search. Anything stored in the attic symbolically weighs down on you, so that's not the best place for these records. Keep these documents stored in a file cabinet or in a closet, so you don't have to look at them every day. Better yet, scan the documents so you have an electronic record, then shred the originals if you not legally required to keep them.

Q: My personal finances are a disaster. How can Feng Shui help?

A: Keep a healthy plant in the area where you pay your bills, along with a water feature like a fish tank or a fountain. If you don't want to use actual water, hang artwork that depicts a waterfall to represent an abundance of wealth flowing into your life. You can also display the stone citrine (called the cash stone) in your Wealth area, or tie three Chinese coins together with a red string and keep them next to your bank statements or pay slips. Each month when you pay your bills, give thanks for what you have already received and ask that it will be returned to you multiplied.

Q: My finances are in the dumps. Will a new stove assist me with new financial opportunities?

A: The Chinese believe that the more people you can afford to feed, the wealthier you are, so that's why the stove is an important Feng Shui wealth symbol. Whether or not you get a new stove, hang a mirror behind it to symbolically double the burners and to increase wealth. Or, if you can't do that, display a shiny teakettle on the stove to accomplish the same thing.

SUCCESS STORY

*Jerry Receives
Multiple Job Offers*

Jerry wanted a home consultation because he was thinking about a career change, and he was intrigued by the possibilities that some Feng Shui changes could help attract job offers. Jerry's bedroom was in the Wealth area of his home, but he hated the furniture. He asked me whether that was having a negative effect on his ability to accumulate wealth. He could afford a better set, but he never got around to looking for one.

Here's what Jerry wrote:

❝ You really opened my eyes when you pointed out that the hand-me-down furniture set that had been in the family for years was showing too much wear. What a perfect analogy for what had been happening in my career, and never making the time to take the steps to improve it. I followed your recommendation and made it my priority to find a quality bedroom set that made me feel prosperous. Within a week of the new furniture arriving, the resume I posted on an online career site started to pay off. I had interviews, received three great offers, and now I'm happily working for a new company at a higher salary with better benefits. Next, I'm working on updating the other rooms in my house as you suggested. ❞

CHAPTER TWO: WEALTH, HARMONY, AND LOVE

Q & A

HARMONY

Achieving Harmony

Q: I've been watching your videos about Feng Shui because I'm getting ready to buy a new unit, and I want to know: what's the first thing I should bring into it to assure harmony and happiness?

A: Congratulations on getting ready to buy a home! I recommend bringing a new broom into your home and symbolically sweeping throughout the house to clear out any stale or negative chi from the previous occupants, and to make room for your own positive energy. Sweep out toward the door, not in toward the room. Next, bring in objects that mean something to you personally in regard to wealth, harmony, and love. Leave behind anything that's broken, ripped, stained, or has lost its positive meaning for you.

Q: What precious stone is good to display to help me calm down and bring more harmony to my home? Some days it feels like we're always arguing.

A: We are all searching for ways to encourage peace and harmony these days. In Feng Shui, precious stones can be used to deflect bad energy, as well as to attract and boost good luck. Amethysts are stones related to peace, spirituality, and tranquility. They can promote calmness and reduce anger and irritability. Amethysts can be displayed on a desk or table, worn as jewelry, or carried in your wallet, purse, or pocket.

Celebrating Holidays

Q: I don't celebrate Chinese New Year, but in the spirit of bringing in positive energy and harmony at the beginning of the year, can you suggest one thing I could do?

A: Whether you say Happy New Year in January or gung hei fat choy in February, it's good Feng Shui to start your year out on the right foot. Buy a new plant and place it in the Health area of your home or workplace to ensure a healthy beginning to the year. Or, display a bowl of nine oranges in the kitchen, or a bouquet of fresh flowers in the family room to symbolize healthy new energy coming into your home or office. Replace the flowers as soon as they die.

Q: Is there any special advice about arranging the house for Easter?

A: If you color Easter eggs, display the results in the Creativity area of your home, which is the bagua area that's activated by round shapes. Display the palms from Palm Sunday in the Family area, because that area is enhanced by the Wood Element and the color green.

Q: Any Feng Shui tips for the Passover Seder table?

A: Arrange the Seder plate according to the Feng Shui bagua. Put the egg on the far left of the plate, the shank bone on the top right, the bitter herbs in the middle, the vegetable in the lower left, and the *charoset* in the lower right. Place the Seder plate in the center of the table.

Q: Are there any Feng Shui animal symbols that are especially appropriate to display for Halloween?

A: Owls and ravens are the most often used Feng Shui animal symbols for Halloween. Outdoors, display owls by your front door facing out toward the street, and inside, place them in the front windows facing out. The black color of ravens represents mystery, and their legendary powerful yet macabre presence makes them a typical Halloween symbol. Owls act as guardians and symbolically keep the roving spirits from entering your home and causing mischief on Halloween night. Display them pointing out, not into, your home.

Q: I have invited my entire family for Thanksgiving dinner, but they don't always get along. Any suggestions for promoting family harmony and reducing conflict around the table?

A: If your family is prone to arguments, keep the yang (or active) energy to a minimum by keeping the lights low and decorating with soothing earth and wood tones, like gold, green, and brown. Keep shiny surfaces to a minimum, and stow the carving knife out of sight to avoid sharp words at the table. Avoid displaying plants with sharp or pointed leaves, and if you choose roses for your centerpiece, remove the thorns. If all else fails, keep this in mind: whoever is seated nearest to the door will be the first one to leave. That means you might want to consider a seating plan.

Fast 5

Create Harmonious Holidays

We all love the bounty of holiday food and the joy of seeing friends and family, but we dread the cooking, cleaning, and entertaining. These five tips can help assure harmonious family gatherings:

1. **Dining Room.** The dining room is considered to be a place of wealth in Feng Shui, so use it instead of eating in front of the TV during the holiday season.

2. **Crystal and China.** Bring out the "good stuff" for your meals— the china, crystal, silver, and all the other special pieces you have been hiding in your cabinets and closets. What are you saving them for if not for the holidays?

3. **Centerpiece**. Use a centerpiece of orange-colored flowers to encourage conversation, or fresh fruit and veggies to represent good health and longevity.

4. **Seating**. Avoid seating an overbearing guest (you know who that is) at the head of the table where he or she could monopolize the conversation.

5. **Photos.** Remove photos of deceased relatives or pets from the dining room, because these could create health problems if you dine in their presence.

Q: Can I Feng Shui my Thanksgiving menu? Every year, I cook the same thing, and this time, I want to do something more purposeful, but without giving up the family favorites.

A: Thanksgiving is the ultimate foodie holiday, and the colors, aromas, and tastes of food are strongly related to Feng Shui. Since we need to balance the darker yin side of the winter energy, your cooking can include strong yang energy food for the holidays. Cooked foods, spices, and hot foods, such as chile peppers, ginger, and garlic, are yang energy (sounds like my Thanksgiving menu!). Foods like raw vegetables, potatoes, and fish are yin and are served in moderation during this period. But that doesn't mean you have to totally give up yin foods for the winter, especially a little bit of chocolate. The dark sweetness helps us to appreciate the holiday season.

Q: Do you have any color suggestions for decorating for a New Year's Eve party? We really need to bring some good luck into our house this coming year.

A: Decorate your home for New Year's Eve with gold and silver, the colors of valuable coins, symbolizing your intention to attract wealth in the coming year. You can also scatter some chocolate coins wrapped in gold and silver foil around the table to represent new wealth for you and your guests.

Q: We have always placed our Christmas tree in the family room, which is near the front of the house. Would it be better to locate my Christmas tree according to Feng Shui principles?

A: The ideal location for a Christmas tree is in either the Wealth, Fame, or Family area of your home, because these are supported by the Wood and Fire Elements. The Wealth area is the room in the upper left-hand corner of your home, or the upper left corner of any room. The Fame area is located at the back of your home across from your front door. Triangular shapes like a pine tree displayed in both of these areas enhance finances, abundance, and prosperity. The Family area is on the middle, left-hand side of your home, and it's activated with the color green.

CHAPTER TWO: WEALTH, HARMONY, AND LOVE

SUCCESS STORY

*Adele Does a Whole
House Makeover*

One of the joys of my work is getting to help people from all over the world through off-site consultations. Adele, who is in the UK, first contacted me about her missing Love and Marriage area, and our email conversations led to changes in many other bagua areas of her home to bring a sense of peace and harmony to all aspects of her life.

Here's what Adele wrote:

❝ I want to send you an update on how your book has helped me. I have made a number of changes, and I have been absolutely amazed by the results. I found making small changes had big results, simply by having a thorough understanding of how it all works. I targeted the areas where I most needed support, which was feeling grounded, stable, and calm, and everything in my life now seems easy. Before, I struggled with conflicts such as back-stabbing at work and lack of recognition, and my emotions were in turmoil. My life is the complete opposite now. Before I found your book, I had it so wrong. I had left the main room in my house neglected, which in turn I realized was the center of my home, the Grounding area. It has had the most beautiful face-lift now, and I can't believe I had it the way I did and still wondered why I was struggling so much! Most interestingly, I have left my Love area until very last. This was an area I thought I was desperate to sort out, but for some reason, I made no changes to it until last week. That's when I finally realized that I would like love in my life. I think before that, I was wishing for love to make me feel

(continued)

> better, but for all the wrong reasons. I have now completed all the corrections you advised for the missing Love area, and it's now full of life, wind chimes, windmills, plants, and lights. It looks taken care of now, while before it was full of weeds, dirty and empty—it was a place even my cats avoided. I am currently having my living room, hallway, and bathroom decorated professionally. Most of it has been chosen to correspond with your advice, then my kitchen will be renovated. It's amazing how I seem to have found the money to do all this! Isn't it fascinating how making a big change to the center of my house could have such a huge impact on my well-being? It is a bit like the Fable of the Magic Geranium in your book about the lady whose colorful plant changed her whole house. I always knew something was wrong in my house, and now it just feels peaceful, with a very happy and content owner... finally. 🙂🙂

Q: Can you give me some tips about using colors to raise my mood, especially around the holiday season when I'm sad. I celebrate Hanukkah, and the Feng Shui advice I've found only deals with Christmas.

A: Celebrate Hanukkah by decorating in the traditional colors of the Water Element (blue) to make your holiday flow smoothly, and the Metal Element (silver) for strength. If you suffer from seasonal winter sadness, especially around the holidays, counteract feelings of loneliness by surrounding yourself with the color orange, which encourages communication.

Q: Hello! I have a quick question for decorating for the holidays. What if you have a white ceramic Christmas tree? What would be the best area to put that in?

A: You can use the Feng Shui bagua to decide where to place the tree in your home. The color white represents the Metal Element, which helps to activate the energy of the Creativity/Children and Helpful People/Travel areas. Place your white tree in one of those areas.

CHAPTER TWO: WEALTH, HARMONY, AND LOVE

Q & A

LOVE

Attracting Love

Q: I'm trying to attract a new relationship. What things do you recommend for romance?
A: Here are my top suggestions for making room for love to find you:

Clear out space in the **bedroom closet** so there will be room for a partner's clothes and accessories.

Make room in the **pantry and refrigerator** for his or her favorite foods.

Leave an opening in the **bathroom** vanity for a lover's toiletries and personal items.

Get rid of items that remind you of a **past lover**, including your ex's photo, old sweater, or gifts that could remind you of a love that went bad.

Remove the **extra pillows** from your bed because they send the message that you have no room for anyone else to join you.

Replace **artwork** from your bedroom that shows a solitary person or a lonely scene; instead, put up images of happy couples to make you more receptive to a relationship.

Q: I'm a single woman and want to be in a relationship. I have a favorite painting with a deep, rich red background, but it shows only a single female draped in black. I don't want to move the painting from my bedroom. Is there anything I can do to complement it, rather than get rid of it, and still invite a relationship into my life?

A: Feng Shui principles recommend that when you're trying to attract a relationship, it's best to remove all art and images that show single people, and to replace them with images that show couples, romantic scenes, or objects in pairs. This is especially important in your bedroom and in the area of your home that occupies the Love/Relationship area. Sorry, that means you need to move the image of a single female out of your bedroom and replace it with art that will help attract a partner.

Fast 5

Make Room for a Relationship

If your marriage or long-time relationship has hit a snag and your love life is in the doldrums, try these five simple Feng Shui adjustments in your bedroom:

1. **Photos.** Remove photographs of your children, parents, and friends. (You don't want them watching you in bed, do you?)

2. **Art.** Choose art showing couples and romantic objects in pairs.

3. **Bed.** Make sure you have the right size bed for your relationship. If the bed is too big, partners can drift apart; if it's too small, partners might feel trapped.

4. **Furniture.** Get rid of furniture from a previous relationship, especially in your bedroom, because keeping it asks the question, "who are you sleeping with tonight?"

5. **Night Tables.** Add matching night tables. For singles, the second night stand invites a partner into your bedroom, and for married couples and committed partners, it encourages equality in the relationship.

CHAPTER TWO: WEALTH, HARMONY, AND LOVE

Q: I am a single mom and sleep in the master bedroom with my daughter. She does have her own room but prefers mine. Does this affect my prospects of finding love?

A: The Feng Shui recommendation is that a bedroom should be reserved for rest and romance only. If your daughter sleeps in your bedroom, symbolically that doesn't allow room for a lover to find you. The place for your daughter to sleep is in her own bedroom. If she needs to feel close to you, place a similar item in both bedrooms—like a throw pillow or blanket—and display a current photo of the two of you in her room.

Q: My sister lives in a tiny studio apartment and has photos all over of the three of us from very early childhood (we're triplets), and even more of our mother who passed in 2008. She's 54 and single and hasn't dated in years. I know she should remove these from her Relationships area, but I've wondered if having them all over her apartment can also affect her "love life" (or lack thereof). Her relationships area has a small table with a lamp on it, next to an old ugly chaise lounge. She has always loved antiques and had plenty of room for them in her last apartment, she has stuffed many of them into this tiny apartment and everything feels crowded. How can I help her?

A: It sounds like your sister is holding on to the past and is reluctant to let go, symbolized by keeping the "ugly" chaise and the extra furniture that fit in her former home. To attract a relationship, your sister needs to make sure both her bedroom and her Relationship area have items that are paired, romantic, and coupled. That means removing the family photos from these rooms. She can keep a few old photos in the living room, surrounded by several new ones to represent growth and harmony among family members.

SUCCESS STORY

*Natalia Replaces
Single Girl Art*

Natalia called me because her relationship had been on the rocks since she moved into her new condo. Everything had been fine in her previous apartment, but soon after buying the condo, her relationship with her long-time boyfriend Rob went downhill and he stopped coming over as often. Natalia said she bought new artwork to fill up the walls of her larger space. When I arrived at Natalia's home, the problem was immediately clear: she had hung too many "single" images on the walls, because there were prints of solitary, lonely-looking women in every room. Making this solitary message even stronger was the large painting of a woman Natalia had hung above her bed. All this single-image art was sending the message to her boyfriend that there was no place for him in Natalia's life. I recommended that Natalia remove the single art and replace it with romantic scenes and paired images.

Here's what Natalia wrote several months later:

❝ I removed all the solitary artwork from my condo, especially the painting from over the bed. Rob and I picked out some replacement pictures together. We hung a picture of a scene in Tuscany over the bed. That's where we want to go for our honeymoon because... we just got engaged! Thank you for your simple Feng Shui solution. ❞

CHAPTER TWO: WEALTH, HARMONY, AND LOVE

Enhancing Love

Q: What is the best thing to hang on the wall above my headboard? Landscapes, silhouettes, family photos, black and white photography, abstracts, etc.? I am married and would like to improve my relationship with my husband.

A: A bedroom should be reserved for rest and romance only, so the ideal art to have over your headboard is anything that feels romantic, coupled, paired, and connected. For example, it could be a romantic scene of a couple holding hands on a beach or sitting in a garden, or even a simple print of a pair of tulips in a vase leaning in the same direction. I recommend color artwork and photography rather than black and white or silhouettes to symbolize a relationship filled with color and passion. You can display a current photo of you and your husband in the room, but avoid pictures of family, children, friends, or pets.

Q: I've been dating a guy I really like, but the relationship never seems to move beyond the "just dating" level. My friend said to check what I have in the areas of my home that are related to love and marriage. I have one chair in that corner of my bedroom and one small table in that corner in the living room. Now that she pointed it out, I'm thinking I'm sending the wrong message with these things.

A: Yes, the placement of single objects in the critical Love/Relationship area of these rooms could be sending the wrong message. I recommend you add a second chair to the corner of your bedroom and add a pair of chairs to accompany the single table in that corner of the living room. If there's not enough room for a pair of chairs, surround these single objects with pairs of smaller objects to balance out their single energy. That will send the message there's room for a lover in your life.

Q: My husband and I sleep in separate bedrooms because he snores so loudly that I can't get any sleep. This is putting a strain on our marriage. Any suggestions?

A: Use the same bed linens, comforters, paint color, artwork, photos, etc., in both bedrooms to pull together your energy. Also, create an intimate place for the two of you where you can be together daily, like a sitting area where you can share coffee as you begin the day, or wine as you end it. [See prior questions for other ideas.]

Q: My daughter has been engaged to her fiancé for over a year now, and I was wondering if there is a Feng Shui cure to move this along? She wants to "do the deed," but he is very slow-moving about everything (he's a lawyer!). I know they are very much in love. Could it have something to do with de-cluttering their house? Thanks for taking time to ponder this.

A: Your question is one I get frequently, either from the would-be bride or from her mother. Clutter clearing will always help, especially in the bedroom and in the Love area of their home. Also, make sure she removes any images that appear single, solitary, or alone, and replaces them with images that show paired things. She can also place a few objects in pairs in these two areas. Be sure to keep the pairs of objects together; for example, two candles on the mantle should be kept together rather than at opposite ends. Take a good look with your own "Feng Shui eyes" and you might see some single images and split placements that your daughter is overlooking. She could leave a copy of a bridal magazine in the Love area, unless you think that might be too over the top. A good question for you to ask your daughter is, what's keeping her from talking with her fiancé about this?

Q: I just became engaged, but my fiancé is going to be working overseas for several months. How do I keep the communication between us as clear as possible while we are separated by an ocean? While he is gone, I will be living in a small temporary apartment and I can't decide if two nightstands are better than one.

A: Congratulations, I wish you both much joy and happiness! The classic Feng Shui adjustment for sustaining love is to place two nightstands in your bedroom to represent equality in the relationship. This would be especially important for each of you to do in your individual spaces when you're in a long-distance relationship. Also, decorate the bedrooms in your locations with the same art and images so you're "present" in each other's bedroom, no matter how far apart you are geographically. For example, hang the same romantic print in both bedrooms and display the same current photo of the two of you, and use the same linens. If you can repaint, use the same color paint on the walls. Knowing that you're looking at the same things in your bedroom helps enhance communication while you're separated.

Fast 5

Set a Place for Love

If you're planning a romantic dinner for two, here are five Feng Shui suggestions to help set the mood and create the perfect romantic setting:

1. **Chairs**. Place only two chairs at the table, at right angles to each other, and avoid sitting across from your dining partner because this is considered a "confrontational" position.

2. **Decoration**. Decorate your table with objects in pairs, rather than single items, to symbolize a coupled and paired relationship.

3. **Color**. Wear something red to activate your own personal Fire Element energy.

4. **Roses**. Display roses on the table, but remove the thorns to represent a smooth relationship.

5. **Clutter**. Remove all clutter from the room, because it symbolizes postponed decisions and the inability to move forward—something you certainly don't want to encourage.

Q : I just moved in with my fiancé, and while I used to sleep soundly, now I can't fall asleep. He's been divorced twice, and we sleep on the bed he has had since college. Does that have anything to do with it?

A: When you sleep on a bed from a past relationship, you're sleeping with all the negative energy from those relationships. It's time for you and your fiancé to get a new bed, mattress, and linens. Also, make sure there aren't any mirrors aimed at you when you're in bed.

Q: Are there a few simple adjustments I can make in my bedroom to bring romance back into my marriage?

A: The primary thing to do is to make sure the room is comfortable for two people. Your bed should be centered in the room so neither person sleeps in the corner against two walls, and each of you should have a night table. Make sure the artwork in the room is romantic and shows images of pairs of things, and especially avoid sad images. Move out the photos of parents, pets, children, and friends and replace them with a current photo of you and your partner. Remove all work-related objects, especially computers, because a bedroom should be for rest and romance only.

Q: I read in one of your newsletters that you shouldn't paint your bedroom lavender if you want to attract a relationship. What about actual lavender? I have several framed postcards that show lavender. Is that OK?

A: The Feng Shui recommendation is to avoid using the color lavender on the walls in an adult bedroom, and instead to choose a color that's a "skin tone." Lavender wall color is considered "virginal" and should be reserved for the walls of a young girl or young teen. If you look at a color and it reminds you of healthy skin—including the blush on cheeks or the color of lips—it's a good choice to encourage rest and romance in the bedroom. It's certainly okay to display lavender, either fresh or pictures of fresh lavender, since it is a relaxing aroma that helps restful sleep. But, avoid displaying dried lavender, real or as an image, because it represents dead energy.

CHAPTER TWO: WEALTH, HARMONY, AND LOVE

SUCCESS STORY

*Michelle Finds
a New Love*

My client Michelle told me that she had been single for too long. She had lots of dates, but no one special was coming "out of the crowd" for her. Many months later, I heard from her again, and her love story speaks for itself.

Here's what Michelle wrote:

❝ Following some of your online tips and those in your book, I made several changes, especially moving the photos of my family from the bedroom to the living room and cleaning out the closet. Boy, did I clean out the closet. I found a painting online that spoke to me of romance and passion, and I hung it next to my bed. Looking at your bagua map, I realized that my Romance/Love area was occupied by the dollhouse I bought when I was 13, which was mostly gathering dust and serving as a nice perch for my two cats. Out went the dollhouse (to a high school friend's two young daughters, who love it), and up went two photos of pink and red flowers from my 2007 trip to Peru. Here's where the story gets interesting. Sometime later, I met an amazing man through an online dating service. Where is he from? Peru. It was love at first sight when we actually met, and things moved quickly from there. We have since moved to Peru, painted our bedroom pink, and hung up that same painting, which he also loves. Thank you for your advice about love. ❞

Q: I have a refrigerator in my love/relationship area and a washer and dryer in my wealth area. I am in a panic that I am freezing out my love and drowning my wealth.

A: I'm a big believer in the saying, if it ain't broke, don't fix it. So, ask yourself these questions before you panic: Does your relationship seem chilly? If so, you do need to balance the energy created by the refrigerator in your Love area. Remove some of the cold by adding heat to the area around your refrigerator in the form of the Fire Element. For example, hang artwork in the kitchen near the fridge that has red or orange images or triangular shapes. Are you drowning in bills? It could be a result of the overabundance of water in the Wealth area. Add a healthy, bushy plant, or a picture of trees to symbolically sop up some of the water. Also, add a touch of the Fire Element to dry up some water and melt some of the Metal Element created by the washer and dryer.

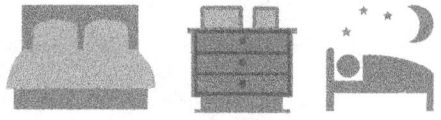

CHAPTER 3

BEDROOMS, BEDS, AND BLISSFUL SLEEP

According to Feng Shui principles, one of the most important spaces in any home is the bedroom. An adult bedroom should be reserved for rest and romance, but all too often, it's crowded with stuff that's not conducive to either. When you're surrounded by work-related reading, an electronic device tempting you with unread emails, and stacks of books or magazines you never read, your mind can't focus on either relaxation or romance, and you can't sleep.

Many people are facing complex times right now because of a chaotic society and all of its potential ramifications. According to the American Psychological Association, Americans report these causes of sleepless nights: work (74%), money (73%), workload (66%), children (64%), family duties (50%), your health (55%), spouse's/child's health (55%), parent's/other family health (54%), housing costs (51%), and intimate relationships (47%). Making Feng Shui changes will help you deal with these worries because you can't solve problems until you get a good night's sleep. The questions I get about bedrooms, beds, and sleep fall into these major areas:

Above: Anything weighing down from the ceiling can detract from sleep. For example, a ceiling fan is certainly useful to circulate the chi in a room, but if it's located directly above your bed, the cutting "corkscrew" chi could lead to poor sleep or illness. Plus, it could symbolically "cool down" your relationship.

Under: Storing things under your bed restricts positive, sleep-inducing chi from flowing all around you. For example, if you sleep with workout equipment under your bed, you're symbolically "running" all night. Or, if you sleep with shoes under the bed, you feel tired when you wake because you were "walking away" from a good night's sleep.

All Around: When your bedroom walls are the wrong color, your sleep will be disturbed. The most restful wall color for bedroom walls is a skin tone, ranging from ivory to mahogany. If you look at a paint color and it makes you think of the glow of healthy skin or the warm blush on cheeks, it's the right color for your bedroom. It's also important to keep all work-related items out of your bedroom. Limit electronics, surround yourself with peaceful artwork, and limit the number of mirrors.

> *The best cure for insomnia*
> *is to get a lot of sleep.*
> *— W. C. Field*

Q & A

MASTER BEDROOM

Look Above

Q: We have a ceiling fan over our bed, and I read somewhere that this is considered bad Feng Shui. We don't want to stop using the fan because it makes such a difference, and there is no other location for the bed. What do I do?

A: I hear this question frequently, especially in the summer. One option is to hang a round, faceted crystal from the center of the fan. This represents the Water Element and reduces the cutting, metal energy of the fan. You can hang a small crystal with fishing line or similar invisible filament so it doesn't show, or buy a pull chain with a crystal at the end. There's usually something on the fan housing that you can hang it on, like the switch that reverses the direction. Another option is to place a red dot on the top side of each of the blades where it won't show. The red represent the Fire Element, which symbolically melts some of the metal energy and therefore reduces its hardness.

Q: There is a skylight in our bedroom. Is that good or bad Feng Shui?

A: A skylight can represent a hole cut into your roof where the chi can escape. If you can't move your bed to avoid sleeping directly under the skylight, cover it with translucent electronic shades or curtains that you can close at night. Avoid hanging sharp-edge blinds on the skylight. Or, hang a faceted crystal under the skylight to deflect any negative energy and to prevent the chi from leaving the room.

Q: I sleep in a bedroom with sloped and slanted ceilings. This is the only place for the bed. How is this affecting me?

A: When you sleep under a sloped or slanting ceiling, negative chi presses down on you. These ceilings can cause imbalance, sometimes resulting in headaches and sinus problems. If you must locate your bed under the low ceiling, you'll need to symbolically raise the energy of the ceiling. You could try creating a canopy over the bed by draping fabric, or place floor lamps in the sloped corners of the room to symbolically lift the ceiling in those locations. Other remedies include hanging strings of tiny lights on the ceiling, painting the ceiling a lighter color than the walls, or stenciling images of clouds, vines, or birds on the ceiling. Anything that symbolically lifts the ceiling will work.

Q: We love the beams over the bed in our new home, but I have heard that they can be negative. What do you think?

Q: We are house hunting, and I have fallen in love with a house that has exposed ceiling beams over the bed. I think they make a room look cozy. If we buy the house, are the beams going to cause us problems?

A: The Feng Shui concern about beams over a bed is that they represent too much weight over your head while you're sleeping. If you have a high ceiling and the beams are rounded, they aren't going to cause any problems. However, if the beams have sharp edges, or if they hang low over the bed, this can challenge your relationship and your health. Some remedies include the following: painting or staining the beams the same color as the ceiling to help camouflage and lift them; aiming spotlights at them to scatter any oppressive chi; weaving silk vines and flowers around them to simulate sleeping outdoors; draping fabric over your head like a canopy; placing upright furniture, floor lamps, or floor plants in the corners of the room to symbolically raise the ceiling; hanging art in the room with a strong image to pull the focus across to the walls rather than up to the ceiling. Another option is to hang a ceiling fan to cut across the beams to lessen their weight, and to spin the chi up and away from the bed. Only use this remedy if the room is big enough to keep the fan from hanging directly above the bed.

Q: I'm trying to buy a new home and found one that's almost perfect, except for the exposed beams in the bedroom over the bed. I read that's not such a good thing in Feng Shui and that I should hang bamboo flutes from the beams. I have no interest in doing that, so should I keep looking?

A: Bamboo flutes were originally used in classical Feng Shui to "cut" the beam and to keep it from "weighing down" on you or splitting a couple in bed. If you don't want to use them, there are modern ways you can reduce the negative effects of exposed beams. [See previous question for several contemporary ways to symbolically lift the pressure.]

Look Under

Q: What do you think about having a treadmill in the master bedroom? I used the bagua from your website and discovered the equipment in my Relationship area. My love life isn't so good and now I'm thinking there's a connection. Can I trade it in for a new one that folds up, so I can store it under the bed? I use it only occasionally, but I like having it available when I get motivated.

A: Move the treadmill out of the bedroom because all that "walking to nowhere" could symbolize working too hard at a relationship. Every room should have a purpose, but when we add the yang energy of working out with the yin energy needed for rest and romance in a bedroom, things can go wrong. Storing a hard metal treadmill under the bed isn't a solution, because that area should be open so the chi can circulate around you and support your relationship and health. Here's the question to ask yourself: *Do I actually use my treadmill enough to make it worth keeping?* If every time you look at the treadmill you feel guilty about not using it, it's better to sell it and put the money toward a gym membership.

Q: My husband and I downsized last year, but we are still struggling with storage issues at our new home. The main problem is shoe storage. I am considering purchasing a plastic, under-the-bed storage box that will hold all our shoes. Is that okay, Feng Shui-wise? I already keep a small suitcase under there.

Q: Can you store shoes in their original shoe boxes under the bed?
A: The best Feng Shui answer is to avoid storing anything under your bed, so the chi can flow all around you at night to assure a peaceful night's sleep.

Unfortunately, shoes are especially inauspicious choices for under-bed storage because they symbolize "walking away" or "moving away" from a relationship. If you can't part with any of your shoes (something I understand!), consider what else you can move out of your bedroom closet to make room for the shoes. If you must store things under your bed, choose soft, seasonal clothing. Avoid sharp or hard metal objects since they can "cut" into your sleep.

Q: I keep my suitcases under my bed because I travel quite a bit. Is that OK from a Feng Shui perspective?

A: The answer also depends on whether you like to travel. Keeping suitcases under a bed symbolizes being ready to "pack up and move out" on a moment's notice, especially if you keep them packed with your travel necessities. If you want your travels to continue, your suitcases can go under the bed. You can even keep guidebooks, photos, and other items related to the places where you'd like to go. But if you're tired of travel—especially if it's work-related and interfering with your relationships—it's time to move those suitcases out of your bedroom and into a closet. If you want to stop traveling but have no place for your suitcases other than under the bed, put a rock in each one and cover it with a blanket to help them stay put for a "rest," and to keep you grounded at home.

Q: It isn't advisable to store moving boxes under your bed, is it? I'm assuming this can block the flow of energy, but does the fact that they're moving boxes make it worse? I have no plans to move, but don't want to have to buy them when I do decide to relocate

A: Storing moving boxes anywhere in your home sends the message that you aren't settled, and it's especially inauspicious under your bed because it can lead to sleepless nights. Holding on to things you're saving "just in case" represents a *poverty mentality*, in contrast to the *prosperity consciousness* of letting things go and trusting you'll always have money to replace them. I recommend getting rid of the boxes. Resale stores like Habitat for Humanity's ReStore will usually take them, so you can get a tax write-off while making room for good things to find you in your home.

Fast 5

Arrange Your Bedroom for Romance

Whether you're looking to attract a new love or want to rev up the love you already have, here are five of my favorite Feng Shui bedroom tips:

1. **Door**. Make sure your bed is not directly across from the room door or you'll feel vulnerable because you are easily seen by anyone entering the room. If you can't move your bed, add a substantial foot board or place a trunk or bench at the foot of the bed for protection.

2. **Mirrors**. A mirror in a bedroom can make you restless, especially if you can see yourself in it when you're in bed. Replace all mirrors with art or beautiful wall hangings. If you must keep your mirror, drape it before going to sleep.

3. **Work**. Reminders of your work responsibilities can keep you awake and negatively impact your love life. If you must work in your bedroom, keep your office area as far from the bed as possible, and use a screen or plants to hide the area. Keep your night tables clear of work-related reading, especially your computer and other electronics.

4. **Toilet**. Toilets are associated with waste in Feng Shui, and looking at one from your bed disrupts restful sleep. Keep the bathroom door closed, or position plants to create a screen in front of the bathroom.

5. **Bed**. Position the bed for a couple with the head against a wall and ample room to walk around it, even if this means switching to a smaller-size bed. When a bed for two people is positioned against two walls, in a corner, one of the partners can feel symbolically "trapped" in the relationship because he or she can't get out easily.

CHAPTER 3: BEDROOMS, BEDS, AND BLISSFUL SLEEP

Look All Around

Q: Is it OK to keep a cell phone on your nightstand when you sleep? It's my only phone, plus it's my alarm clock.

A: A bedroom should be reserved for rest and romance only. If you use your cell as an alarm clock, then it's acceptable to keep it nearby, but you'll need to resist the temptation to use it to catch up on e-mail before you go to bed. Try keeping all electronics as far from your head as possible because they can interfere with peaceful sleep.

Q: I live in a small apartment and have a computer and desk in my bedroom because there is no other space. Is this OK?

A: In Feng Shui, it's best not to mix the purpose of a room. When you keep work in your bedroom, it may be hard to separate your work time from your relaxation time. Try screening off the desk area so you can't see it from the bed. Use a curtain, standing screen, or floor plants to hide the desk after you finish working for the day. Or, consider keeping your computer in a cabinet that you can close at night.

Q: I keep putting off clearing out my bedroom closet because I don't want to give away clothes that I'm not wearing right now but might come back into style. Any advice?

A: The Feng Shui answer is that you should keep only three types of clothes in your closet: clothes that fit, clothes you love, and clothes that bring compliments when you wear them. Holding on to clothes you don't wear symbolizes living in the past, but getting rid of them represents making room for new things to find you. And the "new things" you attract won't be limited to clothes; it will also include new opportunities to wear those clothes.

Q: We are considering buying a house where the master bedroom is located over the kitchen and the only place for the bed is directly over the stove. I've read this is not a good position. Should we pass on the house?

Q: I read that it's not such a good idea, Feng Shui wise, to sleep in a bedroom over a kitchen stove. Is that true? My bed is in that location and I'm worried.

Q: Our bedroom backs up to the kitchen. Is that a good or a bad thing?

A: A bed located above or near the kitchen stove isn't considered a positive location because the Fire Element represented by the stove can disturb peaceful sleep. If you can't move the bed, try grounding your bed by placing an earth-tone color rug under it, or by using earthy colors in your linens. For a bedroom above a kitchen, place a small round mirror under the bed with the mirror side facing down. Mirrors represent the Water Element, and in this location, the symbolic water will cool off some of the fire from the stove. Having a stove on the other side of the wall with the head of your bed is a bigger problem than being above a kitchen. Since the cooking area is active yang energy, and a bed is quiet yin inactivity, you'll need to avoid adding the Fire Element to the bedroom (red, orange, deep purple colors; candles or triangular accents). Instead, add the Earth Element (brown, yellow, or terracotta colors; granite and clay accents), and artwork with Water Element colors (dark blues and lack) to reduce the overheated energy from the stove.

Q: We recently moved into a house where the master bedroom is located at the end of a hall. We don't sleep well in the room, and my husband and I are arguing a lot in this house. I have read that this is not the best location for a bedroom, and wondered if that is contributing.

A: A bedroom located at the end of a hallway is exposed to the straight, rapidly moving energy known as a *poison arrow*. This harsh energy aimed directly at a bedroom can feel like there's an arrow pointed at you when you sleep. This discomfort could certainly contribute to arguments. The best solution is to slow down the fast-moving chi by hanging artwork or a mirror on one side of the hallway. This will add depth to the corridor and slow down the chi. Avoid using a long runner in the hall since this will accentuate the arrow effect. Also, make sure the hallway has good lighting.

CHAPTER 3: BEDROOMS, BEDS, AND BLISSFUL SLEEP

SUCCESS STORY

Nancy Recovers After Her Divorce

My client Nancy went through a nasty divorce and was living a solitary life while she healed, and her too-small twin bed reflected her isolation. Her only bed partners were her three dogs. Nancy reconnected with a past love online, and she wanted to see if she could rekindle the relationship. I recommended that she trade in her childlike bed for an adult bed, move out some of the furniture, and repaint her room from girlish lavender to a skin-tone color more suitable for an adult relationship.

Here's what Nancy wrote:

❝ The same day we spoke, I bought the new bed and consigned the old twin. My new queen bed feels great, and I have no dogs in it. I brought in two matching antique bedside tables from another room and lamps from storage. I removed a lot of unnecessary furniture as you suggested, and that made the room feel bigger. I saw both the wisdom and the necessity of what you told me, and I am sleeping better than I have for a long time. That gave me incentive to redo my home office, library, and a closet. It feels cleaner and more airy all throughout the house. I am taking two boxes of pottery and ornaments to the resale place along with 58 items of clothing I no longer wear. I picked out a more natural color for the walls, and the painter will be here soon. I received an actual written love letter from my friend two days after the bedroom changes were in place—a big change from our usual e-conversations. ❞

Q: I have a small bedroom with a king-size bed. Unfortunately, it faces the bathroom door as well as the room entrance door. How can I remedy this problem?

Q: Our bedroom door directly opens to our bathroom, and I see the toilet from the bed. Is this a bad-luck position?

A: A bed facing the bathroom in not in a peaceful location, and facing the bedroom door is considered inauspicious. If you see into the bathroom from the bed, keep the bathroom door closed at night. If that's not possible, hang a crystal in the doorway of the bathroom. If your feet point directly out the door when you're lying in bed, you can give yourself some protection by placing a solid footboard or piece of furniture at the end of the bed.

Q: I don't know where to get started in purging my bedroom closet. Any ideas for how to tame this beast?

A: At the start of the new season, tie a ribbon on a hanger and hang it at the beginning of that season's clothes. After you wear something, hang it in front of the ribbon. At the end of the season, you'll easily see which clothes you have worn, and which you have not. If you haven't worn something for an entire season, remove it from your closet and donate it.

Q: My bedroom is directly above the garage, which I have heard is bad Feng Shui because of the empty space below it. What can I do to cure this problem?

Q: We are house hunting, and we've noticed the style of house we like usually has the master bedrooms located over a two-car garage. I know it's not the best placement, but should this be a deal-breaker? We have a wonderfully loving relationship (our bedroom now is in the marriage area), and I wouldn't want to jeopardize that. If we do find our dream home and the master bedroom is over the garage, how can we manage it so we have the most auspicious Feng Shui?

A: The Feng Shui issue with a bedroom over a garage is that your relationship is unsupported because there's a void underneath, rather than an actual room. Plus, the real and symbolic fumes from the cars below aren't conducive to good health. It's not necessarily true that most homes have a master bedroom in this location, but it might be the particular style of home you have been looking at, or a popular regional design. Look for a home with the master bedroom in the Love/Relationship area, like your current home. But, if you do choose a house with a garage under the master bedroom, some of the corrections include putting a thick rug on the bedroom floor, avoid keeping trash and junk in the garage, and placing a mirror under the bed to deflect any negative energy. The mirror should face down to push away anything negative.

Q: I have trouble falling asleep since I moved into my new condo, so I am constantly tired. It's a small unit and I don't have as much storage space, so are lots of things that don't have a place yet (like the laundry) end up in my bedroom. Any suggestions?

A: Without seeing your space, it's impossible to determine exactly what is contributing to your sleeplessness. But, there are three classic problems I find in bedrooms that have a negative effect on sleep: piles of laundry, stacks of books, and a mirror at the foot of the bed. Since you have at least one of these sleep-stealers, remove the laundry and see what happens. A bedroom should be a place reserved for rest and romance, with no distractions.

Q: I recently purchased a small jade plant and put it on my desk at work because I heard it was a good-luck symbol. I was wondering if this is also the kind of low-maintenance plant I can put in my bedroom?

A: A jade plant is ideal in an office because its round leaves symbolize coins, and therefore, wealth. Any plant with rounded leaves is also a good choice for a bedroom. Avoid plants that have sharp or spiky edges since they send harsh energy that could disturb your sleep. While living plants are always the first choice, if you can't grow them because of limited lighting, it's acceptable to use high-quality silk plants, photos of plants or trees, or fabrics with leafy patterns in your bedroom.

Bedroom Mirrors

Q: We moved into a new house and love everything except the mirrored closet doors in the master bedroom. I have read this is not considered good Feng Shui, but we can't afford to replace them for a while. Any other options you can suggest?

A: Hang a curtain rod at the top the mirrored doors and hang lightweight solid curtains that match your wall color. Tie back the curtains during the day so the mirrors can reflect light into your room, but keep them closed at night to calm the yang energy of the mirrors while you sleep.

Q: I have just bought a bed frame that has a book case with a mirror in the center. Please tell me what to do. It is too late to return it. Could I cover the mirror up with pictures?

A: A mirror in the headboard above your head can keep you from having a peaceful night's rest and affect your health because it activates energy. If you can't remove the mirror, you can cover it with art that shows a restful scene. This isn't the place for art that's too colorful or too busy. Or, you can drape the mirror at night with a cloth or a scarf.

Q: I want to hang a full-length mirror in our bedroom, but I'm not sure where to place it. I read some things about Feng Shui saying not to face it directly towards a door, so I was thinking of attaching it to the front of the master bathroom door. What do you think?

A: You're right that a mirror shouldn't be placed across from a doorway because it sends the positive energy right back where it came from so it never reaches you in the room. Also, a mirror shouldn't be placed at the foot of a bed because it interferes with peaceful sleep. A mirror on a bathroom door is fine, as long as you can't see yourself in it from the bed, and if it's not in a location where it's the first thing you see in the morning.

CHAPTER 3: BEDROOMS, BEDS, AND BLISSFUL SLEEP

SUCCESS STORY

*Lydia Fills Her
Empty Nest*

Lydia's only child had left for college, and her daughter's bedroom quickly became a place for Lydia to dump things. She called me for a consultation for her apartment because she was missing her daughter and wanted to find a new use for the room that might help her with the transition to an empty nest. Just a few weeks after our session, I received this e-mail from her:

Here's what Lydia wrote:

❝ First of all, I want to tell you how much I am enjoying my new reading room! I can't believe it was so simple to move out all the junk I was storing in my daughter's former bedroom to create a peaceful space, as you suggested. Now I miss her less, because I am using the room as a library where I can keep the books that we both have read. I followed your suggestion to replace the bed with a sleeper sofa. It's a place for me to read and for her to come home to! This is so much better than using the room as a storage dump. The images you suggested for the walls make a big difference, because the view of city rooftop air conditioner units from the window is uninspiring. Now, I look at walls that are covered with prints of lush green forests and a bubbling stream. I'm so glad I engaged your services and followed through. This is an exciting process. Next step: I am going to tackle the mess that I call my office. ❞

Q: In your newsletter, you've been answering a lot of questions about mirrors in your bedroom, and I hope you don't mind one more. I have two mirrors in my bedroom that face each other. Is this a bad thing, and should I move or get rid of one of them? Can't wait to hear back from you. Also, I love your blog and book!

A: It's not considered good Feng Shui to have mirrors facing each other, because the chi bounces back and forth between them and never settles down. This over-active chi can be especially unsettling in a bedroom when you're trying to sleep. I recommend you remove one of the mirrors. If you must keep the two mirrors in the same location, drape one at night with scarves or fabric.

Q: In one of your newsletters, you said, "When you hang a mirror on the wall, you no longer see the wall, but rather, you see what the mirror reflects." We have a mirror on one of our bedroom dressers, and I've always been afraid to put anything such as a picture of us or a tray of coins or bills on it for fear it would reflect against that and would be harmful. Do you mind clarifying?

A: Feng Shui principles recommend limiting the number of mirrors in a bedroom to no more than one, and that one should be placed so you don't see yourself in it while in bed or the first thing in the morning. That's because mirrors activate the chi in a room, and we want the chi in a bedroom to be less active so it supports rest and romance. A mirror on your dresser that reflects a photo would symbolically double whatever energy you're experiencing in your relationship, while a mirror reflecting money would symbolically double it. Make sure the photo near your mirror is current, and if you want to keep money on the tray, include at least one high-value bill. If the mirror is reflecting the bed, move the dresser to another location.

CHAPTER 3: BEDROOMS, BEDS, AND BLISSFUL SLEEP

Beds

Q: We just moved into a new house and placed the bed with the window behind it. We haven't slept well since the move. Do you recommend we move the bed over so the window is not behind it? We do have other options for placing it.

A: The Feng Shui recommendation is to avoid placing the head of the bed in front of a window. Move the bed where you can place the head against a solid wall, with a clear view out of the door but not facing directly out the door.

Q: Do I need a footboard? My husband and I have gone back and forth on this because we like the look, but we're dealing with an older home's master bedroom and space is limited. Is it essential?

A: There are two things to consider about a footboard. First, you need a footboard to give you protection if your feet face directly out the bedroom door when you're in bed. If that's not an issue, a foot board isn't essential. Second, if a footboard makes your room seems too crowded, the chi won't flow around you. Here's something else to think about when deciding about a footboard: it's easier to make the bed without one, and it's less likely you'll stub your little toe—I speak from experience here!

Q: I am looking for a new headboard and want something different this time. Do the different shapes have different meanings in Feng Shui?

A: The main reason for a headboard in Feng Shui is to ground and support you while you sleep, but the shape you choose can also affect your relationship and prosperity. A square headboard represents the Earth Element, which symbolizes stability and balance, nurtures a relationship, and stabilizes finances. A rectangular headboard is also a good choice because it symbolizes the Wood Element that brings growth and expansion. A triangular headboard has a point that represents the Fire Element. Although you do want to add Fire to relationships, this shape for a headboard could cause arguments and disputes. A semi-circular headboard represents the Metal Element, which symbolizes elegance and an abundant lifestyle. A curvy headboard represents the Water Element, which is constantly moving, so it's not recommended because it could mean instability in your prosperity and relationships.

SUCCESS STORY

Karen Replaces Her
Mirrored Bedroom Furniture

• •

When I walked into Karen's bedroom and saw the mirrored black lacquer headboard and matching dresser with a mirrored front, I knew the mirrors were the explanation for her sleep problems and inability to relax, not to mention what she called a "lackluster" love life. Mirrors activate the chi in a bedroom, and Karen's mirror arrangement created a bouncing of reflections back and forth across the room, which was interfering with peaceful sleep. But Karen was not about to give up her furniture, or even agree to drape scarves across the mirrors at night, arguing that she had the furniture for more than a decade. I persisted, she resisted, and we finally agreed to disagree. Then I received a welcome surprise.

Here's what Karen wrote:

❝ It was a delight to meet you last Saturday. You'll be extremely proud of and excited for me. After you left, I agreed with you that the mirrors had to go, since I realized my sleep and relationship problems started long ago when I bought that furniture. I went shopping the next day. It actually didn't take me long to find what I can live with for another decade: a unique, classy, and elegant new wood bedroom set. I chose wood, like you suggested, to grow a relationship. They delivered it the next day. I also hung a print of a man and woman in a loving embrace. I have been on an emotional and psychological high since then because I'm already sleeping soundly and having wonderful dreams. Now, I'm ready for that new man in my life, and as you said, the mirrors aren't reflecting him away. ❞

CHAPTER 3: BEDROOMS, BEDS, AND BLISSFUL SLEEP

Q & A

CHILDREN'S BEDROOMS

Q: I've heard that bunk beds are considered bad in Feng Shui. What cure can help a bunk bed for my daughter who doesn't like sleeping in the bottom bunk? My two girls like sharing a room, but the younger one doesn't like being on the bottom.

A: The Feng Shui concern with bunk beds is that the energy around the lower bed could be compressed, creating heavy chi and difficulty sleeping for the child who sleeps in the bottom bed. Also, the weight of the top bed pushes down and can cause health issues. What's worse, the child on the bottom may feel inferior. If you have to have bunk beds, first be sure they are sturdy and solid. Place a mirror facing up on the bottom of the top bunk (that is, your daughter in the lower bunk will see the back of the mirror) to symbolically push away the top bunk. I recommend dime-, nickel-, or quarter-size lightweight mirrors that you can find at a craft store. Paint the underside of the upper bunk with images of the night sky or of a blue sky and puffy clouds so the child on the bottom doesn't feel trapped. Or, cover the bottom of the upper bunk with a solid piece of wood and paint it a sky-blue color, tack a piece of fabric to it, or hang a poster of constellations. The fabric will shield the child from the harsh energy of the sharp edges projecting from the slats of the top bunk. If you can replace the bunks, consider a trundle bed where one bed is stored under the other and pulls out for sleeping, so both girls will be on the same level.

Q: My 5-year-old daughter doesn't like to sleep in her room in our new house. My friend told me that the problem may be the mirrored closet doors, but we don't want to replace the mirrors because they make her small room look bigger.

A: Mirrors in a bedroom can interfere with sleep, especially for a young child. If you can't replace the mirrored doors with solid ones, hang curtains from a rod attached above the doors. Keep the curtains open and tied back during the day, then close them and hide the mirrors at night. Another way to help a child feel comfortable, especially if their room isn't located near their parents, is to place current photos of parents, grandparents, or godparents in the room near the bed.

Q: Do you have a foolproof system for dealing with all the toys and games in children's rooms?

A: *Foolproof?* Nope! *Useful?* Yes! The Feng Shui solution for clutter in a child's room is to sort, store, and simplify. First, sort out your children's clothes and toys to see what they really need. Next, store out-of-season clothes. Simplify by removing extra toys and clothes until what's left fits into the available space. Remember that closets and cabinets that are made for adults don't always work for children, so modify what you already have. For example, for young children, you can remove the closet doors, lower the rods, and buy child-size hangers to make the closet more accessible. Use containers or baskets on the floor of the closet for toys and clothes.

Q: My daughter's bedroom is very small, so the only options for her bed are under a window or on the wall that backs up to the bathroom pipes. Which location is better?

A: While neither location is ideal in Feng Shui terms, it's better to place the bed under the window. The other location, sleeping with her head against pipes, could result in health problems. Whichever location you choose, be sure to place a solid wood or fabric headboard behind her. If she has to sleep against the pipes, hang a mirror on the wall over the bed, with the mirror side facing the wall to "push away" the negative energy. Decorate the back of the mirror or cover with fabric so it doesn't look unattractive. If she sleeps under the window, make sure you have solid window treatments on the window, and remember to close them each night.

Q: I am re-decorating my daughter's room. Would you suggest a metal headboard or a wooden headboard?

A: I recommend wood headboards for children because they are both the Wood Element material that symbolizes growth and expansion, and the Earth Element color that helps ground the child.

Fast 5

Position Your Child's Room for Success

If you want your child to succeed at school, try arranging his or her bedroom according to these five Feng Shui guidelines:

1. **Bed.** Position the headboard against a wall where your child can clearly see the door, but avoid a location where your child's feet point directly out the door.

2. **Computer.** Locate the computer away from the bed and shut it and other electronic devices off at night to reduce the electromagnetic frequencies (EMFs) in your child's room.

3. **Display.** Hang a bulletin board or white board to showcase achievements, and use it to display your child's awards and citations, as well as artwork, report cards, and special papers to remind your child he or she is succeeding and moving forward.

4. **Storage.** Remove under-bed storage to encourage a good night's sleep. If you must store things under your child's bed due to space limitations, choose soft items like out-of-season clothes or linens. Anything else is considered too stimulating and detracts from peaceful sleep.

5. **Family.** Display current photos of parents, grandparents, and happy family gatherings to help communicate love and security to a child. With all that family support around the room, your child is sure to succeed.

Q: My son is ready to move into his first "big-boy" bed, and we want to buy one that will grow with him. Many of the beds we're looking at have a built-in storage drawer underneath. Is this good or bad Feng Shui? I do store thing in boxes below our own bed so using drawers makes good sense to me.

A: The Feng Shui recommendation is to avoid storing anything under your bed to allow the chi to circulate completely around you, which in turn supports restful sleep and good health. Choose a bed for your son that doesn't have drawers or built-in storage underneath. If you must have extra storage under his bed, use it for soft things only. That also goes for your own bed.

Bedroom Colors

Q: I want to repaint my 9-year-old son's room to assure he has a good year in school. What colors are best for the walls in a child's bedroom? His favorite color is blue, is that OK for his room?

A: My general recommendation for a bedroom color for a child's room is to choose one that most closely resembles a skin tone to encourage peaceful sleep. That means a range of colors from ivory to mahogany. Soft, warm colors create a sense of stability for a child, so avoid cold colors like pure white or gray. A lot of people want to use blue for a boy's bedroom, which is also good because it's a restful color. Just be sure you avoid an icy or cold shade of blue.

Q: My teenage son wants to paint his bedroom ceiling black, but I'm thinking that's not a good idea. My gut says to stick to a white ceiling. What does Feng Shui think about this?

A: A black ceiling will make it seem like there's no ceiling or roof over your son's room, and that will leave him symbolically "exposed" to the elements. His health could be compromised, and he could be more vulnerable to accidents. Also, this would bring too much yin, or heavy, energy to the room, which could negatively affect his studies. Go with your gut and paint the ceiling a soft white color.

CHAPTER 3: BEDROOMS, BEDS, AND BLISSFUL SLEEP

Q: What colors are best for the walls in a child's bedroom? My daughter is choosing between light pink and teal/aqua.

A: The most restful colors for the walls in any bedroom are skin tones. For your daughter's room, I recommend the light pink instead of teal/aqua. Avoid white or any icy variation of a color because these are too cold and discourage restful sleep.

Q: My shy 6-year-old daughter is starting school and is uncomfortable meeting new people. Is there a specific color I can add to her bedroom that will help her better adjust to new people and new surroundings?

A: Start by adding some green to her bedroom, the Feng Shui Wood Element that represents growth and supports people who feel unsettled in a new environment. Another good color is a light pink, the gentle version of the Fire Element and the color of universal love, to help reassure her that she is loved at home. Pink and green is an especially soothing combination of Feng Shui Elements. You could also add some blue, the Water Element, to calm and relax her, and to lessen her anxieties.

Q: I'm doing a major renovation of my master bedroom. I love the idea of decorating it in only black and white. But, I've been reading a lot about Feng Shui colors and now I'm thinking it's not such a good idea. I don't sleep well as it is. What do you think?

A: Using only the colors black and white, a combination of the Water Element and Metal Element, will be too sharp contrast and high energy for your bedroom. Black is considered the color of a void, and for some people, it's associated with fear and dark energy. White is considered a cold and hard color. The combination of the two would contribute to your sleep issue rather than solve it. Instead of black and white, I recommend choosing neutral or skin tone colors like cream or beige for your bedroom. For interest and to encourage romance, you can add accents in Fire Element colors, like red, orange, or deep purple.

SUCCESS STORY

*Melissa Helps Her Child
Find Peaceful Sleep*

I received this encouraging note from my client Melissa, who was having trouble getting her young daughter to stay asleep in her own bed for the whole night. The child would start out in her own room, but sometime in the middle of the night, she would end up in her mom's bed. Neither one of them was getting a good night's sleep.

Here's what Melissa wrote:

❝ Thank you for the fact sheet on children's room. Right after our consultation, I started making some of those changes in my daughter's room to help her sleep better, and my efforts had an immediate payback: she is going to sleep earlier, staying in her room the whole night, and sleeping later! One thing I know helped was your suggestion to put a photo of the two of us in her room as a reminder to her that I'm always there for her, even when we're in different rooms. Also, as you suggested, I bought a storage unit with doors, and each night, we make it part of her routine to put away the toys she has been playing with. It works! I appreciate all the information you gave me. I can't tell you how excited I feel about the next steps. Seeing my house through your eyes has finally given me direction on what to do. I am looking forward to moving on with changes for the rest of my home. ❞

CHAPTER
4

ROOM BY ROOM

I love my job! People invite me into their homes, offices, and businesses. They show me their stuff. I tell them where to put it (where to put their stuff, that is), and they thank me for it. Then, they send me their success stories. What could be better?

We all have a lot of stuff, but we don't always know where to put it. That's why I was fascinated by data showing that changes in specific rooms can make you happier. According to the research by *Money* magazine and Lowe's home stores, 75% of people who had made home improvements within the past two years were happier, compared with 66% of people who hadn't made any changes. The study shows what we Feng Shui practitioners have long known: the rooms that affect happiness most are the living and family rooms, the master bedroom, and the kitchen. The study found that changes made in the garage, patio, and deck affected happiness least.

What's happening in your own rooms? Is your kitchen or dining room table so covered with paper that you can't serve a meal there? Are the kids' rooms so disorderly that you close the doors and try to ignore the chaos? Is your family room so overflowing with games and toys that there's no place to sit? Is your guest room accumulating so much junk that you put your visitors up in a hotel?

If you answered yes to even one of these questions, don't worry, you're not alone, as you'll see from the questions in this section. In most cases, the Feng Shui *cures* or remedies for these rooms are simple and involve things like re-arranging furniture, changing wall colors, replacing artwork, and removing clutter. As we go room by room, you'll find that other people are struggling with the same issues in their rooms that you're experiencing. When I show up for a consultation, clients sometimes want to skip their attached garage, or basement, or attic. Sorry guys, every room counts. If it's an attached structure,

CHAPTER 4: ROOM BY ROOM

it's considered a room of your home, and it should be treated with the same care you give to all other rooms.

Wait, Carol, you're telling me I have to give some thought to the extra bedroom where I keep all the stuff I don't know where else to put?

Yup!

I get the most questions about bedrooms, and that's why I put the bedroom-related questions in their own section. In this chapter, I've arranged the rest of the rooms in alphabetical order, rather than by the number of questions I've received about each room.

> *The reality of a building*
> *is the space within.*
> *— Frank Lloyd Wright*

Q & A

ROOM BY ROOM

Attics

Q: How does an attic affect the Feng Shui of a room below it? The entrance to my attic is a pull-down stairway in the ceiling of my bedroom. There's a lot of junk up there. Is there something I need to do?

A: In Feng Shui terms, what's in an attic weighs down on the occupants of the house. *What* you keep in your attic is even more important. An attic that's crammed full of items that are unneeded, unused, and unloved not only represents stagnant and stuck chi, but it also represents the weight of the past on your shoulders. This is especially negative when the attic is located above a bedroom. Clear the clutter in your attic and you'll lighten your load and make room for new things to find you. Paint the entrance to the attic stairs the same color as the bedroom ceiling to help it disappear.

Q: Can I ignore my attic when I use the bagua? It's a mess with all of our unused stuff right and we hate to go up there. We don't use the attic like a real room.

A: The good and bad news is that every room in your home counts, and you do have to pay attention to it. If a part of your home is messy and filled with objects you don't need, don't want, and don't use, you're sending a message of neglect to that area of your life. It's time to declutter and get rid of everything in the attic that you don't need. Clutter is especially negative when it's located above your head, and it symbolically weighs down on you.

**Q: I enjoy your monthly tips and reading about people's successes using Feng Shui. I'm trying to transition from a full-time job to a part time position closer to my home. I cleared the attic and move up a desk to use as my base for job hunting. I'm rereading your book and checking each of my room to see where I have something that resists change, and

I'm wondering how critical is the attic for career moves because my office is up there?

A: There are a lot of issues rolled into your question about finding a new job. What's above you in the attic symbolically weighs down on you, so if those areas are cluttered or filled with things that have negative meaning, it could symbolize being held back and weighted-down in your job search. This is especially important if you're working amidst all these unwanted and unneeded items every day. Clear out everything from your attic that you no longer need, and watch your job situation improve.

Basements

Q: We are renovating our basement to put in a home gym. What color should we paint it? I'm thinking about yellow or blue with red accents to perk thing up.

A: Yellow, which represents the Earth Element in Feng Shui, is good for a basement workout room because it's both cheerful and energizing. You could also consider green, the Wood Element, which is the color that represents growth. On the other hand, blue, the Water Element, might not work in a basement gym because it calms the body and makes it work harder to elevate heart rate. You should also avoid using too much red, the Fire Element, because it could add too much fire to an already heated activity. [Also see *Workout Equipment* section.]

Q: My husband and I started a major basement clearing project. We made great progress in one area, and then we got stuck and couldn't decide what to keep and what to throw out. I am afraid I will need the item somewhere down the line. Any advice?

A: In Feng Shui, holding on to items you think you may need in the future is considered a symptom of living in the past and a fear of moving forward. As you clear clutter in the basement, pick up each item and ask yourself this question: *If I were moving, would I pay a mover to take this item with me?* Specifically, I'm asking if you would pay the cost to wrap it, box it, load it on a truck, transport it, move it into a new home, unbox it, unwrap it, and put it in place! If the answer is no, you can safely toss, donate, or sell the item.

Q: I am a firm believer in getting rid of clutter. Things like unused clothes and broken electronics are banished from my house regularly. However, I do have "stuff" that I want to save that I store in the basement, like extra rolls of wallpaper, furniture that is not currently being used (including the floor length mirror you had me remove from my bedroom!). It turns out I am storing these things in the Wealth corner. Does this explain why I haven't made much money this year??

A: Great question, which I will answer with more questions: *What are you saving all this stuff for?* Nothing new flows into your life until you make room for it, so it's time to sell or donate the mirror and the other furniture. *Are you ever going to need the wallpaper?* If the paper has been on the walls for some time, it is probably faded and won't match the rolls you're saving. If you're storing unneeded stuff in your Wealth area, think about the message you're sending out into the universe about the prosperity you want to flow into your life. Plus, what's stored in your basement acts as a foundation. But, a foundation of things you don't need isn't a supportive one. A good rule of thumb is this: if you haven't used an item within the past year, get rid of it.

Bathrooms

Q: My master bathroom is in the wealth part of the bagua. I know this isn't good but there's no way I'm going to renovate the whole house just to move it. Ideas, please!

A: In contemporary Feng Shui, I like to think there's almost always a remedy for an inauspicious situation. Water is associated with wealth, but in bathrooms, there's too much negative water—it goes down the toilet as waste and down the drains as dirt. To balance this, you need to symbolically dry up some of that water by adding the appropriate Element to the room. To remedy the draining effect of the bathroom in the center of a home, paint at least one wall in the Earth Element (yellow or brown) to absorb the water. If the bathroom is in the Wealth area, add the Fire Element (red, orange, or deep purple) to the walls or accessories. Or, you can place ceramic objects in the room to balance the overabundance of water. Depending on what it would reflect, you could also hang a long mirror on the outside of the door to deflect the chi, so it won't drain out of this area. As with all bathrooms, keep the toilet seat lid down.

Q: We are building a new house and just started working with an architect who is open to Feng Shui. Where is the best location for bathrooms?

A: The ancient Chinese who developed Feng Shui didn't have indoor plumbing, so they didn't have to deal with locating the bathrooms. The contemporary answer to your question is to draw the floor plan of the house and then divide it into the nine guas (or areas) of the bagua, then locate the bathrooms on the line between the guas so they aren't totally in one gua. It's also good to think about any areas of your life that are weak, and try to avoid placing the bathrooms in the gua associated with that aspect of life. In general, avoid locating a bathroom in the center of the home, which is the Grounding area. This area is activated by the Earth Element, and it would be an especially inauspicious location for all that water.

Q: I am an avid reader of your ezine and blog and have a question for you. I'm buying a second home and the front door opens directly to the staircase, and directly at the top of the stairs is a bathroom, then you need to turn right to get to the living area. I know that a bathroom at the top of the stairs isn't good, and that putting a lush plant at the landing would help, but since it is a second home and I won't be there to care for the plant, that's not an option. What other choices do I have?

A: Sounds like you have a bunch of issues going on with the home. First, you were on the right track when you thought about placing a lush plant on the landing to pull up the chi. The good news is that a high-quality silk plant is an acceptable alternative to a living plant because it's made from a fabric. Avoid using dried flowers or plants in this location. Second, when you do use the house, check your silk plant and replace it when it's too faded and dusty to rescue. Keep the bathroom door closed so the chi coming upstairs doesn't symbolically get flushed down the toilet.

Fast 5

Dry Out Your Bathroom

Is your bathroom the last room you want to think about? Is it situated in a less-than-ideal bagua location for your home? Try these five tips:

1. **Door**. Keep your bathroom doors closed to prevent the positive chi from co-mingling with the negative energy coming from bathroom waste.

2. **Crystal**. Hang a round faceted crystal from the ceiling halfway between the door and the toilet to continue to break up the chi from going down the drains.

3. **Plants**. Grow plants in your bathroom to represent the Wood Element, which helps to reduce some of the excess negative bathroom energy.

4. **Color**. Add a touch of red, like candles, towels, or silk flowers, to increase the Fire Element.

5. **Toilet Seat**. Develop the habit of putting the toilet seat and lid down when not in use, to keep the positive chi from going down the drain.

Q: We bought a house that has a bathroom right in the center on the first floor, which I know is considered negative in Feng Shui. We're doing extensive renovations before we move in, and I want to convert the bathroom into a closet. Will this remove the negativity, or will the plumbing underneath continue to be a problem?

A: Water represents wealth in Feng Shui, but in a bathroom, water is symbolically contaminated because it goes down the drains as dirty water and is flushed down the toilet as waste. Therefore, we make adjustments in

CHAPTER 4: ROOM BY ROOM

bathrooms to symbolically dry up some of the water. If the room is no longer a place where water is flowing down the drains and where waste is going down a toilet, there's no reason it should have a negative effect on the house. Paint the inside of your new closet yellow—the Earth Element—to balance any residual effect from when it was a bathroom.

Q: I have been looking for a new job with little success. I have tried to use a Feng Shui bagua, and I think the bathroom is in my career area. What should I do?

A: A bathroom in your Career area could symbolize "flushing away" all your career luck. Keep the toilet lid down and the door to the bathroom closed at all times. Find an image that symbolizes successfully finding your new job, and hang it in the bathroom, preferably in the Helpful People area of the room.

Q: We have found a home that we would love to buy, but the bathroom is located in the center of the home. We hate to pass on this house. Can this situation be cured?

A: To remedy the draining effect of the bathroom in the center of a home, paint at least one wall in the Earth Element colors (yellow or brown) to absorb the water. You can also place tile or ceramic objects in the room to balance the overabundance of water. Depending on what it would reflect, you could hang a long mirror on the outside of the door to deflect the chi, so it won't drain out of this area. As with all bathrooms, keep the toilet seat and lid down.

Q: I downloaded a bagua map from your website and realized that there is a bathroom in my prosperity area. Help! How do I fix this, so all my wealth doesn't go down the drain?

A: Water is associated with wealth, but in bathrooms, there's too much negative water because it goes down the toilet as waste and down the drains as dirt. To balance this, you need to symbolically dry up some of that water by adding the appropriate Element to the room. With a bathroom located in the Wealth area, you have several options. You can paint the room or one wall in a Fire Element color (red, orange, or deep purple). Or, you can choose towels in those colors. It's especially important to hang artwork with images that make you feel wealthy, abundant, and prosperous. Resist the urge to decorate with watery beach scenes in this room because you don't need to add any more water.

Q: How do I balance the energy in my bathroom that's near the kitchen? The fixtures are all old and cruddy and the faucet leaks, but we can't afford to renovate it right now.

A: Bathrooms present some challenges since they have an overabundance of wet, cold chi from the excess Water Element in the room. According to classical Feng Shui, when we started bringing bathrooms indoors, we created an imbalance of water in our environment. Too much water isn't advisable, especially water that's "contaminated" by the waste and dirt that goes down the drains. This is especially inauspicious when the bathroom is located near the kitchen. Decorate the bathroom in colors and objects that represent the Wood Element to symbolically soak up the water and grow your wealth, especially the colors green and teal and images of flowers and forests. Display plants (natural or silk) that have an upward shape, and hang artwork with images that make you feel wealthy, abundant, and prosperous. Fix the leaky faucets immediately, because this represents a slow drain on your finances, and start budgeting to upgrade the fixtures as soon as possible.

Q: The door to my powder room is directly across from the front door. I read that this is bad Feng Shui and that I should hang a mirror on the door, but I've also read that I shouldn't have a mirror directly across from the front door. Major confusion going on here.

A: The front door is called the *mouth of chi,* where positive chi enters your home. The concern about a bathroom directly across from the front door is that this positive energy flows right into the bathroom and down the drain. That means its positive power is lost before it reaches the rest of the house. You're right that a mirror across from the front door is negative because it sends the positive energy right back out the house. Hanging a mirror on the bathroom door isn't a good choice for your situation. The simple solution is to keep the bathroom door closed all the time. Also, you can create a diversion or focal point near the bathroom door to direct the energy away from that room and toward the rest of the house. This could be something like an especially compelling piece of art or a floor plant.

Q: I keep my toilet lids down in my home, but my sister likes to keep the toilet lids up in hers for what she calls "quick access" by the men in her family. She is always in debt. Is there a Feng Shui solution to stopping her money drain other than closing the toilet lid?

A: If your sister is always in debt and she always keeps her toilet lids up, she could try keeping them down and see what happens. In addition to the Feng Shui symbolism of wealth "going down the drain," open toilets are unattractive. There could be many Feng Shui adjustments she could make to help stop the flow of wealth out of her life, but it won't hurt to start by teaching the men in her family the simple habit of keeping the lids down.

Q: I live in a small condo with a windowless bathroom. Is that bad Feng Shui? It also has an old fluorescent fixture above the sink.

A: Although a windowless room isn't a bad situation, it's certainly not the most ideal. Connect with the natural world outside by hanging artwork that depicts the real world, like trees, flowers, rivers, etc. Make sure the room is well-lit, using full-spectrum bulbs that simulate natural daylight. Replace the fluorescent lighting, because it represents the hard Metal Element.

Q: Please help me. Every book I read says you should not have the bathroom in your SW corner if you want a fulfilling relationship, however, I cannot afford to move and mine is located there. I have just lost my relationship and am devastated.

A: On a classical Feng Shui bagua, the SW corner would be the Relationship area. So, if that's where your bathroom is located, yes, you could be symbolically flushing your relationships away. Place something red in the bathroom to represent the Fire Element (red candle, ribbon, towel, etc.), keep the toilet lid down, and hang a romantic picture in the bathroom that shows two people in a happy situation. Avoid adding any water images to the room.

SUCCESS STORY

*Ana Opens Up
Her Dining Room*

I was happy to receive the good news from my client Anna that she got engaged. But the bad news was that she and her fiancé had been having difficulty with his ex-wife meddling into their affairs. She called me for a consultation because it looked like the wedding was on an indefinite hold. We made a lot of changes in their home, including getting rid of almost an entire storage shed of stuff she was holding on to for her family members. Inside, there were overhead shelves on all four walls near the dining room ceiling that displayed pottery and knick-knacks. I explained the shelves were symbolically weighing down on the couple, and I recommended removing them.

Here's what Ana wrote:

❝ Immediately after you left, I removed the pottery and stuff from the overhead shelves, and then we took down all but one shelf. But, about a month later, I realized that I still had pottery on the remaining long shelf on the wall over the window in the dining room. I had removed all the others as you recommended, but I'm not sure why I hadn't removed that one. When I finally got up there to take it down, I remembered that my fiancé had acquired all these things with his ex-wife! He didn't care about them now, so I got rid of all of it. I was surprised how much bigger and more open the room felt. It's amazing how that also opened up our relationship, and everything changed after that. His ex has calmed down and has actually been nice. I guess it was

(continued)

CHAPTER 4: ROOM BY ROOM

> like she had been watching us from above (which was kind of creepy now that I think about it). The opportunities in my life have opened up, and I was able to finally start the online business I told you about. Oh, I also sent emails to all four of my brothers and told them to come take their stuff from the shed within the next month or I'm calling a junk removal service. 〞

Dining Rooms

Q: I was planning to host a family dinner in my newly-redecorated dining room, and thinking of wearing red because I read that was lucky. But, after reading your tip about avoiding red at family gatherings because it could lead to arguments, I wonder if I should choose another color. Since I had the dining room table refinished and added stained wood details, there is a lot of wood in the room.

A: You were probably thinking about wearing red because you instinctively felt there was too much of the Wood Element in the dining room. Red, the Fire Element, will reduce the Wood Element in the same way that actual fire will consume any wood in its path. But, it could also add too much heat to the conversation. Instead of adding Fire by wearing red, add the Metal Element instead, because it will symbolically "cut" Wood and reduce it. You can do this by displaying actual metal objects or wearing metallic and pastel colors like silver, white, or pastels. Enjoy your gorgeous table!

Q: There are two entrances to my dining room. Which one do I use to orient the bagua map?

A: When there's more than one doorway or entry to a room, orient the bagua from the entrance you primarily use to enter that room. In the case of a dining room, this would typically be the entrance your guests would use, rather than the entrance from the kitchen.

Enclosed Porches

Q: We have an enclosed screened porch off our family room that we use all spring, summer, and early fall, but it isn't heated so we don't use it in the winter. Should we treat it as a room when using the bagua to map our house?

A: Yes, an enclosed porch that's connected to your house and that you use on a regular basis is considered part of your home and should be included in the bagua. Be sure to decorate the porch with the same care you use for other rooms in your home, rather than storing the old furniture in this area. And, try to enter the porch occasionally during the winter months when you don't use it, even if it is only to dust the furniture and sweep away the cobwebs. You could also keep a brightly-colored silk flower display on the porch in the off-season to bring some life to this area. Match the color of the flowers to the bagua area your porch occupies.

Foyers and Entries

Q: Can I place a mirror in my foyer next to my front door?

A: Yes, next to the door is fine, as long as it reflects an attractive view. Avoid placing a mirror directly across from your front door because it reflects the good energy that enters your home right back out the door.

Q: What is the best shape rug for an entry area? There's a hallway from the front door that leads to the patio door.

A: I prefer octagon, oval, or round to slow down and circulate the chi as it enters your home. Avoid a long runner from the foyer down the hall, especially if your front door lines up with the back door. Doors that line up represent a *poison arrow* pulling the chi out of your house, and a long runner will accentuate the problem.

CHAPTER 4: ROOM BY ROOM

Garages

Q: I looked at the bagua chart in your book, and my garage is in the Helpful People/Mentors area of my house. We keep so much stuff in the garage, I can't even park one of the cars there. What can I do? I run a business from home and need more clients.

A: Treat your garage with the same care you give to the rest of the rooms inside your home. Specifically, you can activate the energy in that area by first clearing all the unnecessary items out of the garage, then decorating it with images and objects that represent being supported by others. Don't be afraid to hang artwork in your garage!

Q: I am trying to help my elderly mother clear the clutter out of her garage, but she is being resistant to getting rid of anything. I keep setting aside a whole day to work on the garage, but she won't budge. The most frustrating part is that the garage takes up the entire right side of the house, which I know includes the love, creativity, and helpers areas. I put a mirror inside the door reflecting it all back into the garage. Was that the wrong thing to do?

A: My concern about the mirror is that it's reflecting the clutter back into the garage, and therefore doubling it rather than reducing it. Plus, the placement of the mirrors is keeping the positive energy from entering three critical bagua areas of your home that the garage occupies. Try removing the mirror and see if that opens up your mother's ability to deal with the clutter.

Q: My husband enters our home from the garage and rarely uses the front door. I use the front door 60% of the time. How should I position the bagua?

A: No matter what entrance you or your husband use, position the bagua from the front door because that's where the energy will enter. Stand at the front door facing into your home and hold the bagua chart in front of you, draw the shape of the home, and map out the different areas. See if you can convince your husband to use the front door occasionally.

SUCCESS STORY

Ted Decorates His Garage

My long-time client Ted had made many Feng Shui changes in his home and office in the past that resulted in good things flowing for the entire family. However, when he called me for a return consultation, things were tense at his home because the company he worked for had started to lay off employees. Ted feared that his division would be hit next. He was taking the obvious steps of sending out resumes and activating his network, but he wanted to make a few more Feng Shui changes to move the positive energy toward finding a new job quickly. Ted's Helpful People/Mentors area was in his garage, and it was a mess. I recommended he activate the energy in that area by first clearing all the unnecessary items out of the garage to open it up to possibilities, then decorating it with images that represented a peaceful job transition.

Here's what Ted wrote:

❝ At first, I was hesitant to hang some job-related things in the garage because it seemed silly, but my wife reminded me that Feng Shui had worked for us before. So I took your advice and hung up the business card from the head of the company that I had interviewed with, and I put up artwork with a flowing river image, along with some other career-related items. Wouldn't you know it, the day before I received my "pink slip," the new company offered me a great job! And I had enough leave accumulated that I could take a short vacation before starting the new job. Feng Shui saved the day for us, again. ❞

CHAPTER 4: ROOM BY ROOM

Home Offices

Q: I work from a home office. Where do I keep a paper shredder?

A: The general recommendation is to avoid keeping a paper shredder in the Wealth area of your home where it symbolically shreds your money. Beyond that, the best location might depend on how you view the purpose of the shredder. For example, if you think of a shredder as something that helps keep you safe by destroying data that could be stolen, you would locate it in the Helpful People corner of your home office, or wherever you pay your bills.

Q: My question is what to do about my home office in the guest bedroom now that we have a guest coming for a 2-month stay? I'm thinking I want to move my laptop and current papers to the unused dining room temporarily. I'm feeling a bit dislocated, so maybe there's a Feng Shui fix to help me feel settled. Also, will the desk and chair left in the guest room with other office stuff bother my guest?

A: The key words in your question are "unused dining room." Since it sounds like you don't eat meals there, you have control over alternative uses for the space. Can that room become your office? Depending on how open the dining room is to the kitchen and/or family room where everyone gathers, you might need to screen off your work area with a floor screen or standing plants. That way you can symbolically open up your office in the morning by moving the screen and close it down for the night by replacing it. It will also help to move as many work-related items as feasible from your current office to the new location to make you feel more settled and less temporary. Considering that you'll only be in there for two months, is there room to actually move the desk and chair into the dining room temporarily instead of using the dining room table? Even if you don't move out the desk and chair, I hope your guest will be thankful for your generous offer of a room for two months, which would more than make up for any small inconvenience of extra furniture.

Q: I have a desk in my home-based business that came from my late father's accounting office, and I love it because it reminds me of him. But, I have to admit it's too huge for the room. Sometimes I like sitting

behind it, but sometimes, it makes me feel small because it's so big, and it's the wrong height for my laptop. Should I get rid of it?

A: The size of your desk influences your success at work, so it's important to choose the right one. A desk that's too big can make you feel like you aren't up to the challenges of your work, while a desk that's too small makes you feel overwhelmed by the work you have to do. Just like Goldilocks, you need to find the desk that's "just right." I recommend you honor your father's memory by keeping the desk, but move it to another room where it can be a showpiece instead of a work space. Then, treat yourself to a new, appropriate-size desk as a symbol of success.

Q: I don't have a problem keeping clutter under control at home, except for the small desk in my home office that is a disaster. I love my work, and I think I'm organized, but the stacks of paper just grow and grow. I'm heading into my busy season when I generate the most paper. Are there Feng Shui tips to help me get a grip on this before it gets out of control?

A: Office clutter issues relate to either having too much stuff, having too little storage space, or both. If your shelves, cabinets, and drawers are filled to capacity, clear out old files and supplies to make room to store those things that are on your desk but you don't use frequently. Another issue is the size of your desk. Is it adequate for the work to be done? If your desk is too small for the work that you do, it can make you feel overwhelmed and can lead to accumulation of piles of stuff. It's time for a new desk and storage options to help you control clutter.

Q: I work out of a first floor room in my home with floor-to-ceiling windows behind me. I love all the light, but sometimes, I feel like I am too exposed.

A: Windows behind you can make you feel exposed, vulnerable, uncontained, and consequently, overwhelmed. To remedy this situation, simulate a solid wall behind you by hanging window treatments like shutters, or shades that rise from the bottom up, to cover the bottom half of the window. Another option is to position a "wall" of plants on the floor behind you. You'll still be connected to nature and get the benefit of the light, but you'll also have privacy and protection.

SUCCESS STORY

Janis Triples Her Income

My client Janis hated going into her home office, and consequently, her business wasn't flourishing. I recommended she clear out everything that wasn't supporting her in order to make room for new business to find her.

Here's what Janis wrote:

❝ I followed your suggestions and cleared out everything that didn't remind me of success. This is only the short version of what I did, but I cleared the clutter, removed all the knick-knacks except for those that remind me of success and accomplishment, and moved some of the family photos to the den. I hung my framed certifications and awards, and put elegant things on the bookshelf and desk. I added living plants. I took out all the light-blue stuff and replaced it with silk flowers, vases, a soft throw, and pillows in rusts, reds, and browns. I have a green candle on my desk in a gold-rimmed platter with golden "coins" (they are really dark chocolate). I removed some of the chairs to make the room more spacious. Now, I love, love, love spending time in my office because it reflects my authentic, empowered self and inspires me to succeed. I spoke at the women's networking group where you and I first met, and they told me afterwards that I had the record attendance. As a result, my business has soared. Thank you for helping me to enjoy going to work again and for helping me to triple my income. ❞

Q: I have started to telecommute from my home office 3 days a week. My home office desk is much smaller than the one in my other office. Is that OK? Thanks!

Q: I work from an office outside my home for three days a week, and from home the other two. I have asked for a large desk at my office to offset the tiny one in my home workspace. Is that suitable to balance out my workload? Thanks!

A: Ideally, you would have the appropriate size desk in both locations, because your work from both offices. Wherever you have control over the size of your workspace, choose the largest one you can work at that fits in the room. The closer you can come to having the same size desk at the office and at home, the more successful you'll be at your job.

Q: I started a new job this week, and I will be working two days a week out of an extra bedroom that I am turning into a home office. What color should I paint the room to assure success?

A: The choice of color often depends on what kind of work you're doing. For example, red and burgundy (Fire Element) are energizing and good for people in sales and marketing; blues and greens (Water and Wood Element) are inspirational and support writing and creative professions; warm, earthy colors like yellow and gold (Earth Element) encourage collaboration; white and gray (Metal Element) are important for work that needs intense focus, but only use them as accents rather than on all walls, or they will make the room feel too cold.

Q: How can I create a sense of balance in my home office space?

A: Computers and all the other electronic equipment in the office are considered to be the Metal Element, which can be hard. To balance all this harshness, try adding the Water Element in the form of actual water like a fountain or a small fish bowl, or representations of water such as a mirror, curvy or patterned shapes, or the colors blue and black.

Q: My husband and I run a family business and share a home office. Lately, we seem to argue about every business decision. Could the problem be that our two desks face each other?

CHAPTER 4: ROOM BY ROOM

A: Placing two desks across from each other is considered to be a "confrontational" seating position. You're literally and figuratively going head-to-head when you're sitting at your desks. Move the desks so that each one occupies what's called the "command position" in the room. That is, place each desk in a corner diagonally facing the office door. This placement gives each of you a commanding position in the room.

Q: I am a writer who appreciated your Feng Shui for writers article in your ezine, but I have a follow-up question. My desk faces my home office door, but my computer is on a separate table. So, when I am writing at my computer, my back is to the door. I face a window and see a beautiful view of trees and flowers. Am I sabotaging my writing by having my back to the door, or does the positive view balance that out?

A: You may not be sabotaging your writing by sitting with your back to the door when you're at your computer, but you're certainly working harder at it than you need to because you're not sitting in a secure position. For people who spend most of their time at their keyboard (many of us), I recommend rearranging your office so you're facing the room's entrance door when in front of the monitor. If it's not possible to reposition your desk, place a mirror in front of you so you can glance at it and see the door behind you. You can either place the mirror on your desk, on the wall in front of you, or get a computer mirror. It's a special mirror that looks like the rear-view mirror in your car, which you attach to your computer.

Q: I just bought an electric fireplace for my home office. I love it, but the only place I think it fits is in my career area. My desk is in the power position and I do not think there is enough room behind it. It is portable and will be moved out of the space in the spring. It's possible that I could rearrange the furniture and put it on the right wall to the door, which is the Children/Creative area. What are your thoughts? I just started my favorite and most interesting job a few weeks ago. Your advice for changing the Career wall behind me worked wonders.

A: Congrats on getting the job! It's wonderful to know the changes you made to the art on your wall helped make it happen. An object that represents the

Fire Element, even "faux" fire, can go anywhere along the Power Wall, which includes the Wealth, Future, or Love areas of the room. Avoid putting it in any Water Element areas—Harmony, Career, or Helpful People areas—where it symbolically dries up the flow of water in those locations. You definitely don't want to impede the flow of good energy now that you have a great new job.

Fast 5

Get Rid of Desk Clutter

Can you actually see the top of your desk? Whether you work in a corner suite, a cubicle, or a home office, here are five tips for your desktop to assure that your career will flow smoothly:

1. **Stuff.** Get rid of anything that's driving you nuts: drippy pens and markers, the mechanical pencil where the lead always breaks when you try to write with it, and the outdated cartoons and jokes on your bulletin board that no longer make you laugh. Why are you saving these?

2. **Files.** File the excess paperwork that's on your desk, like bills, receipts, or client folders.

3. **Folders.** Look in your "To Keep" or "Save" folder and throw away what's obsolete.

4. **Business Cards.** Sort the stack of business cards, then enter or scan the information into your address book and toss the cards.

5. **Tools.** At the end of the day, put away any specific tools and equipment you needed today only, and set out the tools you'll need for tomorrow's agenda.

CHAPTER 4: ROOM BY ROOM

Kitchens

Q: I read that I should hang a mirror over my stove to attract wealth, but this is frustrating me. I want to increase my wealth, but there is no place to hang a mirror in that area. Is there anything else I can do?

A: According to classical Feng Shui theory, the more people you can afford to feed, the wealthier you are considered. Hanging a mirror over a stove will double the number of burners you see, symbolically doubling your ability to cook, and therefore doubling your wealth. If you don't want to hang a mirror over your stove, try what I did: keep a shiny teapot on a back burner. It's functional art that does the same symbolic job of reflecting burners!

Q: I just moved into a new apartment where the stove faces the sink, and I realize there is nothing I can do about that. But how can I solve the problem of the opposing forces of fire and water?

A: An oven facing a sink can result in hostile energy because of the conflict between the Fire and Water Elements. You can place a small, nickel-size mirror on the stove (Fire) to reflect away the energy of the sink (Water). You should be able to find these mirrors at craft stores or websites, and they usually have a self-stick backing. Or, place a green rug on the floor between the stove and sink, which represents the Wood Element that will balance the other two opposing Elements.

Q: The fame area in my house is the kitchen sink. What can I do to improve this situation?

A: The Fame and Future area of a house should be activated by the Fire Element. However, in your kitchen, the sink represents the Water Element and it could be putting out the Fire and negatively affecting your future prospects and reputation. To balance these two Elements and to symbolically dry up some of the excess Water, decorate in the colors and shapes of Fire Element. That means using the colors red, orange, or deep purple, and adding things that have a triangular shape. Also, avoid adding blue things or displaying artwork with images of water in your kitchen.

Q: I love to display my children's art on the fridge, but they bring home new things all the time. I hate to throw them out, but the refrigerator door is getting pretty crowded.

A: You love all the adorable drawings your children create at school, but if you save everything, it diminishes the value of those special ones since they get lost in the clutter. Instead, each week, collect all the papers in a folder and have each child select one paper or piece of art to place on the refrigerator or to display on a bulletin board. After a week, date the paper, take a photo of it, and store it electronically. You can share these files with grandparents. As your children get older, they can create their photo files.

Q: My husband and I independently came to the conclusion that we need to remove the bookshelf full of cookbooks near the door in our kitchen to make more room for a table, but we can't agree on where to put the books. He suggested building shelves all around the back door, on both sides, and over the top for the books, but this sounds a little intimidating to me.

Q: I love to cook, but I have too many cookbooks cluttering my kitchen counter. Any ideas?

A: I agree that placing cookbooks on shelves over the door is going to be impractical at best and intimidating at worst to have them hanging over your head. Instead of trying to find a bookcase big enough for all those books, first weed through your collection and make three piles: those you use regularly, those you use occasionally, and those you no longer use. For example, if you no longer follow a Paleo diet, or the last time you made fondue was in college, you don't need cookbooks with those recipes cluttering your kitchen. Donate the books you don't use and store the ones you use occasionally in a kitchen cabinet or in another room. No matter how many cookbooks you have, I bet you only use a few recipes from each book, especially from the older books. Scan the recipes you use frequently and store them electronically or print them and place them in a three-ring binder. That way, you can donate some of your books but still have access to your favorite recipes, all while releasing the clutter from your kitchen. Replace the current bookshelf with a smaller table or shelf and use it to display frequently-used cookbooks.

CHAPTER 4: ROOM BY ROOM

SUCCESS STORY

Alice and Jim
Move Forward

Alice and Jim were living in a house that was in need of updating. Jim had inherited it from his grandparents, but the couple had made only a few changes in the nine years they'd lived there. When their last child left for college, they decided it was time for a serious Feng Shui makeover that included renovating and redecorating. One issue I found was their family room, which was lined with built-in shelves on three walls. Not only had they accumulated a lot of unnecessary stuff on the shelves, but these tall shelves were hard to clean and were coated with dust and cobwebs near the ceiling. I explained that cobwebs represent being stuck and unable to move forward. The heaviness of the shelving weighed down on the room, and its sharp edges pointed at the couple wherever they sat, making it an uncomfortable room. These edges are called poison arrows in Feng Shui, and they represent harsh energy pointed at you like an arrow aimed at a target. No wonder they couldn't relax in the room!

Here's what Alice wrote:

❝ I am happy to report that we finally took down all of the built-in shelves in the family room. It was a lot of work and took a lot of repairing, but the room immediately looked bigger, better, and cleaner. We gave the whole room a coat of paint in the warm color you recommended. As you pointed out, the room is in our Future area, and as you know, Jim had been having trouble with his supervisor. The very next day, after we finished repainting, an

(continued)

> announcement came out that Jim's boss was transferring to another division and Jim was being named director. Was it cause and effect? I don't know, but we certainly lightened the heavy load aimed at us, and an unexpected promotion came our way. I'm thinking it had more to do with Feng Shui than with luck. More of your recommended Feng Shui changes are planned and who knows what else will manifest in our lives. 🙶

Q: I'm trying to use Feng Shui to bring balance into my life, and I'm starting with my kitchen. I have a set of steak knives that I don't use and would like to get rid of, but I don't know how to do it. I don't want to donate them if they have negative energy that will harm someone else.

A: The negative issue with knives refers to giving them as a gift, because it symbolizes cutting a friendship. However, I don't see any problem with donating knives to a nonprofit that will resell them, as long as they are in good condition. However, if the knives are damaged or are especially dangerous for any reason, it would be better to wrap them securely and dispose of them according to your community requirements, rather than donate them.

Laundry Rooms

Q: My laundry room is in the center of my home. More money is going out of our lives than coming in. Is the location of the laundry the problem?

A: There are many reasons why prosperity that flows into your home could be draining out, and a laundry room in the center (Grounding area) of your home could certainly be one of them. Water is associated with prosperity, but in the laundry room, is goes down the drain as dirt. You can correct this imbalance by adding adequate amounts of the Earth Element around your washer and dryer, including the colors yellow or brown, images of mountains, tile floors, etc. Make sure your washer and dryer are stable and balanced. Keep the area clutter-free. Clean the filter after every load, because a full lint filter represents clutter, and it's also a fire hazard.

Q: Is it possible to have good Feng Shui in a laundry room? Mine is in the basement and it's small, drab, and dim. It only has one hanging bulb for light. I hate going into it so I let the laundry – dirty and clean – pile up. Can Feng Shui help?

A: You know I'm going to give you the expected advice to keep your laundry room clutter free. That usually involves things like adding more storage so you can put away the laundry detergent and softener, adding a table so you can fold laundry as an encouragement to put it away as soon as it's dry. But, I understand that doesn't always work in a small space. Instead, try decorating your laundry room to attract positive chi. Use the bagua map to determine the Element for the location of your laundry room, then hang art that activates that Element. Look for art that's fun and upbeat, maybe even whimsical. Also, upgrade the lighting. At the very least, find a fun covering for that solitary light bulb.

Living Rooms/Family Rooms

Q: I have a staircase in the family bagua area of my house, and our family life definitely has more "ups and downs" than I would like. Are these stairs the cause, and what is the cure?

A: A staircase can represent a hole in the bagua area where it is located, so it's possible that yours is symbolic of the family situation you describe. To remedy this situation, hang current family pictures in this area and be sure they're hanging level and not stair-stepped, like the stairs themselves. If possible, hang a crystal from the ceiling above the stairs. Make sure you clear the clutter in the Family area of each room. Pay special attention to what you display in the family room, or wherever your family tends to gather, and only keep what you love and still use.

Q: I love jigsaw puzzles. I'm almost finished with a puzzle that shows a mountain, and I would like to frame it and hang it in my living room. Is that a good idea? It does have all those lines through it.

A: You raise two conflicting issues. Mountains are Feng Shui symbols for support, and it's good to display them in your home. But, an image that appears broken, chipped, or cracked is considered negative in Feng Shui. Jigsaw puzzles have so many "hidden" cracks that it's not a good idea to display them. You can continue to enjoy doing puzzles, which are good stress-reducers, but I recommend against mounting and hanging them.

Q: We don't use our living room all that much because we tend to spend our time in the family room. It's a beautiful room with plenty of light coming in through the windows, but it never feels as comfortable as the other room. What can I do to make the room more inviting?

A: It's good to hear that your living room has lots of natural lighting. But, it's important to also make sure the artificial lighting in your room feels just as comfortable. Modern halogen lighting can be harsh, so look for bulbs that are tipped toward warm colors that mimic natural sunlight, rather than stark blue-white bulbs. Put a table lamp on a timer to come on at dusk and go at night so there will always be light to welcome you into the space. Next, consider painting the walls in neutral, Earth Element colors like the beiges, yellows, or shades of brown. Once you have a neutral color on the walls, you can add blue (Water Element) and green (Earth Element) accessories to bring positive chi into the room. I suggest limiting the amount of red you use in the room if you are want to create a relaxing space. For the furniture, try to place all seating so it has a view of the door. That way, you can see who is coming into the room. This is called "command seating" because it makes you feel secure. If you can't place all seating in that position, position a mirror so you can see what's behind you. For art, choose pieces with uplifting images and themes. It's important to only display art and objects that you love. If something no longer appeals to you, don't display it. If you have a lot of artwork, you can rotate it and display different pieces as the seasons change. And of course, keep the room clutter-free.

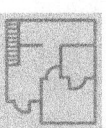

CHAPTER
5

REARRANGING, SHIFTING, TRANSFORMING

Do you ever feel stuck? Your surroundings have a powerful effect on what you attract into your life. When the positive chi flowing into your home or workplace is blocked, your prosperity, relationships, health, and well-being can be affected. Feng Shui rearrangements work to shift energy and to assure that good things naturally find you.

I often say that good design is good Feng Shui. And to get to that good design, the first step is usually to move your stuff. This will help you shift your thoughts and ultimately improve your life. Here are a few ways that simple Feng Shui rearrangements can help increase harmony in your household and transform your life:

Sit in the right spot. Your go-to sofa or chair should be positioned in "command position." That is, facing where you can see the door to the room, but not directly across from it. That's because when you sit in the non-command position, facing away from activity, your brain produces cortisol and adrenaline, which are the stress and anxiety hormones.

Add storage. Messy rooms can cause anxiety, but a minimalist setting isn't ideal either. One correction for this is to add shelves to display your favorite objects, and include closed cabinets to contain all of your necessary but less attractive things.

Hide the TV. Researchers have found that the more TV you watch, the more you overestimate the affluence of other people, with the result that you become less happy. To help control how much you watch, conceal the screen in any way that makes you less likely to turn it on.

CHAPTER 5: REARRANGING, SHIFTING, TRANSFORMING

Let the sun shine in. Sunlight boosts your mood, so the more natural light you bring into your rooms, the better for the people inside them. Choose lightweight window treatments, and hang draperies far enough outside the window opening so the daytime view is unobstructed.

Vary indoor light sources. Choose a mix of task lighting, diffuse ceiling lighting, and hanging fixtures with dimmers rather than uniform lighting. When a room has unchanging lighting, it's harder to connect with the people around you. Replace all outdated fluorescent bulbs with warmer or full-spectrum bulbs to reduce fatigue. You don't still have any of those corkscrew, mercury-filled, CFL bulbs, do you? Out they go!

> *There is nothing like returning to a place that remains unchanged to find the ways you yourself have altered.*
> *— Nelson Mandela*

Q & A

REARRANGING, SHIFTING, TRANSFORMING

Apartments and Condos

Q: I moved into a new apartment with all white walls, white appliances, and even white indoor shutters (ugh!). I can't paint, so how can I balance all of this blandness?

A: All that white is called the Metal Element, which can make everything feel hard and cold. Since you can't add color to the walls by painting, add it by hanging artwork that represents the Water Element, which will balance it. Look for art that depicts outdoor scenes and movement, like rivers, lakes, streams, etc., with lots of greens and blues. Be sure to choose images that show the water flowing *into* your apartment, rather than *out of* the windows and doors. Mirrors, glass, and blue objects are another way to add the Water Element to balance all the white in your apartment.

Q: Any Feng Shui suggestions for correcting the feeling of low energy in my basement apartment?

A: A basement apartment can be a Feng Shui challenge because of the limited natural light; plus, you can feel like you're living underground, disconnected from the growing world outside. Also, your unit can be affected by the occupants above you. Simple Feng Shui adjustments to get the chi moving include adding air-purifying plants that tolerate low light, choosing lighter color wall paints made with light reflecting pigment, and adding art with active outdoor themes to get the chi circulating. If your building allows, place a plant in the hall near your front door to help represent a connection to the natural world. I've included a list of Feng Shui-friendly house plants in an article on my website at bit.ly/FengShuiPlants.

Fast 5

Downsize, Even If You're Not Moving

Get rid of thing you no longer like, want, or need, and you'll make space for better things to find you. To decide if an item is clutter or a "keeper," ask yourself these five questions:

1. Can I **borrow** or rent this object when I need it instead of owning it?
2. Am I keeping this only for **sentimental** reasons, even if it doesn't fit my decor?
3. Do I have the storage space to buy in **bulk**?
4. Do I really need all my holiday **decorations**?
5. Will I ever use these dried-up and expired **spices**?

Q: I live in an apartment and all I have is a balcony, so your gardening tips don't work for me. With my limitations, how do I implement some of the cures?

A: When you live in an apartment or condo, you can still have a garden on your balcony or patio by using the appropriate bagua colors and shapes for each area of your small outdoor space. Map out your outdoor space using the bagua, then decorate with flowers, small potted plants, or garden ornaments in the specific colors and shapes of each bagua area.

Q: We are downsizing to a lovely new apartment, but our closet space will be comparatively limited. What do I do about all the stuff I have saved over the years, such as my children's artwork, my wedding dress, household files, and memorabilia from my parents?

A: Many of us have trouble letting go of things that have deep emotional attachments. You can take gentle steps toward downsizing by limiting what you take to your new home. First, convert paper files to electronic, keep only one or two items from your children's school days, take photographs of your parents' antiques before selling or donating them, and cut a small piece of fabric to save from your wedding dress. Next, remove what I call "guilt clutter." You know what I'm talking about: the birthday blouse from your mom you're never going to wear; that wedding gift your girlfriends chipped in to buy (15 years later and it's still in the box); the poster from the gallery opening you went to with your boyfriend (your ex-boyfriend); the 144-piece tool set you still haven't used to fix anything; the expensive treadmill that's now a clothes rack. As you let go of physical items, you'll make room for positive energy to flow into your new home.

Q: I live on the 20th floor of an apartment building in a major metropolitan city where we are not allowed to put welcome mats outside our apartment door or hang anything like dried flowers or a wreath on the outside of the door. Bummer, since I'm trying to find a new job, and this is part of my career area. Is there anything you can recommend to spruce up the door? Weekly, I clean the outside and the inside of the door, hoping that it will help the energy flow.

A: I share your frustration that you can't decorate the front door, which is the *mouth of chi* where positive energy enters your home. Is there any way you can hang something small and discreet on the door frame or from your door knocker without it being too obvious? For example, it could be a small piece of ribbon, or an image or emoji that relates to your career field. The goal is to mark your door differently from all the others so that symbolically, the chi coming down the hall will be attracted to your door first. You're already ahead of most people because you're paying attention to cleaning your door—that's something I rarely hear that from apartment dwellers.

CHAPTER 5: REARRANGING, SHIFTING, TRANSFORMING

SUCCESS STORY

Jo Witnesses an Apartment Miracle

My client Jo was living in an apartment complex that wasn't being maintained by the landlord. She was suffering from cigarette smoke rising from her neighbor's apartment, and there were also issues with a low ceiling. This negative energy was making it difficult for her to attract the wealth, harmony, and love she was seeking. I gave her a Feng Shui plan that started with simple things like replacing the old-style harsh CFL light bulbs that were zapping her energy, to moving her bed to a location more conducive to sleep, to asking the landlord to remove the rotted wood trellis and decayed vines that surrounded her front door. We also did a dowsing of her apartment to clear the predecessor chi, which is the energy from previous occupants. As soon as she started down her Feng Shui path, Jo began to see changes immediately, all around her.

Here's what Joe wrote in a series of emails:

❝ All the light bulbs are changed, and my eyes are more at ease, I must admit. The bed has been moved and the mirror removed from the dresser across from it. My significant man is scoffing at Feng Shui, but I notice he is more attentive and affectionate. How does this work? Really?

Another interesting development: I moved the old iron table and chairs from my patio to the common area as a contribution to the smoking community. The neighbor has become more diligent

(continued)

about avoiding smoking near my windows because he has a place to sit now way over across the way. It's opening up my patio area.

I forgot to tell you that I immediately moved my son's ashes and trunk of related memorabilia out of my bedroom, and it improved my sleep immediately.

This morning at sunrise, I installed a convex bagua mirror on the back porch facing the school, and already I feel a general flow of good energy. Thrilling. How does this work?

Just letting you know, Carol, a miracle is afoot: seven people showed up and cleaned up the mess around the community storage shed that I see from my window. In addition, I met with the head office manager, and now they are tearing out the dead wood, trimming back the rose bush, and adding a wood-colored lattice all around. This is really difficult to believe but most welcome. Amazing that changing out some objects from my apartment started all this in our lives. ♪♪

Q: I'm moving into an apartment with a balcony, which I've never had before. Are there any special Feng Shui tips?

A: Avoid overcrowding your balcony, and don't store broken or unwanted items out there. In season, grow bright flowers in colorful planters. Be sure to check your planters after a cold winter and replace if they are cracked. Avoid growing spiky cactus or pointed-leaf plants on the balcony because they could repel any positive chi that's trying to flow into your home. Sweep the balcony frequently to get rid of dirt and dead leaves. If you have an unattractive view, place tall plants in the corners to hide it.

CHAPTER 5: REARRANGING, SHIFTING, TRANSFORMING

Aromas

Q: How can I use different aromas to improve my environment?

A: Freud said that the quickest way to trigger an emotional response is with scent. In Feng Shui, we use scents throughout a home to encourage balance and harmony. Try mint or lavender if you need to de-stress, lime to improve your mood, basil to cheer you, rosemary for memory, and geranium for self-esteem. Here are a few other recommended scents for some critical locations around your home:

> **Front Door:** Vanilla to create well-being
>
> **Living Room:** Cinnamon to maintain harmony and conversation
>
> **Kitchen:** Citrus to stimulate your mind
>
> **Dining Room:** Mint to encourage appetite
>
> **Bathroom:** Cedar or sandalwood to balance all the water
>
> **Child's Room:** Lavender to bring relaxation
>
> **Master Bedroom:** Rose, ylang ylang, musk, or jasmine to enhance love
>
> **Workout Room:** Strawberry to encourage exercise
>
> **Office:** Peppermint to attract prosperity, rosemary to strengthen memory, bergamot for wealth

Beams and Sloped Ceilings

Q: There is an exposed overhead concrete beam right in the middle of the room I use as my home office. It's a support beam, not just decorative. I read that the Feng Shui cure for this is to hang bamboo flutes, but that's not something I'm interested in doing. I love the light in this room and do not want to relocate my office to the basement, which is the only other option in the house. What can I do?

A: The Feng Shui concern about exposed beams is that they carry the weight of the roof, symbolically pressing down on you. Also, the edge of an angular beam can symbolically cut into your body when you sit under it. In classical Feng Shui, the correction was to hang a pair of bamboo flutes with a red tassel and red cording at the end of each beam at a 45-degree angle with the mouth piece on the bottom to symbolically cut the beam and lessen its impact. You're not alone in resisting this correction, because it's not appealing to everyone. A ceiling fan can sometimes accomplish the same thing as bamboo flutes, because its blades symbolically cut across the beams and lessen their weight. But, this correction only works if the fan is not directly over your work area or bed. Or, try any of these contemporary ways to symbolically lift the pressure:

Paint or stain the **beam** the same color as the ceiling to lighten it;

Aim **light** up at the beam to raise it;

Drape **fabric** over the beam to round the edges and blunt the cutting energy;

Wrap the beam in silk **vines** to simulate being outside under a natural canopy;

Hang quarter-sized **mirrors** on the beam with the mirror showing to symbolically raise it; or

Place tall **plants** in the four corners of the room to lift the energy.

Q: I am remodeling an older home that has sloped ceilings in almost every room. I am new to Feng Shui, but can you give me some general hints about dealing with these?

A: Similar to exposed beams, the issue with sloped ceilings is that they symbolize downward pressure on the occupants of the room. And similar to the correction for beams, you need to symbolically lift the area where the ceiling is lowest. I like to do this by placing a floor plant in the low corner or corners of the room to lift the energy. Or, you could place a tall chest or vertical furniture in the low area. [See previous question for more options.]

CHAPTER 5: REARRANGING, SHIFTING, TRANSFORMING

Cemeteries and Graves

Q: My son just moved into an apartment near a cemetery. Is this an acceptable location according to Feng Shui? His door is painted red, does that help?

A: In Chinese Feng Shui, a cemetery is thought to have the strong yin (low) energy of death that draws chi away from the surrounding homes. It's possible that living near a cemetery over time could deplete your son's energy. A red door is helpful as an adjustment for this location, but only if it's directly across from the cemetery. He could also accent the interior wall across from the cemetery with bright red art or decoration. He should make sure the apartment is well lit to balance the dark chi from the cemetery. And, he can hang a convex bagua mirror on the outside of the apartment pointed at the cemetery to send back any negative energy. A bagua mirror is a Chinese octagon-shaped mirror with a yellow wood frame. If that isn't possible, he can hang a round, flat mirror in the window pointed at the cemetery. He can also conduct a space clearing or house blessing, which is good to do to clear residual energy whenever moving into a new residence.

Q: I put a very nice silk flower arrangement on my parents' headstone and change it each season. The flowers are still in excellent condition, and I would like to use them again when the season comes. When I bring them home, where and how should I store them until it's time? I thought about having an arrangement made of greenery that would not be seasonal, so I wouldn't have to bring home flowers that have been on a grave. What is your take on this? Right now, the arrangement is in our garage, which is the Helpers area.

A: I recommend against bringing arrangements home from a cemetery because they could carry yin or low chi, which would accumulate in the area of your home where they are stored. Instead, consider choosing fresh flowers for the headstone. And, if it's not possible to visit the cemetery often enough to change the flowers when they die, consider using a maintenance or perpetual care service to tend the site. Ancestors play an important role in Feng Shui, and their grave sites benefit from frequent attention.

Clearing Rituals and Remedies

Q: Can you ever over-do it and place too many Feng Shui cures? Will it have the opposite effect of what I really want to attract?

A: Feng Shui is all about setting the intention for something to enter your life, and you can do this by making simple adjustments in your home and workplace. I worked with a client who was desperate to find a relationship and had placed all kinds of pairs of red objects in his Relationship area: two red candles, two red tassels, two red hearts, two red hats, and even a pair of red socks (don't ask!), but he wasn't meeting anyone. I recommended he remove all that and replace it with one simple piece of art with a romantic theme to open up his energy to the possibility of a relationship. It worked!

Q: Is there something else I can use instead of fu dogs as a cure near my front gate? I'm not having luck finding a pair that I like. They all look mean to me.

A: Feng Shui recommends placing a pair of objects flanking the front door or front gate to create a threshold to protect the home and to attract positive chi. But in contemporary practice, you don't need to use fu dogs—those lion-dog looking sculptures used in classic Chinese Feng Shui remedies. The goal is to frame the doorway with guardians, and the choice of objects is yours. I recommend a pair of cobalt blue or black ceramic planters, because these Water Element colors represent the flow of abundance to your door. In the warm months, you can grow red flowers in the pots, and in the colder months, fill them with pine cones, colored glass balls, or other artful objects. The beauty of the planters can also be enough. Another option is to choose two matching outdoor sculptures or garden ornaments.

Q: I read somewhere that you are supposed to use cinnabar as part of the rice blessing ceremony for a house, so I was so happy to find the article on your website with alternatives. I'm really concerned about the mercury in cinnabar, especially since I have a golden retriever who is a "garbage disposal," and I'm concerned for his safety. Will my ritual still

be as effective if I substitute paprika? In my research, I read that cinnabar is mined from lava, which has "magical properties."

A: My Feng Shui approach is Western and practical, so I don't use cinnabar for the same concern about mercury. Personally, I feel the *intention* of a Feng Shui remedy or ceremony is more important than what you choose to implement that remedy, so paprika should work fine. Other options are red chile powder or red chalk. If you're specific about what you want to clear and use positive affirmations, you'll be more successful in your efforts and you won't need any kind of "magic" substance.

Colors

Q: I don't get this yin-yang stuff. Do you mean I have to decorate everything in black and white, like in the yin-yang symbol, to bring good luck or can I use other colors?

A: No, you don't have to make everything black or white. Feng Shui aims to achieve a balance of the opposing characteristics in the world around you, which are known as yin and yang. These are the everyday opposites we see around us in our homes and offices: soft and hard, cold and hot, dark and light. In most cases, we balance yin and yang naturally and instinctively in our homes. For example, we add soft, yin seat cushions to hard, yang wooden chairs. If the bathwater gets too hot, we turn on the cold. We paint one wall a darker accent color to keep an all-white room from looking too bland. That's because when these two equal and opposite forces are in balance in our interior surroundings, we feel comfortable, secure, and at peace. Mix up your color choices around your home and you'll feel balanced.

Q: Which of the Five Elements includes white plastic? I have a lot of it around me, especially on my desk.

A: While the white color of a plastic object does represent one of the Five Elements (the Metal Element), the material itself does not have life and isn't considered an Element. If you have lots of items surrounding you that are plastic, they're not attracting a flow of positive chi. Replace as many as you can with objects made of natural materials. For example, replace the plastic accessories on your desk with wood, glass, or metal; exchange the plastic trashcan for a wicker or metal one; and choose ceramic or metal containers for your plants.

Doors

Q: I have a huge mirror across from my front door. Why is that considered bad luck in Feng Shui? We have never felt settled in this house, and I'm starting to question whether the mirror is part of the problem.

A: Yes, it's likely that the mirror placement is making you feel unsettled in the house, because a mirror across from the front door reflects away the positive energy as soon as it enters. That means the chi never spreads throughout your home. Try replacing the mirror with art that has a happy, upbeat image that feels warm and welcoming.

Q: My question is, which door is the primary...the front door we never use or the door from the garage through the laundry room that we use all the time?

Q: We rarely use our front door. Do I still use it to orient the bagua when I am mapping out my entire house?

A: Yes, you orient the bagua map at the front door of your home, even if you enter through the garage, side door, or back porch. This is the architectural entrance that was created by the architect and builder, and it's the way the positive chi enters your home, even if you don't. The front door is called the *mouth of chi*, so it's a good idea to use it frequently. Try opening this door every day, even if it's to get your morning newspaper or to greet the day. Avoid taking out the trash through the front door. If you come home through the garage and laundry room, make sure that entrance is as pleasing as your front entrance. Paint the door between the garage and house the same as your front door, use the same door mat, and if you decorate your front door for holidays, do the same with your garage entry door.

CHAPTER 5: REARRANGING, SHIFTING, TRANSFORMING

Q: I have a lovely front door that opens into a beautiful foyer and a grand view into the house. But here's the thing, it's never used. We enter our house 100% of the time via the garage. When family and friends visit, they also come through the garage entry after leaving their cars in the driveway. I assume making our garage lovely and clean is very important, but does our garage become our "Mouth of Chi" since we never use the front door?

A: Yes, an attached garage is considered a room in your home and should be decorated according to the bagua area it occupies, but no, it's not the *mouth of chi*. It's time to start entering your home through the front door, even if only occasionally, especially since you say you have such a grand view. Tell your guests about this view, and urge them to start using the front door. Maybe you can landscape in a way that directs your guests from the driveway to the front door.

Q: I read your newsletter with the answer to the question about whether it's OK to have a glass front door. WOW... I have a new house and my front door is very nice, but there is a large leaded glass pane in the door. You can literally "see" into my house. I find there are just some very strange things that cost me money that go on with the house, and now I'm beginning to associate that with the door. I will put up at least a mini-blind this week to block the insight into my house some, but I really don't want to buy a new door. Thoughts on how to fix this?

A: In Feng Shui terms, the glass in your front door is letting money symbolically flow right through your house, and that could be resulting in those unexpected expenses. The fix for the problem is exactly what you're already figured out: covering the glass. It doesn't matter whether you choose translucent or opaque curtains, mini-blinds, or another kind of draping; as long as you cover the glass, you'll help stop the energy loss.

Q: We always enter our house through the back door; is this OK? I read in your newsletter that I should try to use my front door every day, so I do go out that way every morning to get the newspaper. But, the back door is so much more convenient for entering the house.

A: Of course, it's OK to use your back door as an entrance, as long as you occasionally enter your house through the front door. Make sure you treat the back door with the same care you give (or should give) to your front door. Keep the door clean, and paint or stain it as needed. Use the same door mat here as you do at the front door, and if you decorate your front door seasonally, do the same for your back door. Make sure the area behind your back door is clutter-free so the door opens easily and completely.

Q: I really want a new front door that is mostly glass. I live in a split foyer house, so you really can't see anything beyond the stairs. I just love the look and feel of a glass door, but I have heard that it is not good Feng Shui to have a door like this installed.

A: A glass front door can be considered inauspicious in Feng Shui because it represents weakness and lack of protection. This weakness can also affect your wealth, because you can literally see through the door into your house. This is even the case in a situation like yours where you only see the stairs. There are some adjustments for an existing glass door, but it's always better to avoid creating a problem, rather than having to fix one. Plus, split foyer homes have a special set of Feng Shui issues, and some typical adjustments to balance the energy of a glass door can't be made in this style house.

Q: We live in a center hall colonial where the front door is positioned directly across from the stairway. I read somewhere that this is not good Feng Shui. We love the house, but we certainly don't want bad Feng Shui.

A: This location for a stairway is considered inauspicious because the good energy comes in the front door and races right up the stairs without flowing to the rooms on the entry level. The traditional adjustment for this situation is to hang a crystal from the ceiling between the bottom step and the door. The modern equivalent is to hang a crystal chandelier or a cut-glass light fixture in the foyer. Another option is to place a plant in the foyer or to hang lively artwork prominently in the rooms off the foyer to direct the chi away from the stairs and into the other rooms.

Q: I read that I'm not supposed to keep things behind my door. Why? I really need that storage space in my small house. For example, I have to hang my robe on the back of the bathroom door.

CHAPTER 5: REARRANGING, SHIFTING, TRANSFORMING

A: When your doors don't open fully, stagnant energy lurks behind them, and just like the door, opportunities won't "open" completely for you. This is especially important for your front door, but it also applies to your back door, room doors, and your closet doors. A hook on the back of the bathroom door is fine if all you hang is a frequently-used robe or a towel, as long as the door can still open all the way. But, avoid hanging heavier items on the backs of your doors, like an ironing board. Remove objects from behind your doors, and watch your future prospects open.

Q: Do I have to paint my front door red to bring in some good luck?

A: The color red represents the Fire Element that symbolizes prosperity in Feng Shui, which is why it is often a recommended color for your front door. However, you can paint or stain your front door any color and still attract good energy into your home. The key is to make sure your door is clean, attractive, and in good repair. Choose a color that makes you feel good when you approach your door. For example, try red for wealth, blue or black for relaxation, green for growth, or brown for stability. The front door sets the tone for the rest of your home, so keep the area around the door clean and well lit, and make sure you have a house number that can be easily seen from the street.

Q: Is it a problem if you have more than one entrance door to the house?

A: It's only a problem if the main entrance isn't clearly defined. Even if you most often enter your home through the "working" entrance, such as the back door, garage, or porch, the front door that the architect designed is the main entrance for your home. Keep this door clean and neat, place healthy plants in decorative planters on both sides of it as "greeters," and add a fresh doormat at this entrance to clearly designate it as the front of the house.

Q: Hi, I'm a reader in Australia. I'm concerned about the two bedrooms in my hallway where the doors are directly across from each other. I read that this is bad Feng Shui.

A: The situation in your hall is called "clashing doors," because the doors symbolically confront each other. This situation can lead to hostility between the occupants of these two rooms. The solution is to hang a red drapery tassel on the outside doorknob of each door to lessen any potential antagonism.

Fast 5

See What's Lurking Behind Your Doors

In Feng Shui, doors represent opportunities, so if all your doors open fully, your life will be fully open to opportunities. To maximize your potential, ask yourself these questions about your doors:

1. **Condition.** What does your front door look like? If it's faded, stained, chipped, or peeling, it could be repelling, instead of attracting, positive chi.

2. **Across.** What's across from your front door? If it's a mirror, a blank wall, a struggling plant, or a less-than-inspiring piece of art, your positive chi will languish right there and never reach the rest of your home.

3. **Behind.** Is something behind the door keeping it from opening completely? When your doors can't open fully, your energy becomes stagnant and opportunities may not open for you. Remove objects from behind your doors, and watch your future prospects open.

4. **Dirt.** When's the last time you cleaned your front door? Neglect for your door represents neglect for your finances, and it keeps you from attracting new wealth.

5. **Use.** Do you ever actually use your front door? Open your front door daily, even if it's only to symbolically greet the day.

CHAPTER 5: REARRANGING, SHIFTING, TRANSFORMING

Q: I am researching options for replacing my front door, which is in very bad condition. Should the interior side of the front door be the same color as the exterior

A: The exterior side of the door should be a color that symbolizes what you want to attract into your home. However, the interior side of the door can be a color that harmonizes with the entry area walls. The most important suggestion for a door in poor condition and beyond repair is what you're already doing: replacing it with a new one! [See prior answer for door color options.]

Q: I love your tips and regularly read your monthly newsletter. I recently noticed creaking of my bathroom door. Next thing you know, I open my kitchen cabinet door and it creaks. Then, I remembered a cabinet door in my bathroom, which I use daily, has been creaking for a while now. Now I'm wondering what creaking doors denote, and I will get out the oil to fix them. Thank you for your energy, your sharing, and the light you shine on the world.

A: I'm flattered by your praise! In general, doors represent opportunities, so whenever they are blocked, stuck, or creaking, it symbolizes restricting new opportunities. There's also some thought that creaking door hinges relate to creaking in your joints. I wouldn't read too much symbolism into the fact that you have more than one creaking door, especially since one has been creaking for a while—unless your body is feeling achy. It could simply be the effect of weather or aging wood and hinges. The Feng Shui solution (and practical one) is to get a can of WD-40 and lubricate the hinges regularly. In fact, that's just what I did in my home this weekend! When your doors open and close smoothly, it symbolizes that nothing can hold you back from receiving new opportunities.

Q: More of my doors squeak than don't squeak, and it's driving me nuts. Does this also have a Feng Shui meaning?

A: When doors don't open and close smoothly and quietly, it represents blocked opportunities. Squeaky doors are specifically associated with petty arguments because they represent restricted flow into your life. A squeaky front door means you're fighting your way through life. Fix your squeaky doors and you'll start to fix what's not working in your life.

Q: How can the Compass Feng Shui Bagua and the Front Door Bagua method both work if they position the door in different ways?

A: My practice of Feng Shui is Western in approach, so I use the front door to orient the bagua rather than a compass. All schools of Feng Shui are valid, but it's best not to mix them. Think about Kung Fu and Tai Chi—both work, but if you try to do them at the same time, you might pull a muscle. Picking an approach to Feng Shui is similar: pick one that resonates with you so you don't strain your Feng Shui muscles.

Dorms and Shared Spaces

Q: I've always suspected there is some funny business about dorm rooms, when your bed and computer are in the same room, like there is some bad energy to that... Do you have any thoughts on an issue that most college kids like me have to face?

A: Ideally, you would never keep any work-related material in the area where you sleep. However, college students often live in less-than-ideal dorm or shared-apartment situations. Try to screen off your study area from your sleeping area by using plants, a floor screen, or a curtain. I know I'm asking a lot, but try to power down your computer and all your electronic devices at night before you go to sleep. Trust me, you'll sleep better, and your tweets will be waiting for you in the morning.

Q: We dropped our daughter off at college this weekend, and I hate her dorm room. Mainly, it's the location of the bed. Her roommate arrived first and claimed the other bed. The only place for my daughter's bed is with the side against the wall that's adjacent to the door. That means her feet point directly out the door, which I've seen written somewhere is considered the death position in Feng Shui. This is not the way I wanted her to start off her college life. Please help!

A: Try not to panic. You're right that this isn't the most auspicious position, and it could make it difficult for her to sleep soundly because she's so close to the door, but there are remedies for a bed in this location. See if she can find something to position at the end of the bed to symbolically protect her from the chi coming in the door, like a short bookcase, a padded bench, or a floor plant (silk is acceptable). Or, maybe she can hang a lightweight curtain from the ceiling to separate her part of the room from the entrance area. Anything that acts as a separation between the door and the bed will help her sleep more.

Q: I moved to a new state and have been staying with friends while I find a permanent place to live. I feel like I live out of my suitcases because in addition to living in "borrowed" space, I travel for work. I feel like there's no point in unpacking.

A: It's always good Feng Shui to unpack when you stay in a temporary space, so you can feel as settled as possible. For business travel, put together a kit containing a few special things to put in your room wherever you're staying. Your kit could include a picture of your loved ones to help you feel connected, a precious stone to feel grounded, a scented candle to make your space special, a scarf to drape over an inconveniently-hung mirror, and other similar items to make your temporary location feel more like your own. In your room at your friends' home, hang a picture of the type of house or apartment you're looking for as a symbol that you're ready to move in to your own space.

Family

Q: I recently remarried and moved into the house where my wife lived with her 8-year-old son. My relationship with my stepson is good, but I would like to make it even better. My wife is a little bit resistant to Feng Shui. Is there one change we can make to help further blend our family?

A: One way to help create a blended family is to take a recent family photo of all of you doing something you love, and place a framed copy in your stepson's room and another in the Family area of your home. Choose a wood frame to represent the Wood Element, which encourages growth and harmony in your family relationship.

Q: Can I do a cure in my home for someone who does not live here? My daughter has some health problems, and I would like to do something to help.

A: Unfortunately, Feng Shui doesn't work that way. Changes that you make to your home will only affect the people who are living in that home. The Feng Shui remedies that could be helpful for your daughter will depend on the arrangement of furniture and objects in her home and her readiness to make changes. Perhaps you can help her understand the basics of Feng Shui, and together you can make some changes in her own space.

Q: I was wondering, is it possible to improve the success or love for your children with Feng Shui? I have two sons. One son doesn't live with us anymore, but I want to help with his love life. He doesn't believe in Feng Shui. Can I do it in my home for him? Also, another son still lives with us but is going to college next year. Can I do anything in his room to help him with luck and success but in a way so he doesn't find out about it?

A: Making Feng Shui changes is all about setting intentions for what you want to flow into your life. It's not possible to make adjustments in your own home on behalf of someone else's home. These adjustments would need to be made by your son in his own home. You can make changes in your home that will have an affect on the son who is stilling living with you, but he would have to be a willing participant in those adjustments.

Q: My family does not talk—we argue. Are there any quick Feng Shui tips to help improve our communication?

A: It's impossible to know without seeing your home, but there could be something about the objects, colors, and images you have around that are blocking conversation. Try making some changes in color and see if that helps. The color orange encourages communication, so start by adding orange accents like flowers, placemats, and an orange ceramic bowl to the kitchen or dining room table. Food brings people together, so if you're all eating in various places around the house, start eating together at the same table. A round table encourages equality in a family.

CHAPTER 5: REARRANGING, SHIFTING, TRANSFORMING

Fashion

Q: Can I Feng Shui the way I dress? Some days, I think I pick the wrong color or pattern to wear because it never seems to match my mood.

A: The Five Elements is the Feng Shui name for colors and shapes. When you go to your closet to pick your outfit for the day, first ask yourself what kind of energy you need, then try choosing clothes that symbolize the Feng Shui Element you need to activate. For example:

If you need to be **creative**, wear the **Water Element**: dark blues, wavy or abstract designs, and fluid fabrics.

If your goal is to feel **energized**, try the **Wood Element**: greens, plant-based fibers, floral patterns, and relaxed styles.

If you need to be **empowered**, choose the **Fire Element**: hot colors, textured fabrics, and dramatic styles.

If you want to feel **grounded**, wear the **Earth Element**: browns, earth tones, and traditional styling and patterns.

If you want to feel **sophisticated**, wear the **Metal Element**: luxurious fabrics and metal jewelry and accents.

Q: I'm changing my wardrobe for the new season, any thoughts on how I can bring Feng Shui into this process?

A: Think about the color of your clothes based on the Five Elements in Feng Shui, because when you wear a specific Element, you project its attributes:

Purple is associated with royalty and luxury. Wear purple clothes or accessories when you are in the midst of transition, want to attract new opportunities, or are in a spiritual setting.

Red is the ideal color when you want to draw attention to yourself. Wear red when you speak in public or want to stand out from the crowd, but avoid red if you're nervous or self-conscious. Wear something red—even if it's hidden—and you'll feel powerful and lucky.

Pink is the color of romance and fun. Wear pink if you want to resolve a situation with a loved one, because it is soothing and helps dissolve feelings of anger.

Yellow conveys stability, so you can wear it when you have an important decision to make. Avoid yellow when you're feeling tired, because it might drain your energy levels.

Green projects growth and advancement. This is a great color to wear when learning new skills, taking classes, or when you need to be energized. Green is a stimulating color, so avoid wearing it when you're already restless.

Brown is a comforting and grounding color that you can wear if you feel scared or insecure. Brown makes you feel safe, but avoid wearing it when dealing with stubborn people.

Black conveys authority and power, and promotes a sense of depth and strength. Wear black if you need to command leadership or exude mystery. Black makes you stand apart from the crowd, so avoid wearing it when you need to be seen as an equal.

Q: I am applying for a new position that will essentially be a promotion. I have been using Feng Shui principles in my home with fruitful results. I'd like to know if I should wear a specific color when I submit my job application (online). Thanks for your time.

A: The classic Feng Shui recommendation is to wear something red—the Fire Element—for a job interview, so it wouldn't hurt to wear some red when you submit your online application. It can be as simple as a red or burgundy accessory, a piece of jewelry, or even something else that doesn't show like red underwear. Good luck!

Food and Diet

Q: I want to lose weight. Is there a particular place I should use Feng Shui to enhance my house to help me with my goal?

A. Focus on the kitchen first when you're trying to lose weight. You want to create a clutter-free room that has a sense of lightness to it. Choose a calm color like blue, which can help curb your appetite, or a healing color like green. Avoid the Fire Element colors like red, orange, and deep purple because they heat things up. Keep a bowl of fresh fruit on the counter, and grow fresh herbs or plants. The second place to lighten up is your bedroom closet, where you should get rid of old clothes you can no longer wear. Overstuffed closets represent holding on to things, especially weight.

Q: I'm on a diet but I'm having trouble resisting temptation. Any Feng Shui tips to help?

A: Switch to small, blue plates. Studies have shown that the color blue, which is the Water Element, slows down the body by reducing blood pressure and pulse. The term *Blue Plate Special* was popularized during the Great Depression when restaurants found that patrons were satisfied with smaller portions of food when it was served on a blue plate. Also, if your kitchen is the first thing you see when you enter your home, this could encourage overeating. Place a plant or object near the kitchen where you'll be forced to walk around it, creating a disincentive to enter the kitchen.

Q: Is there anything I should do in my dining room to help me eat less and stick to a diet?

A: Hang a mirror in the dining room and sit facing it when you eat. Your reflection will remind you to slow down.

Q: I've gained a lot of weight since I moved into this house, and my clothes don't fit. I had to buy new clothes, but I'm keeping my old clothes because I hope to get into them again. By now I'm wondering if my cluttered closets are actually contributing to my weight gain?

A: Clutter in Feng Shui represents the inability to move forward, and when your closets are cluttered with clothes that no longer fit, it symbolizes holding on to old behavior patterns. The Feng Shui recommendation is to get rid of clothes you can't wear now to make room for new clothes (in smaller sizes!) to flow into the space you open up in your closets.

Fast 5

Clear the Way for Weight Loss

Whether you're trying to improve your health, get rid of a few excess pounds you put on from eating too many holiday cookies, or anything in between, these Feng Shui changes can help:

1. **Colors**. To slow down your eating and help stick to a diet, switch to blue plates. Blue is the color of the Water Element, and it has been shown to slow down the body by reducing blood pressure and pulse rate. Red is the color of the Fire Element that stimulates the appetite, so avoid using red dishes, tablecloths, or placemats.

2. **Table**. Try to eat all your meals at a table to make each meal a positive and pleasant experience. Place fresh flowers on the table.

3. **Clutter**. Clutter keeps you stuck in a rut, no matter where it's located in your house, and a cluttered kitchen can psychologically add weight. Lose the clutter in your cabinets and on your counters and you'll lose the weight.

4. **Foods**. Display healthy foods. When the first thing you see when you enter your kitchen is a bowl of nourishing fruit, it will be the first thing you eat.

5. **Closets**. Get rid of old clothes you have been saving for "when I lose weight." If you hold on to clothes that don't fit, it symbolizes holding on to the past.

CHAPTER 5: REARRANGING, SHIFTING, TRANSFORMING

House Shapes and Styles

Q: We live in a one-level ranch home that is shaped like an L. How do I align the bagua with this shape?

A: The bagua is always aligned standing at your front door looking into your home. The ideal shape for a home is a square or rectangle because it includes all the areas of the bagua. When you live in an L-shaped home, you need to anchor the missing area of your home to bring back these areas. Stand at your front door looking into your home, hold the bagua in front of you, then draw the shape of your home. Divide this into the nine equal areas of the bagua to determine which rooms occupy the specific areas of the bagua, and to see if any bagua areas are missing. You'll find detailed directions for making this correction in Chapter 6 of the *Feng Shui Quick Guide For Home and Office: Secrets For Attracting Wealth, Harmony, and Love.*

Q: I live in an L-shaped house that's missing the Helpful People area of my home. The missing corner is on the concrete driveway. How do I make this kind of correction on a hard surface?

A: You can make the correction by painting a small design on the driveway to mark the missing corner. Paint the design where the walls would come together if your house were a complete rectangle. I like to match the color and shape of the design to the Element that activates the bagua area you're missing. For example, the Helpful People area is activated by the Metal Element, so you could paint a simple silver circle on the concrete. In fact, that's the correction I made on the driveway for my own missing Helpful People area. Just be sure to check your correction frequently, and if it's been worn away by the weather, immediately repaint it.

Q: How do I use the bagua for a duplex? Both entry doors are in the center of the building, which means when I enter my side, all the rooms on the first floor are to the right of the entry, which is a long hallway with living room, dining room, bathroom, then kitchen.

A: If you only occupy one side of the duplex, you use the bagua only on your side of the building. This is similar to how you would only use the bagua for your apartment if you lived in an apartment building. Stand at your front door looking into your home, hold the bagua in front of you, then draw the floor plan for of your home. Divide this into the nine equal areas of the bagua to determine which rooms occupy the specific areas of the bagua, and to see if any bagua areas are missing.

Q: How do I use the bagua map for a split level? If I can't map the house as a whole because it is a split, do I use it room by room?

Q: We live in a bi-level home and something feels off-balance. Nothing I have tried seems to help. What do you suggest?

Q: Does a tri-level house warrant any special consideration when using the bagua?

A: A multi-level home represents a Feng Shui challenge because the levels are incomplete. You'll need to make corrections on several levels to symbolically bring the missing areas back into the home. On a subconscious level, entering into a half-up and half-down situation creates an imbalance. You use the bagua on each level of your home to determine which rooms are located in specific life goal areas, and then to decide how to place the furniture, art, and objects to move out walls and activate the bagua areas. On the main level, stand at the front door looking in and hold the bagua in front of you and draw the shape of that level of the house. Then, go to every other levels of your house and stand with your back to the equivalent of the front door, hold the bagua in front of you, and draw that level. Be sure to map the basement and attic. The correction for these missing areas is to symbolically move walls and thereby complete the level that's missing from the home. This is done by placing either a mirror or artwork that depicts a landscape or natural scene near the stairway that marks the split.

Q: I have been reading your blog with much interest and enjoying my study of Feng Shui! It is so interesting and confusing at the same time! But, you explain everything in your book so well, it truly helps. My question: when you draw out the bagua of your home and place it over the rooms, what do you do if there is empty space where there needs to

CHAPTER 5: REARRANGING, SHIFTING, TRANSFORMING

be an area? Also, what if you have an attached garage at the back of your house with rooms for storage and a home office? Do you treat that as a separate bagua schematic?

A: I'm glad to hear that you're enjoying your Feng Shui studies. In Feng Shui, the ideal shape for a home is a complete square or rectangle, because all areas of the bagua are equally represented. That means all attached parts of the home, including the garage, should be included when you draw the floor plan and lay the bagua over it. Most of us don't live in perfectly square or rectangle homes, so there's often a missing area. It's necessary to find the spot where the walls would come together if the house were complete and mark it to symbolically return the missing areas—and the missing attributes—to your life. [See prior questions for more information about making corrections.]

Q: I am thinking of purchasing a mid-century home and have seen two that I like. One of the homes has five steps down to the living room, two steps up to the dining room, and two steps more up to the kitchen. The other home has two steps down the long hallway, and another two steps down the hallway, and two more steps down the rest of the hallway. Then the rest of the house is on one level. I heard in Feng Shui that the kitchen should be the highest room in the house. Does this really matter?

A: I'm not familiar with the recommendation that the kitchen needs to be the highest room in the house. I practice Western Feng Shui, and it's possible this comes from another school of Feng Shui. However, for me, the issue with the houses you describe is that the steps create levels of the house that are incomplete according to the Feng Shui bagua. You'll need to make numerous corrections to complete each level to assure balance. My recommendation is to keep looking at houses until you find one that feels more complete on each level. [See prior questions for more information about making corrections.]

Q: I live in the UK in a semi-detached house where the prosperity area is missing. I have heard of cures such as putting a plant outside to fill out a missing area, but the outside area is not ours, so I am unable to do this. Short of moving, I don't know what to do.

A: No need to move. The correction for a missing bagua area when you don't have control over the outside space is to hang an object inside, on the wall adjacent to the missing area, to symbolically move the wall and bring the missing bagua area back into your own space. You have two choices in how to make the correction. First, you can hang a mirror on the wall, because it makes the wall symbolically disappear. Just be careful about what the mirror reflects. Or, you can hang art or photos of things you would see in nature, like trees, flowers, meadows, rivers, or mountains to symbolize seeing through the wall to a beautiful scene.

Q: My husband and I just bought a new home. As you enter the front door, there is a brick wall separating the front hallway from the dining area just behind the wall. Is this a bad thing? If so, how will I remedy the situation?

A: If you enter the front door and immediately face a wall, it stops the chi from flowing into the rest of your home. In your case, the chi symbolically crashes into a brick wall. To correct the situation, hang artwork on the wall that shows an image that's bi-directional, or flowing out in both directions. This will direct the chi away from the wall and into your home. Avoid hanging a mirror on the wall because it will reflect the chi out the front door.

Landscaping

Q: Our driveway has a pronounced slope to it. I read that a sloped driveway can cause our wealth to flow out. What landscaping would you suggest to stop this problem?

A: You can stop the flow of wealth out of the driveway by installing a light or reflectors at the top of the driveway or along the sides of the driveway. This lighting draws the energy up the driveway and reduces the draining-away effect. Also, you could place planters or other solid decorative objects at the bottom of the driveway to "catch" any escaping chi.

Q: The path to our front door is very straight and I know that is not considered good Feng Shui. What do you suggest?

A: A straight path to your front door is considered a *poison arrow* that brings harsh energy. However, a meandering path to the front door simulates the flow of water and encourages a more natural flow of good energy and chi to your home. To give the illusion that the pathway curves, plant bushes and flowers along the sides, either in the ground or in round pots. Avoid planting them in a straight line, and vary their height and size.

Q: We are planning to build a pool. Does it matter where the pool is located in the backyard and what shape it is? Is there a special way to landscape around a pool?

A: One of my clients referred to her pool as the hole in the ground into which she threw money. A bit of Feng Shui planning can help make your pool a positive part of your life and not a symbolic drain on your finances. The most important consideration is to keep the traffic pattern from inside your house to the pool as easy as possible. If it's a chore to get to the pool, you won't use it and it will symbolically drain your wealth. A curvy shape for the pool is best, but if the pool has to be rectangular, place large planters in groups of three on the concrete deck to soften the hard edges of the pool.

Q: We have a storage shed in the wealth area of our backyard. It's not part of our house, but does it still have a negative effect because it's filled with junk?

A: The shed is outside of the bagua of your home, so it doesn't have a direct impact on the energy inside your home. However, the fact that you're concerned about all the junk you have stored in there means it represents negative chi for you. First, clear out the shed and get rid of everything you don't use anymore. Then, consider painting the outside of the shed in a Wealth area color, like red, orange, or dark purple, to help activate that aspect of your backyard. One of my clients painted a beautiful floral scene with red and purple flowers on the outside of her shed.

Q: I've been searching in different books for the best place to put a compost bin in the yard and some say to avoid having one, so I'm confused. My family believes in living green as best we can. Right now, our compost bin is behind the garage in the Wealth area of our property.

To me this makes sense since in time, the food scraps decompose into "rich" dark soil. What do you think?

A: Since you consider the compost bin to be an important part of "living green," it appropriately belongs anywhere in your yard that's convenient, since it nourishes your family and the earth. Behind your garage in the Wealth area of your backyard is fine, or locate it in the Health and Community area. You find these areas by standing behind your house and holding the bagua in front of you, drawing the shape of the lot, and divided it into the nine bagua areas.

Q: I'm getting ready to do some spring planting around my house, and I need to replace some plants and trees we lost in a deep frost, which were located by the front door. Anything I should avoid?

A: Avoid planting prickly plants with thorns and spikes near your front door because they repel visitors and positive energy. That means avoiding cactus and even roses because of their thorns. For the trees, avoid anything with downward falling leaves, such as the weeping willow, because they can make the house look and feel sad.

Q: I read that I should get rid of roses growing in my garden because of the thorns. Is that necessary?

A: If you can, keep roses restricted to around the edges of your property rather than at your front door, where the thorns symbolically repel visitors. Thorns are triangular in shape and activate the Fire Element, so you can plant them in the Fame/Future area of your garden to bring the attributes of this Element into your life. However, I recommend avoiding them in the Love/Marriage and Family/Health areas, where they represent a *thorn in your side* in these aspects of your life.

Q: Is it OK to have cactus growing in front of my house?

A: Prickly plants like cactus can represent negative chi, so it's best to avoid having them in front of your door. I don't now where you're located, but in places like Arizona, where my clients want saguaro cactus near the front door because it's part of the local culture, I suggest planting colorful, fragrant plants near the cactus to blunt the sharpness.

CHAPTER 5: REARRANGING, SHIFTING, TRANSFORMING

Q: I read in one of your newsletters that fall is also a good time to make sure nothing is growing on, or over, your house. We live in an old house, and there is lots of ivy growing near the front door. Does that mean I need to get rid of it? And we have a big tree to the right of that door with large limbs that do hang over the house.

A: The image of an ivy-covered cottage may be romantic, but in Feng Shui, vines growing on your home symbolize something *eating away* at your life. I recommend removing them. You should also consider trimming large limbs that grow over the top of your house, because they symbolize issues weighing down on you.

Location

Q: We are considering buying a house on a cul-de-sac. I have heard that this is not a good Feng Shui location, yet our real estate agent tells us cul-de-sac houses are considered premium locations.

A: I get a lot of questions about living on cul-de-sacs. It's a love-it-or-hate-it situation. In Feng Shui, homes located on a cul-de-sac can present challenges for the occupants because the chi travels around the curve like a sling shot and doesn't stop at any house. Or, if the house is located directly at the end of the cul-de-sac with the main street pointed directly at it, it can receive harsh energy. Some locations on the straight part of the street that leads into the curve of the cul-de-sac are fine because the chi energy moves more slowly. Also, landscaping in the center of the cul-de-sac helps to slow down the energy, which makes living in the house more comfortable. If you buy a house located at the point of the cul-de-sac, make sure you plant bushy plants between you and the street to give you some protection from any spinning chi.

Q: We live in a gated community and have been happy with our neighborhood, until I read somewhere that it's bad Feng Shui to live behind a locked gate. What does Feng Shui say about this kind of living situation?

A: My quick answer is that it depends. Feng Shui is all about intention, so what intentions are you setting for your life in the community? Do you feel that being behind the gate feels secure, protected, and comfortable? Or, do you feel like you're locked away and nothing and no one can reach you? Your answer will reveal whether this is a good Feng Shui location for you.

Q: My home is adjacent to a storm drain that I think might be affecting my prosperity. I'd like to retain more of my income and thought you might have a cure for me. I also have a street light above the storm drain, so at least I feel like I am en-light-ened!

A: You're right to be concerned that a storm drain near your home might be draining your wealth. If the street light is directly in front of your door, it could be having an additional negative effect. Water represents wealth and abundance in Feng Shui, but the storm drain represents *negative* water, because it carries dirt and refuse. Since you can't move the drain, the best remedy is to plant soft, bushy shrubs between the storm drain and your home to symbolically create a barrier. Plants represent the Wood Element, which will draw up the overabundance of negative water. To attract more income, place the Water Element in the foyer or entry, near the front door. This can take the form of a fountain or fish bowl, or artwork that shows a river, stream, waterfall, or ocean flowing into the home.

Q: We're considering building a new house on a street that goes up a hill, and we have our choice of lots. We like the lot at the very top of the hill because the view is fantastic, but I read that this is not a good Feng Shui location. How do we decide which lot to choose?

A: The phrase "top of the hill" has negative connotations in Feng Shui because there's too much chi directed at the house, making you overly exposed. Think about how some people want to "knock off" the person at the top. That's the same situation with a house in this location; plus, there's nothing behind you for protection. The better Feng Shui location is mid-way up, because you have some of the hill behind you for protection. The house at the bottom of the hill is considered the least auspicious. Choose the higher side of the street if that's an option.

CHAPTER 5: REARRANGING, SHIFTING, TRANSFORMING

Q: The front door of the house is lower than the road. I love this lot, especially the view out the back, but I don't want it to have bad Feng Shui.

A: The challenge about a house in this location is that you start each day with an "uphill climb." However, when you make Feng Shui adjustments to lift the chi, you change this to a positive feeling of starting each day by "moving up." Some ways to do this include installing lighting along the driveway to pull up the chi, placing a decorative object such as an outdoor sculpture at the top of the driveway, displaying your house number prominently at road level on a mail box or artful number display, or placing a flag, banner, or wind-sensitive decoration near the front door, as high up as possible. A beautiful view out the back helps to balance any negativity of the slope in front.

Neighbors

Q: The windows in my neighbors' family room face the windows of my living room. They just bought a 6' wide TV, and they have it on all day. It is so BIG, I feel like I'm being bombarded by electromagnetic energy. How can I reflect the negative energy?

A: An article in the *Wall Street Journal* called these huge televisions the "elephant in the room." Not only is the TV distracting for you, but the electromagnetic issues for its owners are substantial. To reflect the negative energy, hang a mirror in the window facing the neighbors. Use a round mirror, around 4"– 6" in size. You can stick it right on the window with double-stick tape, or put a loop or eyelet on the back and attach it with a suction-cup hook. Make sure the mirror faces the offending TV. Also, you may need to invest in some sheer or translucent window treatments, either curtains or shades, that you can keep closed while letting in some light.

Q: I'm fed up with my neighbors. They are noisy, the grass in the front yard is always overgrown, they don't shovel the snow in winter, and they keep a lot of junk in their backyard. Does this bad energy from their house contaminate mine? We can't afford to move right now.

A: You can try to create strong, protective energy around your house with landscaping changes to push away their negative energy. First, place a barrier between you and the neighbors. Options include attractive fencing, a wall of tall evergreens, a rock garden, tall garden sculptures, or wind-sensitive objects. You can plant shrubs with orange flowers between the houses, because this color encourages positive communication. Or, hang a convex bagua mirror on the outside wall of the house that faces the neighbor to push the negative energy back to its source. A bagua mirror is a Chinese octagon-shaped mirror with a yellow wood frame. Make sure you have window treatments on the side of the house that face the neighbors to help block their energy, and if there are any doors facing their house, make sure they are solid and in good repair. For the noise, consider playing soothing music throughout your house or use a white noise machine. Make these adjustments with the affirmation that these positive changes push away the neighbors' negative energy, and subtly encourage them to move.

Q: Our neighbors have just installed a skateboard ramp right outside my bedroom window. Kids are out there from morning until nightfall and we are going crazy. We asked them several times to move it, but they won't. Help!

A: Hang a bagua mirror on the outside of your home facing the ramp. The mirror will send energy back at the skateboarders and make them feel like they are being "watched," pushing them in the right direction, which is away from your house!

Q: We live in a low-rise condo development where all our decks overlook the balconies of other units. We not only lack privacy, but sometimes it feels like we have dozens of eyes staring at us. Is there anything we can do to help?

A: Try defining your space by placing planters near the edge of the deck or hanging planter boxes on the deck railing to separate you from your neighbors. Plant flowers or shrubs in them, or even small evergreen trees if you have enough space. These will not only attract the Wood Element energy to your home, but will also help deflect any real or imagined "prying eyes" of neighbors. On the inside, energize your home against any troublesome neighbors by placing fresh flower arrangements on your windowsill or on a table near the window.

CHAPTER 5: REARRANGING, SHIFTING, TRANSFORMING

Numbers and Symbols

Q: Is any particular house number especially good or bad? My house has the number 4 in the address, and I read that this is an unlucky number in Feng Shui. My life is pretty happy, and I certainly don't plan to move. Should I do anything to keep my luck going in the right direction?

A: The Chinese consider the number four to be unlucky because it sounds like the word *death* in certain dialects. But, the word *four* doesn't have this association in Western cultures. So, if you have this number in your address and you're from a country other than China, try thinking of the word *four* as rhyming with the word *more*, instead of worrying whether it's unlucky. In analyzing a house number, you first need to reduce the address down to a single digit. For example, in the address 9701 you would add 9+7+0+1 to get a total of 17. Then you would continue to reduce the number by adding 1+7 to get 8 as your final 1-digit number. Apartment dwellers use their unit number rather than the building number. No matter what numbers are in your address, make sure they are clearly visible from the street so visitors—and positive chi—can find you.

Q: Where in my house should I keep statues of elephants, and should I choose the ones with the trunks lifted up or pointed down? We're trying to get pregnant.

A: I loved reading this question because my mom collected white elephants with uplifted trunks, which she thought would bring us luck. She bought one every time we went into Chinatown for dinner! This was before I discovered Feng Shui, so I was pleased to learn that elephants are, indeed, considered auspicious symbols of good fortune. With their trunks up, they are said to protect a home and are best placed in your foyer flanking the front door. With their trunks down, they are said to bring "descendants' luck" to the family. If a couple is trying to conceive, elephants with their trunks down are placed in the master bedroom, on both sides of the door, as you enter the room.

Q: What is the meaning of the dragonfly in Feng Shui? Even though I never thought they were pretty, I find myself drawn to images of dragonflies, and I have to surround myself with them. The dragonfly

images started showing up a few years ago after much loss in my family, and since then, there has been huge transformation in my life. It feels like the dragonflies forced me to stop and listen, and they have become a huge part of my healing and ability to help others.

A: In Feng Shui, the dragonfly is considered a predictor of the future, and similar to a butterfly or bird, it carries the energy of transformation. Perhaps the universe is showing you there's even more change and movement coming for you. The world is undergoing quite a lot of transformation right now, so it's good to locate dragonfly, bird, or butterfly symbols near your front door.

Pets

Q: I live in a small condo and the only choices for places to keep my cat's litter box are in my kitchen or in my office where I run my consulting business. I chose the office. I looked at the bagua chart on your website and it seems like her box is in the Wealth area. Is there anything I can do to keep both my cat and my wealth?

A: The ideal place for a litter box is in the bathroom, laundry room, or garage. Keeping the litter box in an office repels wealth rather than encourages it. In other words, you don't want the cat doing her business where you're trying to run yours. The worse location for the litter box would be in the kitchen. Kitchens are associated with food, and the negative chi of the waste litter box is detrimental to your health. Keep the litter box in the bathroom. Buy a covered litter box so you don't see waste every time you enter the room. Whatever kind of box you use, be sure you empty it often.

Q: I'm planning to fence in an area in the backyard for my dog and wanted to pick the best bagua location. How do I use the bagua out back?

A: You can use the bagua for your backyard by standing outside with your back to the house and hold the bagua in front of you. Draw the shape of the lot and then divided it into the nine bagua areas. The best bagua location for pets is either the Family area or the Creativity area of the bagua. Please remember, it's critical to clean up after your dog every time. If you live in a house surrounded by poop, more poop is what you'll attract into your life

CHAPTER 5: REARRANGING, SHIFTING, TRANSFORMING

Fast 5

Feng Shui for Your Pets

*Are you attracting what you want into your life?
If not, take a good look at how you have arranged
your household around your pets:*

1. **Pet waste.** Clean up pet waste in your yard and around your home. A house surrounded by poop, attracts poop (I'm using polite language!). No exceptions here.

2. **Fish tank.** Keep the fish tank or bowl clean since dirty water represents a cloudy financial future. The best combination to bring wealth into your home is nine fish (eight gold and one black).

3. **Pets.** Keep your pet out of your bed if you're having relationship issues. When a pet sleeps between a couple, it represents splitting the relationship and deterring romance. If you must have your pets in the bedroom, give them their own beds on the floor.

4. **Odors.** Ask a good friend to give you an honest opinion of whether your home smells from pet odors. You might be surprised about what "ghost odors" remain. Take care of any problem rooms immediately.

5. **Jumping.** Don't let your dog jump on people, bark, or scare guests when they first enter. This symbolizes struggling with relationships and scaring off love. Consider keeping your pets in another room when you have visitors until you know how they get along with each other.

Q: When we put our bed on risers, one of our Cocker Spaniels started using the space underneath as her nest. She doesn't bring stuff under there or sleep under the bed; she just likes to hide out there. Is there any negative chi from her going in and out and resting under the bed? If anything, it may keep that space active and create more movement there.

A: Pets are considered good Feng Shui because they have active yang energy. It is only when owners let their pets rule the household that they become negative energy. But, that does not seem to be the case here. The chi from your dog nesting under your bed is positive, especially since she doesn't sleep there or store things under you. You described it quite accurately: she brings positive energy to the room and good chi flow under your bed. It obviously works for you, and it certainly sounds like a happy arrangement.

Q: I fell in love with Rufus the moment I saw him at the shelter. I've never had a dog before, and I'm used to keeping a very neat place, and I can't believe the mess. I know I can't Feng Shui Rufus, but are there some tips that could help us adjust to each other while still keeping my home balanced?

A: Lively pets bring vibrant yang energy into your home. The trick is to make sure Rufus doesn't overwhelm your home, which can happen when a pet is too large or energetic for the size of your home. The love we put into caring for our pets represents positive energy, but sometimes, we inadvertently arrange a home around the needs of our pets in a way that upsets the natural balance that's critical to good Feng Shui. You need to make the decisions about the arrangement of furniture and objects in your rooms, not Rufus.

Q: What bagua area should I activate to help bring back my lost cat?

A: The Helpful People/Travel area is the first place to start because it represents safe travel and returns. Place one of your pet's favorite items in that area, along with a picture and the name of your pet. Good luck!

CHAPTER 5: REARRANGING, SHIFTING, TRANSFORMING

SUCCESS STORY

*Linda Turns a Negative
Into a Positive*

Linda is a long-time reader of my Feng Shui newsletter who shared her clutter-clearing story. It all began with my tip to move 27 things in her home to make room for new things to enter her life. Linda was heartbroken after the loss of her German Shepherd, who was her constant companion. A senior who lives alone, she said her family was concerned about her safety after this loss, but she didn't think she had room for a new pet in her life.

Here's what Linda wrote:

❝ I was hesitant to even think about getting a new dog because of the pain I was feeling for my departed pup (he was a senior, too). As fate would have it, I was in the pet store with my daughter when we were introduced to two kittens: a brother and sister who were only 10 weeks old. They were from the Humane Society and were the last two from a litter. I held the little boy and the tears began. Long story short, I left there with both. I was coming from a quiet lifestyle with my senior dog and now transitioning to two very active babies in a compact apartment, so I moved 27 things immediately to kitten-proof my living quarters. Plants had to go except for one, anything glass that didn't have a purpose was put away, etc. The end result was no clutter, which makes cleaning so much easier. I still feel grief over losing my pup, but I now have two youngsters who gave my heart a boost, and they keep me on my toes for what is safe and what is necessary. They show me how to enjoy the moment and not dwell on what cannot be changed. Hope you enjoy my story as much as I am enjoying my reasons for moving 27 (plus) things. ❞

Poison Arrows

Q: After remodeling some areas of the house and opening up the floor plan to an open kitchen, now when we walk in to the house through the front door, we have a straight shot to a window and at an angle with the back door. I read an article about the front door and this direct line, which said it wasn't a positive situation. What are your suggestions to stop this runaway chi? Please help!

A: This is a frequently-asked questions. The situation you describe is called a *poison arrow*, because the chi comes in the front door and runs straight through the house and out the window, like an arrow aimed at a target. What you want instead is for the chi to enter and slowly fill up the home. The general Feng Shui recommendation is to place something between the doors to slow the chi. Options include placing a small rug in the entry area rather than a long runner; hanging artwork at different levels on the walls; or covering the back door with window treatments so the chi must slow down and move in a more flowing manner. The words *feng* and *shui* means *wind* and *water*, and that's the gentle way you want the chi to flow in your home, rather than straight out the back door.

Real Estate

Q: With the help of the information in your book, my fiancé and I found our dream house and will move in a few weeks. Are there any items I shouldn't take with me?

A: Avoid taking anything with you that you don't like, don't use, or don't need. That's because anything that has negative associations for either of you represents stale chi. This is the perfect time to get rid of unwanted things rather than bring their negative energy into your new home. Make sure you don't bring anything from a past relationship (you shouldn't have that around anymore, anyway!). You want to love everything you bring into your new home and make sure it all has special meaning. Get rid of any furniture, plants, or art that the previous owner left behind. Also, I recommend you do a space clearing or blessing ceremony before you move in any of your possessions.

CHAPTER 5: REARRANGING, SHIFTING, TRANSFORMING

Q: I am a real estate agent. My clients' house has been vacant for a while because they moved out of town for a job change. Every time I go inside, the house feels cold and deserted. Any Feng Shui suggestions to make the house feel more alive?

A: When a home sits vacant, it loses vital chi, or life force, and can appear lifeless. I recommend you do a Feng Shui staging to add furniture and artwork. This will bring active energy back into the space. Be sure to add some life to the landscape as well by making sure everything is well maintained. And, consider adding something wind-sensitive to the yard, like a wind chime or a moving sculpture.

Q: We are getting ready to look for our first home. Are there certain Feng Shui problems that we should avoid?

A: The real estate saying "location, location, location" also applies to Feng Shui. These are my top three locations to avoid:

1. Near **power lines or cell towers**, which can negatively affect your health.
2. On the **curve of a cul-de-sac**, where the good chi can bypass your house making the house cold and unfriendly.
3. At a **T-junction**, where the traffic coming at you acts like a sharp arrow hitting a target, making the house difficult to live in.

Q: I'm a real estate agent and I'm trying to sell a house in the $1 million range that had been on the market for several months with very few showings. The home has several challenging issues, and I'm especially bothered by the strong food smells that still permeate the house even though it's vacant, not to mention the stark white walls and awkward floor plan. It has been staged, but it still feels empty and stark.

A: A Feng Shui staging can go farther than a typical real estate staging in correcting a floor plan that's missing bagua areas, and in balancing the Five Elements throughout the house. To keep the house from feeling so cold, try playing music throughout the house during a showing to keep the chi moving. Diffusers in the rooms could temporarily mask the musky smell odor, but, ultimately, you'll need to steam or replace the carpet and window treatments. Repainting the walls will also help with the odor issue, and choosing a warmer shade rather than stark white will help bring some yang energy to warm up the space. You could also add some big plants throughout the house, and when you show the house, direct lighting to them to create yang energy.

Q: My husband built a very expensive and beautiful spec house last year. We have come close to selling it a couple of times, but we lost both customers. Is there anything we can do to counteract this?

A: What's going on around the home? Are there larger buildings, obstructions, or negative energy pointing at the house? Is it located at a T-junction or on a cul-de-sac? Is it near a school or religious building? All these things can reduce the positive energy reaching the home, no matter how beautiful and high-end. Landscape the property to block the view of any of these obstructions.

Q: I am trying to sell a house that has a bedroom painted a bright green. Several potential buyers have commented that the color is uncomfortable for them. What color should I repaint it?

A: Green is the color of the Wood Element, which represents growth and expansion, but it's too stimulating for a bedroom. That's why it doesn't feel right to buyers. The ideal color for a bedroom is a skin tone, ranging from ivory to mahogany. If buyers see a bedroom in a 'human" color such as blush, rose, or peach, they will feel more comfortable in the room.

Q: I'm condo shopping. Is there anything that makes a home un-livable right from the get-go?

A: In the real-world approach to Feng Shui that I practice, there's almost always a remedy for every negative situation in a home. That being said, it's preferable to choose a home that needs the fewest adjustments. First, look at the floor plan of the condo. The closer the shape is to a square or rectangle, the more balanced you'll feel living there. Second, consider the location of the unit. Is anything blocking your view, like a dumpster or a taller building? Avoid a location where a structure nearby monopolizes the chi, like a church or other religious building, a school, or a cemetery. Third, look for a unit where the bathrooms and laundry aren't in the Wealth, Love, or Health areas of the bagua. If you're considering a place that needs a lot of repairs, be sure your budget allows you to finish the repairs quickly, so you won't be living with negative energy.

CHAPTER 5: REARRANGING, SHIFTING, TRANSFORMING

SUCCESS STORY

Erica and Michael Finally Sell Their Home

Erica and Michael were moving out of town because of a job change and needed to sell their house quickly for full price, so they called me to see how Feng Shui could help. They had done all the usual things their agent recommended, including repainting, freshening up the landscaping, and de-cluttering the closets and garage, but they had no offers. One of their main issues was that the front door lined up directly with the back door, and then out to the pool, symbolizing prosperity flowing out of the house. I recommended a few simple Feng Shui changes.

Here's what Erica wrote:

❝ We immediately understood what you meant when you said buyers couldn't tell which of our double front doors was the one to enter, so we placed a fresh, earthy color doormat in front of the main door and a pair of clay pots with red geraniums on both sides of the doors to act as a welcoming greeter to buyers. We replaced the house numbers written in unreadable script that couldn't be seen from the street with large black numerals. We boxed up our very personal modern art collection as a symbol that we were ready and willing to move, and we replaced it with inexpensive, colorful prints with happy family themes as you recommended. We removed the runner between the front and back doors that you said was acting like an arrow directing the chi out of the house, and we placed large evergreen trees in red planters outside on the pool deck keep prosperity from dumping into the pool. Within a week of making these simple changes, we got a contract for full price! Yes, Feng Shui made the difference! ❞

Religion

Q: Is Feng Shui a religion? I'm interested in learning more about it, but I don't want to get involved in anything that's different from my religion and culture.

A: Feng Shui isn't a religion or superstition. It's not magic. Rather, it is the art and science of keeping your indoor environment balanced. Even though the roots of this ancient practice are Chinese, Feng Shui improvements can be made to fit all cultures and all decorating styles. You don't need to decorate your home in an Asian decor to appreciate order and harmony, because Feng Shui-like advice runs through various cultures. Serenity knows no single culture. We experience Feng Shui cultural crossover all around us without even realizing it.

Stairs

Q: We're considering buying a condo, but our hesitation is the spiral staircase in the center of the house from the living room up to the loft. What do you think?

A: The Feng Shui concern about a spiral staircase is that it can act like a corkscrew, removing the core of energy from what's considered the Grounding area of your home. People often feel unstable on a spiral staircase because there's nothing underneath them for support. If you buy the condo, place plants at the base of the staircase to act as a cushion. Choose plants that have soft, rounded leaves rather than pointed leaves or thorns. I would advise against placing plants on the steps themselves because that will narrow the width of the stairs.

Q: Can you provide advice to correct the Feng Shui of an open spiral? There is a mirror the size of a doorway facing the start of the stairway. I have read that this staircase is a very bad situation causing major money leaks (this is happening) and instability (I feel this way).

A: It's hard to know for sure without seeing your space, but it's probably not a good idea for a mirror to reflect the stairs. Mirrors double what they reflect, and

CHAPTER 5: REARRANGING, SHIFTING, TRANSFORMING

this would represent doubling the "hole" in the middle of your home. Remove the mirror. Assure the staircase is always well lit. If possible, carpet the stairs.

Q: I have an open spiral staircase in my house, and I have fallen several times going down, fortunately without really injuring myself. Is there anything I can do to feel more secure on the staircase?

A: With an open staircase, there's nothing at the bottom to make you feel grounded as you climb the stairs. Try placing several bushy plants at the bottom of the stairway to give you a feeling of grounding. Other option specific to your problem of falling includes placing a stone statue at the base of the staircase to ground it (Earth Element), or hanging artwork near the staircase that has outdoor and landscape themes (Wood Element). Also, make sure the staircase has good lighting. [See previous questions for more ideas.]

Trash

Q: Where should I keep the trash can?

A: This is one of my favorite questions because it was the first one I asked my teacher when I started studying Feng Shui. I knew I didn't want to keep the trash in the Wealth, Love, or Health area, but I couldn't figure out which area was best. His answer, and the one I have often repeated, is to choose the smallest trashcan you can live with. Then, place it in the part of the room that relates to the bagua area that's exceptionally strong for you, rather than in the bagua area that you feel isn't working so well in your life. Wherever you place the can, empty it frequently so the negative chi doesn't have time to accumulate.

Q: I live in an apartment, and each night, I put the outgoing trash bag by the front door so that I remember to take it to the trash chute when I leave for work in the morning. Is there a better place to keep it?

A: It's good that you take out the trash every day, but the front door is the *mouth of chi* where all positive chi enters, so that's not a good place for trash. Start a habit of taking out the trash after you do the dishes each night. Or, leave the bag in the trash can until it's ready to go in the morning. You can hang a small sign by the front door that says, *REMEMBER THE TRASH!*

Travel

Q: I am going on vacation. Can I do anything Feng Shui-wise to protect my house while I am gone?

A: In addition to the obvious things of stopping the newspaper and holding the mail, put the radio or television on timers so they will periodically play in the house while you're gone. This will keep some yang, or active, energy in the house so it doesn't become still, or yin, energy. A still house draws more negative energies to it, such as burglars. A symbolic technique to ward off intruders is to turn a broom upside down outside, next to the door. Be sure to remove the broom once you have returned.

Trees

Q: I have a big tree in front of my house and I read somewhere this is a big Feng Shui problem. What do you think?

A: The answer depends on the location of the tree in relationship to your house. If a tree is directly in front of the main door, it's considered negative because it blocks the positive chi from entering the house. One correction for this situation is to hang a convex mirror above the door to reflect away any negative energy. If a tree is to the side of the front door, it's better to have it on the left side of the house slightly higher than the tree on the right side (looking out from inside the house). You can have a tree service prune the tree on the right to lower it. Generally, you want a tree to be far enough from the house that it gives both you and the tree enough breathing room.

Q: Is it ever bad luck to have a tree planted near your house?

A: The basic rule is to avoid planting a tree directly in line with the front door because it blocks the flow of positive energy into your house. It's also recommended that you avoid planting trees so close to your house that the limbs hang directly over the roof, since heavy branches could fall on the house during a storm. If you already have large trees near your house, the solution to these issues is to take care of and nurture your trees. If you keep your trees properly pruned and trimmed, they will represent positive energy sheltering your home. Remove all dead trees immediately.

Q: We have a huge old tree in our backyard that provides wonderful shade, but some limbs are starting to hang over the house. I've heard it's not a good omen in Feng Shui. What do you think?

A: Heavy tree limbs hanging over your roof represent added weight on your shoulders, so the Feng Shui recommendation is to remove those to "lighten your load." It's especially important to allow plenty of room between these limbs and your house. You should consult a professional arborist who will be able to guide you on pruning to keep the tree healthy and your house safe.

Q: We lost a beautiful tree in our backyard after a storm, and now the view out my kitchen window is a tree stump. It's pretty bleak out there. What should I do?

A: Your tree stump represents yin, or inactive, energy that should be balanced by the active, yang, energy of a living plant. The best option is to remove the stump and plant a new tree. If you can't do that, you can bring back the energy in this location by planting ivy or other climbing plants around the stump that will cover it with vines and foliage. You can also display something like a brightly-colored plant in a pot or a metal garden ornament on top of the tree stump to give it more life. I've also seen the remains of dead trees carves into shapes and figures, which is a unique way to bring yang energy back into a yin object.

Windows and Skylights

Q: I'm in a mood to re-arrange furniture in our bedroom, which is a real challenge because of the number of windows and doors. I want to put the head of the bed on a wall where it would be under a window. Could I enclose the window by filling the space with a fitted piece of Styrofoam covered with cloth and then hang a curtain in front of it? Would that be a "real" cure, or am I just doomed to keep the bed in the same location?

A: Your idea for filling the window with fabric-covered Styrofoam is fine, but you don't need to go that far if you don't want to. You can install a window treatment that gives a lot of privacy and protection, and then be sure to close it each night. For example, wood shutters, woven blinds, or lined drapes would work to make you feel more grounded when sleeping in front of the window.

Q: For the last several years, I've been putting plastic on the windows to keep the warmth in my apartment. I am definitely warmer, and I save lots of money on heating costs, but this year I noticed the old plastic looked filmy. I'm wondering if this is not good for my Feng Shui. Is there any way to offset the effects? The landlord will not replace the windows.

A: Windows are considered to be the eyes of a home, so I'm concerned that when you look through filmy plastic on your windows, it symbolizes looking at life through a clouded lens. Instead of the old plastic, hang insulated drapes or shades over the windows. If you must have plastic, at least replace it each year. You could also display a picture of another apartment or house in the Future area, as a sign that you'll move on to a better place (with better windows) in the near future.

Q: Is it OK to have a skylight right over my bed? I love being able to look at the stars at night, but I read this is not a good Feng Shui recommendation. Now I'm concerned.

A: A skylight can be seen as a hole in the room that lets chi escape, so it's not always good to have one directly over your bed. The primary consideration is whether you feel safe and secure under the skylight, or whether you can't sleep and feel exhausted in the morning. Make sure you keep the skylight clean and maintained. Hang electronic coverings over the skylight, so you could close them if needed, but avoid sharp-edged metal blinds. Or, hang a faceted crystal from the skylight to deflect any negative energy and prevent the chi from leaving the room.

CHAPTER

6

OBJECTS OF DESIRE FROM A-Z

Everyone can use Feng Shui to feel connected to the natural world. The good news is that with contemporary approaches to Feng Shui, you don't have to decorate your home like a Chinese restaurant or a Zen shrine to bring the power of Feng Shui into your life. You get to surround yourself with objects that you love.

Buying a Feng Shui object and hoping it will take care of all your problems has been called the "vending machine" approach. That is, the belief that selecting a special object will automatically give you what you want. Unless you bring your own symbolic value to an object, it won't affect your life, no matter where you buy it or place it. All the so-called Feng Shui enhancements—like fu dogs, dragons, laughing Buddhas, red envelopes, bamboo flutes, and red streamers—are part of Chinese culture, but not necessarily part of contemporary Feng Shui. If these objects don't symbolize anything to you, they won't help you attract what you want.

My Feng Shui mantra is *you are what you see*. My favorite image is Dorothy's ruby red slippers, and my often-used phrase is *there's no place like home*. These are powerful reminders of how I help my clients live in harmony with their homes. What are *your* touchstones? When you surround yourself with items that relate to your specific goals, you shift the energy of your space to match your own style.

The most effective way to do this is to choose objects that symbolize your hopes and dreams. For example, if you want to enhance your relationship with your spouse, instead of buying a pair of Chinese fu dogs (those dog-lion looking creatures) for your bedroom, hang a romantic picture of a place you've visited together, or a scene with a couple holding hands.

CHAPTER 6: OBJECTS OF DESIRE FROM A-Z

The most effective way to make adjustments is to choose objects based on how they inspire, encourage, or empower you in a specific aspect of your life, rather than for what they are *supposed* to do for you. Then, put these objects in your home in the appropriate bagua areas as a visual reminder of the positive steps you're taking toward making necessary improvements in that area of your life.

Choose images and objects that represent a clear idea of what you want to bring into your life. Keep in mind that if you don't like a so-called Feng Shui object, it won't fix anything.

Every object tells a story,
you just have to know how to read it.
— Henry Ford

Q & A

OBJECTS OF DESIRE FROM A-Z

Antiques and Previously-Owned Stuff

Q: Is it bad Feng Shui to buy items from antique stores and estate sales? I've been thinking about buying an antique bed, but I can never find the one that I feel good enough about to actually buy.

A: Items from antique stores, consignment boutiques, and flea markets can carry strong energy from previous owners. We call this *predecessor chi*. Some objects, especially beds, absorb more of this energy than others. Reflective objects like glass, silver, and gold will absorb less energy than items made from non-reflective materials like wood or heavy fabrics. If you have any doubts about an item when you're still considering whether to buy it, that's probably your own Feng Shui intuition telling you the object is carrying energy that's not right for your home. If you do buy an antique or vintage object, do a clearing as soon as you bring it into your home. This can be as simple as wiping down the object with a sea salt and distilled water solution.

Q: I hate my sofa. I bought it at a consignment shop because that's all I could afford. Is it bad Feng Shui to buy cast-offs and other second-hand items from a consignment store? My budget is strained these days so I'm trying to save money where I can.

A: The key concept in your question is *cast-offs*. If you have negative feelings about anything you buy, no matter what kind of store it comes from, you'll bring that negative energy into your home. Buying second-hand can be positive Feng Shui as long as you feel good about the object you're acquiring. It will be negative Feng Shui if you feel you're accepting second best because it's all you think you can afford. It's important to love everything you have in your home. Replace the sofa with one that you feel more positive about, whether or not it's from a consignment store. Feng Shui is all about intention, so set your intention to feel good about your purchase, no matter where you end up buying it.

CHAPTER 6: OBJECTS OF DESIRE FROM A-Z

Q: I inherited some beautiful antique furniture from my mother, but it has been sitting in storage for several years. I hate to part with it because it has so many pleasant memories of my childhood, but I don't want to continue to pay to store it. Any suggestions?

A: Take a good, hard look at the furniture and decide if you truly love what it looks like, or if it's only the memories surrounding it that you love. If you still love what you inherited, consider replacing some of your current furniture with these heirloom pieces. If you don't love it enough to surround yourself with it, take digital photographs of the furniture so you'll have the memories, then sell or donate the pieces. This will get your positive chi flowing toward the future.

Q: I've been collecting antique teapots for years and I love them all, but recently, I began wondering if they have good or bad Feng Shui mojo.

A: Antiques and other previously-owned objects do carry *predecessor chi* from their previous owners. That energy can feel positive or negative. My guess is that if the energy in any of your teapots felt negative, you wouldn't have been attracted to them to begin with. As long as you love what you buy, it's okay to continue collecting. Just be sure to avoid buying a teapot (or any object) that's cracked or chipped. If you acquire new teapots, give them a good cleaning with distilled water and sea salt before displaying them in your home. Be careful not to let your collection overwhelm the room you have for displaying it.

Q: I have begun taking piano lessons, and I have located a beautiful small grand piano in the neighborhood that I'm considering buying. It's owned now by a woman whose sister played it for some years before she died from cancer. I'm concerned about the karma that might be associated with the piano, and I didn't want to bring that into my happy, healthy home. Do you have any thoughts on this?

A: Get in touch with the feelings you're bringing to the purchase of this particular piano, and that will help you decide. For example, ask yourself whether you look at the piano and see a woman lovingly playing it and living a full and rich life before she died, or whether you see a woman who died tragically, and a family who must sell the piano because they don't want negative memories. The answers will help you decide. Make sure you try playing the piano in the owner's home and see how you feel.

Art

Q: How can I use Feng Shui to decide what art I pick to hang on my walls to help me feel happier?

A: Because every action has a reaction, we're influenced by everything around us, and in turn, we influence everything. That means the colors, shapes, and images you use to decorate your surroundings influence what you attract into your life. The more you surround yourself with symbols of what you want to attract, the more likely you're to achieve it. For example, if you surround yourself with artwork that's bleak and expresses isolation, you'll attract experiences that make you feel similarly isolated and lonely. But, if the images in your artwork express joy and prosperity, your life will be prosperous and joyous. Match the feeling of the art to the appropriate bagua area.

Q: When you did a phone consultation for my new apartment, you suggested I get a cityscape piece of art for my creativity wall. My question is whether I should pick the DC cityscape since that's where I live, or could I pick any of the other cityscapes, most likely London, because I love it? I don't have any plans or wishes to move somewhere else, so that's why I'm unsure of what to pick.

A: Try to first clarify your intention when choosing and hanging either image, because when you make Feng Shui changes, you get what you need, not necessarily what you think you want. Ask yourself which image speaks to your creativity, playfulness, joy, etc. That's the one to display in your Creativity area. If you do want to travel or move to a new location, hang a picture of that city in your Helpful People/Travel area. Enjoy your new art!

Q: I'm an artist, and I received a painting of a girl as a gift from my drawing teacher many years ago. Now, I'm concerned that because the girl looks angry, it wouldn't be good to have it in a prominent place in the house. Please let me know what would be best. I love this piece of art, and it means a lot to me. The reason I am asking is that it faces the door as you walk into the house, and I wasn't sure if her frowning/angry expression would be unwelcoming or even act as some sort of poison arrow aimed at guests, and at me.

CHAPTER 6: OBJECTS OF DESIRE FROM A-Z

A: The general rule of thumb is that if you're having concerns or second thoughts about any piece of art, it doesn't belong in your home. If your gut is telling you that the angry expression on the subject of the painting is unwelcoming, don't display it in your house. Consider donating the painting to a nonprofit—maybe an arts organization—that can resell it to support their cause.

Q: An artist friend recently gave me a gift of a portrait he drew of me. I read in your book that displaying artwork that shows a single woman reinforces the idea of staying single. I would like to attract the right person eventually (this artist is a friend only). Is there anywhere I should, or should not, place the portrait?

A: Avoid putting the drawing in the Love/Relationship area of your home or in your bedroom. Ironically, people often display art with images that represent *singleness* in these areas, which symbolizes that they're not ready for a relationship. The ideal location for your portrait is either in the Knowledge/Wisdom area, where it represents self-knowledge, or in the Family area surrounded by photos of your family and friends.

Q: I am delighted that I found you on the internet, and plan to hire you to do a remote session in the fall. In the meantime, I have a question concerning using a painting or drawing to bring the Water Element into my Wealth area. I know that the ideal paintings will show moving water, correct? Or will it help if it is a painting of just an ocean, river, lake, etc.? In my particular case, it is going in our laundry room that is, unfortunately, a good portion of our Wealth area. Anything you can do to help or point me in the right direction would be most appreciated.

A: Avoid displaying an image of water in your Wealth area, because that area is activated by the Fire Element. If you add Water here, you'll symbolically reduce the Fire and extinguish your wealth, which is the opposite of what you want to do. You already have too much Water in that area because it's a laundry room where water goes down the drain. I recommend avoiding images of oceans, rivers, or lakes. Instead, choose images that have the Fire Element colors (red, orange, or deep purple) or shape (triangle). This will symbolically dry up some of that excess Water created by the washer.

Q: I have a sculpture made by my daughter that has lots of heads in it. My other family members all agreed that the sculpture is creepy, they have never liked it, and they suggest I get rid of it. I tried to put it somewhere else, but it didn't look or feel right. I have to admit I only sort of like it and I am tired of it. My daughter is dealing with a minor health issue, so I'm feeling superstitious about moving it until the health issue is cleared up and she moves to a new apartment.

A: I appreciate your concern that the image may have some power related to your daughter's health issues. The best solution is to remove it with a ceremony. Wrap the sculpture in a red cloth or red tissue paper and pack it away until your daughter wants it back. This may actually support your daughter and help her move past her health issue. At some point, you may want to ask if she does want it back, because it's also possible she doesn't like it anymore.

Q: We are New Yorkers, now living on the other side of the country. We have a framed picture of the Twin Towers in our bedroom, which is a beautiful night skyline, but it makes me feel sad when I look at it. I worry that the negativity surrounding it could be the reason for our past serious financial woes since this picture is located over the desk in our bedroom. Is this bad?

A: I recommend removing the image from your bedroom. A picture with such an emotional message for you might be too strong for your bedroom. Your bedroom should be reserved for rest and romance only, so move out anything that interferes with that purpose, including this emotionally-charged picture. Art for a bedroom should feel romantic, paired, and coupled. And by the way, it would be better if you didn't have a work area in your bedroom. If you must keep it, screen it off with a floor screen or standing plants so you don't see it from the bed.

Q: I have a painting of a bull and a bull fighter over my bed that my girlfriend hates. What kind of picture should I hang in my bedroom to help our relationship?

A: I agree with your girlfriend; the symbolism of the bull fight is violent and isn't sending the right bedroom signals. The art in your bedroom, especially above your bed, should be romantic and depict what you want to attract into your relationship, like love, romance, marriage, etc. Also, to strengthen the relationship with your girlfriend, place a recent photo of the two of you in the Love area of the room.

Fast 5

Decide Where to Hang It

If you're looking at sad, lonely artwork, that's what you'll attract into your life. Instead, try these five tips for attracting what you want into your life:

1. **Water.** If you want to attract prosperity, choose art showing water images or a waterfall, since both are associated with a prosperous career and increasing income.

2. **Ships.** Images of sailing vessels also represent wealth flowing into your home, especially when the ship is sailing into—not out of—your home or workplace.

3. **Happy People.** If you want to feel more connected to friends and family, choose images of happy people and joyous events.

4. **Negativity.** No matter how valuable the art, think twice about purchasing something with a depressing or negative theme, since it can pull down the positive chi energy in your home.

5. **Value.** Display only what you love, and avoid hanging art just because you paid a lot for it.

Books and Book Shelves

Q: I'm hooked on Marie Kondo and her advice to tidy up and only keep things that spark joy. She says she only keeps 30 books in her home. I'm not convinced that will work for me. What does Feng Shui say about books? And what do you personally think?

A: I've been a Feng Shui practitioner for more than 20 years, and whenever I start talking about downsizing a book collection, I get dirty looks and that arms-folded-across-the-chest body language that tells me to back off. I know it's hard to get rid of books. As often as I advise people to cull their book collection, I would never tell anyone to limit their books to any specific number. In fact, Marie says she has been misquoted when it comes to limiting book collections to a specific number of books. That was her choice to limit it to 30 books. The books we choose to display are the ultimate reflection of who we are, where we've been, and where we are going. That means you have my Feng Shui permission to display books, as long as you can answer yes to all of the following questions:

1. Do the books still have meaning for you?
2. Will you read them again?
3. Will you display them artfully?
4. Do you promise to remove one book every time you add a new book?
5. Do you promise to dust them regularly?

That will help you keep your special books, and at the same time keep Marie Kondo (and me) satisfied.

Q: A friend told me about a Feng Shui article that said you should get rid of all the books in a study and remove the book shelves because they are bad Feng Shui. Is this true, and is there a best way to display books, either horizontally or vertically?

A: Books are considered positive Feng Shui because they represent wisdom and knowledge, but too many books in the wrong place can have a negative effect. Book shelves that are completely filled symbolically prevent new knowledge and information from flowing to you. Remove a few books and open up some breathing space. It's not a good idea to have a lot of unread books in the bedroom because they can over-stimulate your mind and make it hard to get to sleep. On the other hand, your home office or family room is a great place for books. It doesn't make a difference whether you display your books horizontally or vertically, just don't over-crowd the shelves.

Diplomas, Awards, and Citations

Q: I am graduating from college. Where do I hang my diploma in my room to help me find a job quickly?

Q: I have a job in my career field. Where do I hang my diploma in my office to assure continued career success?

A: The most auspicious area to place a diploma—or any award, citation or trophy—is in the Fame, Future, and Reputation area. This is the center back area of your home, or the center back area of an office or any room. If you can't hang it in this area of your home or office, hang it on the wall behind your desk or wherever you do your work or job hunting.

Q: I have several certificates, awards, and trophies from back when I was in school many years ago that I would like to display. I wonder if there is a specific room where I should hang them?

A: Certificates and awards are best displayed in the room that occupies the Fame, Future, and Reputation area of your home. You say that you were in school many years ago. That means when you choose which certificates to display from the past, be sure that you include some current accomplishments, not just those from school. If you only display awards from your past it could keep you from moving forward into the future. [See previous question for more ideas.]

Cars and Commuting

Q: Any suggestions for a good car color?

A: Pick the car color that resonates with you, rather than the one you think you should have:

White – Metal Element symbolizing purity and brightness

Red or Orange – Fire Element representing wealth and power

Yellow or Brown – Earth Element grounding you

Silver, Gold, or Bronze – Metal Element bringing strength and focus

Black or Blue – Water Element symbolizing tranquility

Green – Wood Element helping you expand your horizons

Q: I park my car where it points directly at my bedroom. I don't sleep well, so I'm thinking this is not such a good idea. There is no other place to park that's off the street. Any suggestions?

A: Your bedroom is located where it's getting strong chi from the parked car aimed at you, making it difficult to rest and perhaps affecting your health. To stop the chi from hitting directly, place three large ceramic planters outside to act as a buffer between the car and your house. If you can't do that, hang a mirror on the wall in the bedroom to symbolically expand your room, out and over the car. Place the mirror where you can't see yourself in it from the bed.

Q: My husband says I'm a nervous, over-cautious driver. I hate to admit it, but he's right most of the time. When I'm in heavy traffic, I start worrying about accidents. Anything I can do Feng Shui-wise to feel safer in my car?

A: Print out the words SAFE TRAVEL in a large font on a sheet of white paper and place it in the glove compartment of your car. This will set the intention to drive carefully and return home safely. And of course, only use your phone in hands-free mode and don't text!

CHAPTER 6: OBJECTS OF DESIRE FROM A-Z

Q: My home and office feel comfortable, but the commuting trip between these two places is terribly stressful because of the traffic. Are there Feng Shui tips for driving in rush hour?

A: Treat your car like your home or office when it comes to what you see and what you hear around you. First, clear out the clutter. That means getting rid of all those empty take-out cups, and cleaning out the kids' messes from the back seats. Avoid listening to an all-news or an all-talk channel that could be stressful, and opt for peaceful music instead. Or, try a comedy channel. Take the scenic route home at least once a week. It may take longer, but the resulting stress reduction will be well worth it.

Q: My wife is annoyed because I keep so much stuff in the car. I say if it's out of the house, it's out of our lives.

A: I'm with your wife on this one. You can't move all that stuff out of your house and into your car and assume that it's out of your life. You need to declutter your car, just as you declutter your home. Clean out the glove compartment and all those storages spaces and cup holders. Get rid of old cups, fast food wrappers, parking stubs, and work-related items that you really don't use when in the car. Wash your car frequently. Check those little things that need attention, like a squeaky windshield wiper, and fix whatever else needs fixing as soon as possible.

Q: My kids drive me crazy when I pick them up from school and activities and we're stuck in traffic. If they were just whining about "are we there yet?" I could deal with it, but they are constantly bickering and leaving their stuff in the back. Can I Feng Shui my car to help make my commuting easier?

A: Do your kids have tablets or other electronic devices they could use to occupy themselves when they're in the car? Also, if you get in the habit of treating your vehicle like you treat the rooms in your home rather than like a moving trash can, they'll get the message. When you treat your car with care, the occupants will do the same.

Fast 5

Smooth Out Your Road Trip

Whether you're running errands, commuting, or cruisin', a symbolically out-of-balance car can make the driver and passengers feel uncomfortable. These five tips make your travel enjoyable and safe:

1. **Clear the Clutter.** Treat your vehicle like a room, rather than a moving trash can, and it will move your life and career forward. Remember to clear out the glove compartment, the storages spaces, the cup holders, and the junk in the trunk.

2. **Clean the Windows.** Windows represent eyes, so if you're driving with a filmy, cracked, or broken windshield, your vision toward the future will also be cloudy.

3. **Drink Water.** The Water Element represents a smooth and flowing experience, so sipping water occasionally while you drive may help you smoothly cope with traffic and avoid incidents of road rage.

4. **Play Music.** Choose the music that matches the mood of your trip, like classical when you need to relax or rock when you need to stay alert.

5. **Wash Your Car.** Keep both the inside and outside of your car clean as a symbol that your future path will be clear and easy.

Clocks and Watches

Q: Is there any safe place to put an antique clock that I don't intend to have running? I've kept it in a closet since my dad died. He was the clock collector. I'm thinking about a guest room that's used occasionally for my bodywork clients and regularly for exercise when we don't have a guest. Is there a better room, like the office, living room, or kitchen? Surely not our bedroom?

A: The general Feng Shui recommendation is for all clocks to be running and telling time accurately. A stopped clock represents limited opportunities, since time is not moving forward. You certainly wouldn't want to locate a nonworking clock in your office or a room where you see clients, or where you workout to stay healthy. Fix the clock, then move it to the Helpful People or Family areas to represent a legacy from your father.

Q: How does Feng Shui feel about analog clocks? I recently purchased two new large ones I liked in an Asian store, and want to know where to put them.

A: You can display a clock in your kitchen, home office, or living room, but avoid displaying a large clock in your bedroom. A small clock or clock radio is okay in the bedroom. The bedroom is for rest, so a prominent clock would make you preoccupied with the passage of time rather than with relaxing. It's okay to put a clock in your child's room to help teach about time, as long as it's a small one. Avoid placing a large clock in your foyer or in a place where it's the first thing you see when you enter your home. Avoid giving a clock as a gift, especially to an older person, because it could symbolize stealing time from them.

Q: I'd like to give my young niece and nephews a weather station for Christmas that includes a thermometer, barometer, hygrometer, and a clock. I think the kids would have some fun with this gift, and it would be educational, but I'm worried that I might be making a Feng Shui mistake because a clock is included. Do you think this will be a problem?

A: In this case, because of all the other instruments included in the weather station, the clock becomes an instrument of "science" and a way for the kids to learn, rather than only a way to tell time. It sounds like a great gift that your niece and nephews will be lucky to get.

Q: You wrote in one of your newsletters that gifts like watches and clocks are not auspicious. Well, my boyfriend gave me a watch for my birthday a few months ago, and since then it feels like our relationship has taken a step back because he doesn't seem to have enough time for me anymore. Am I making too much out of the fact that the gift of a watch could have caused this change?

A: According to Feng Shui principles, a gift of a watch can symbolize stealing time and a limited life span. The best thing to do is to offer your boyfriend a token payment for the watch—even a penny—so it's no longer considered a gift, but instead symbolizes a purchase. Feel free to blame me if this sounds silly to him. Then, you can stop worrying and see how your relationship naturally progresses.

Décor

Q: We brought home two tribal masks from a recent trip to Africa. Can I hang them in my bedroom?

A: Masks are considered to be an inauspicious symbol in Feng Shui because they represent hiding or covering up something. However, if your masks have pleasant associations with them, like yours have from a trip, it's okay to keep them. Just avoid displaying them in the bedroom, or in the Love/Relationship or Family/Health areas of your home, where they would symbolize hiding things from each other.

Q: How do you feel about cow skulls?

A: I get this question occasionally from my clients in the Southwest or from clients who want to bring home something from their Southwestern vacation. There was a woman on my flight from New Mexico to New York who tried to carry on a huge, bubble-wrapped cow skull with no luck. Cow skulls have been

CHAPTER 6: OBJECTS OF DESIRE FROM A-Z

romanticized by Georgia O'Keeffe's art, but a skull is the remains of a dead animal. Feng Shui principles recommend against displaying any kind of remains or taxidermy of trophy animals because they represent dead, stagnant energy. If you must add a cow skull to your home, limit its display to your backyard, far away from the door, where it more appropriately relates to the natural landscape.

Q: Are peacock feathers auspicious? I have heard arguments both for and against having these inside the home.

A: Some schools of Feng Shui feel that peacock feathers are auspicious because they signify beauty and dignity, and recommend placing the feathers at the front door because the eye can drive away evil spirits. As with any object, my main concern is your feelings toward the feathers. If you like peacock feathers and you have a positive reaction to them, display them in your home. But, if you feel ambivalent about the feathers, out they go!

Q: I ordered a pair of large, ceramic Chinese dog-like statues to place near my front door for good luck. Which one is which gender, and which one goes on which side?

A: In Chinese Feng Shui, fu dogs are those statues that look like a cross between a dog and a lion, and they're considered guardians and protectors when placed as a couple at the front door or entrance. The male is holding a globe under his right paw, which signifies control over his domain and protection of his home. The female is holding a cub under her left paw, signifying strong maternal protective instincts. As you stand facing your front door from the outside, place the female dog on the left, and place the male on the right.

Q: Do I have to buy Feng Shui accessories to make it work?

A: Fu dogs, money frogs, dragons, laughing Buddhas, red envelopes, bamboo fluids, red streamers and similar objects are part of Chinese culture, but not necessarily part of modern Feng Shui. If these objects don't symbolize anything to you, they won't help you attract what you want into your life. I recommend instead that you choose items related to the area of your life you want to improve. For example, if you want to enhance your relationship with your spouse, hang a romantic picture in your bedroom.

Q: I bought a gold sailing ship from a Feng Shui website and put it in my dining room, which is in the wealth and prosperity area of my home, but my wealth hasn't improved at all. I don't especially like the ship, but I need help in holding on to my money. Did I put it in the wrong place?

A: Buying a so-called Feng Shui object that you don't like but believing that it will take care of all your problems isn't going to have any positive effect. Unless you bring your own symbolic value to an object, it's not going to affect your life, no matter where you place it. Instead of a symbol that means nothing to you, place an object in your Wealth area that symbolizes abundance and prosperity for you. If that object happens to be a ship, make sure it is facing into your home, so the wealth sails in—not out—of your home.

Dried Flowers

Q: What do you think about dried flowers? My friend read in a Feng Shui book that they were bad luck, and now she wants me to get rid of the dried arrangements that I have decorating my front door and my family room.

A: I recommend against keeping dried flowers in your house or hanging them on your front door. Instead, choose a living plant or fresh flowers instead of a dried arrangement in your family room to symbolize growth and expansion of the good things in your life. If you absolutely can't give up your dried flower arrangements or door decoration, make sure you dust them frequently and change your display seasonally.

Q: I'm planning to save my wedding bouquet by letting it dry naturally. What do you think? Is this a good idea?

Q: Is it OK to save the dried flowers and ribbons from my wedding bouquet? I keep the bouquet on my dresser, but we've been married for five years now and the flowers are starting to crumble and make a real mess.

A: I often hear from women who want to hold on to their dried wedding bouquets or dried rose from their first boyfriend. I'm as sentimental as anyone, but dried flowers are considered negative energy in Feng Shui. This is especially the case when they become unattractive. A crumbling wedding bouquet could be turning into negative chi. An alternative is to save ribbons from the bouquet in a scrapbook or keepsake box, and let go of what's left of the flowers. You'll be better off with living plants or fresh flowers to symbolize growth in your marriage, instead of a dried bouquet.

Fireplaces

Q: I read somewhere that because a fireplace is an opening into the room, a mirror above it prevents chi from escaping. We would rather hang the picture we bought specifically for that area.

A: Some schools of Feng Shui do recommend a mirror over the fireplace. However, that would be mixing the Fire Element (fireplace) and the Water Element (mirror). I prefer using art to balance the chi. The artwork you place above the fireplace needs to be appropriate for the area of your home where it's located. For example, if the fireplace is in the Wealth area, the art should feel wealthy, abundant, and rich. If it's in the Love area, it should be romantic. If the artwork you've selected fits with the bagua area of your home where the fireplace is located, go ahead and hang it there.

Q: We use our fireplace constantly in the cold weather, but the rest of the time it feels like a big open space. Are there any Feng Shui recommendations for making this feel as good in the summer as it does in the winter when we have a real fire in our fireplace?

A: You're right that when not in use, an empty fireplace represents a hole in your room where your positive chi can escape. The remedy is to keep firewood or objects like candles, a silk plant, or a decorative object in the fireplace when you're not using the fireplace. Keep the glass doors closed if you have them, or place a screen in front of the fireplace. Keep the fireplace damper closed to help limit the loss of chi.

Fountains and Fish Tanks

Q: Where is the best place to put a fountain in my home? Is bigger better?

A: I get a lot of questions about what I call the "care and feeding" of fountains. Sometimes, caring for a fountain is almost like caring for a pet, so make sure you're committed to maintaining it before you buy it. Fountains are best placed near the front door to attract prosperity into the home, office, or retail space. Size isn't critical. Just make sure you locate your fountain in a place where the water is flowing in (toward your home), rather than out (away from) it. Use distilled water in your fountain so it stays clear. The regular attention required by a fountain symbolizes the regular attention you should give to our own prosperity and finances.

Q: I received a gift of a beautiful blue ceramic fountain. Where is the ideal place for it on my deck, which spans the entire back of my townhouse? Right now, I have it sitting in my Wealth corner, but I am not sure if that is right. I definitely do not want to wash away any wealth or something equally scary.

A: The bagua areas across the back of your house (Wealth, Future, Relationships), are all considered Fire Element areas, and you don't want to add the Water Element here because it could drown your wealth. If there's no other place to put the fountain, you need to symbolically dry up some of this excess water. You can do that by adding more of either the Fire Element (red, orange, purple objects, triangular shapes, candles) or the Earth Element (brown, yellow items, square shapes, actual earth or items made from earth, such as tile, stone, clay) near the fountain. The fact that the fountain is ceramic will help symbolically contain the excess water.

Q: I have a new fountain in my home office and would like to add some stones and other icons to encourage prosperity. What do you suggest?

A: The traditional Feng Shui formula for attracting wealth is to add these four precious stones to the fountain: malachite, citrine, lapis, and peridot.

Q: Good day, Carol. I am from South Africa. I wish to place a water feature in the inside towards the left of my front door. Is this good Feng Shui?

CHAPTER 6: OBJECTS OF DESIRE FROM A-Z

A: How wonderful to hear from a reader in South Africa! Water represents the flow of wealth and abundance into your home, so it's a good thing to have near your entrance. Yes, just inside your front door is an excellent place for a water feature. If possible, place it toward the right side of the door (facing into your home as you come in the door from the outside), because people naturally move to the right when they enter a door. If that's not possible, the left side will also work.

Q: Do I have to have a fish tank or fish bowl in my home in order to attract wealth? Everyone in my family is busy, and we we're not sure we want to get involved with maintaining one more thing, but I want to attract wealth.

A: A fish bowl or tank is considered a sign of wealth in some approaches to Feng Shui, especially when it's located near your front door. Contemporary Feng Shui is all about surrounding yourself with what you love to make you feel comfortable in your surroundings. That means if you don't like fish or don't want the responsibility of caring for them, it's not necessary to have them. An alternative to a fish tank or fish bowl is to display images of fish. If you do decide to set up a fish tank, the ideal Feng Shui choice is a tank with nine goldfish, one of which is a black fish.

Gifts and Re-gifting

Q: My daughter has expressed a need for a set of knives for her new apartment, and I would like to oblige as part of her holiday gifts. I know there's something about giving blades and scissors as symbols of cutting the relationship. She and I didn't always get along, but we are now, and I don't want to do anything to jeopardize that. The kind of knife set she as in mind is the large block with the blades facing inward.

A: You're right that Feng Shui recommends against giving knives as gifts, because they symbolically cut a friendship or relationship. Instead, give her money or a gift certificate for the store that sells the set she likes, and include a picture of the knives so she knows how to use your gift. I know most people

166

want knives out on the counter, but my Feng Shui preference is to keep them out of sight in a drawer or cabinet.

Q: I'm a real estate agent, and I have bought five pricey knife sets to give my clients as closing gifts. There are two knives in the set, and my name, phone number and the name of the real estate company I work for are on the bright red handles. I was hoping that giving a gift with my information would bind me to my clients, but now I'm wondering whether a knife will cut the relationship.

A: I wish I could give you the answer you want to hear, but in Feng Shui, giving knives as a gift isn't the best Feng Shui choice if you want to continue the relationship with your clients. Also, I would be concerned about having your name on the handle, because if you ever move to a different company, your clients would have the name of your previous agency. Red represents the Fire Element and is good for many Feng Shui applications, but in this case, it brings too much hot energy to an already sharp and cutting object. Many realtors give gift certificates for Feng Shui consultations as a symbol that they want their clients to continue to grow, thrive, and prosper in their new homes.

Q: What's the Feng Shui opinion of re-gifting? My mother-in-law always brings me gifts when she comes to visit. She shops in the best stores, but what she buys doesn't always fit my style. Is it OK to give these things to friends?

A: Re-gifting is Feng Shui-friendly because it removes things you don't want from your home and sends them to places where they are welcome. Just be sure to avoid re-gifting if you have negative feelings about the gift or its original giver, since you might be passing along your negative thoughts to the next recipient. And here's another option from my own experience: My mom liked to bring me gifts when she visited, but our tastes were different. I suggested she bring something that belonged to one of my grandmothers that she no longer used. The result was a win-win situation, with no re-gifting required and wonderful memories coming into my home.

CHAPTER 6: OBJECTS OF DESIRE FROM A-Z

Q: I'm following your New Year's advice and gifting myself with a new red wallet and a new tote bag to help attract wealth. But what should I do with the purse and wallet I'm replacing? Is it OK to donate them?

A: If your wallet and purse are in good condition, it's a good thing to donate them to a charity, especially if you leave some amount of money inside to symbolize passing along your wishes for prosperity to the next owner. Or, an inspiring new trend is to fill a donated purse or tote with snacks and hygiene products and pass it along to a shelter for homeless or abused women. However, if your wallet or purse has holes or is ripped or stained, put it in the trash or recycling.

Q: I am planning on the beginning of the next year being the best possible. As I read your list of things to bring with me into the new year, I stopped at the recommendation to gift yourself with a new piece of gold jewelry, but with the price of gold skyrocketing, would a gold and silver combo piece work just as well? As much as I love gold and want to give myself a gift, even a simple necklace has a crazy price.

A: The gift you give yourself doesn't always have to be gold or silver. The most important Feng Shui aspect of buying yourself a gift is to select jewelry that symbolizes abundance for you. How about selecting a lovely piece of costume jewelry that costs a bit more than you would usually spend on yourself? You can determine how much more. Then, every time you wear it, remind yourself that you'll always have more than enough money to treat yourself to fine things.

Q: Greetings, and as always, thank you so much for sharing your fantastic newsletters, I love them. My son and his wife recently got married, and they are moving into their new home next month. What kind of gift should I bring to their open house?

A: Congratulations on your son's marriage. My three favorite Feng Shui-friendly housewarming gifts for newlyweds, or for anyone moving into a new space, are the following: wind chimes because they help draw positive energy to a home; a plant with rounded leaves in a red ceramic pot, which represents wealth and prosperity; precious stones because of their special powers of healing, happiness, inspiration, wealth, and love. My favorite stone for a house warming is amethyst, the stone of change, protection, and enlightenment that enhances serenity and composure. Other good choices include rose quartz for love, tiger's eye to help concentration and clear thinking, and turquoise to dispel negative energy and to provide protection and peace of mind.

Q: Your column about gift giving reminded me that I have a dilemma. A dear childhood friend died recently, and her mother sent me one of her rings as a memento. It's gold with a large amethyst. I don't normally wear rings, although I might wear this one for special occasions if I can do so in a positive way. I would have to get it resized. Is this the best way to honor her memory, or would it be better to display it, put it away, or get rid of it (I hate the thought of doing that)?

A: My condolences on the loss of your friend. How special that her mother thought to send you a memento. It's obvious you don't want to get rid of the ring, so that's not an option. As an alternative to resizing the ring, you could have the amethyst reset into a piece of jewelry that you would actually wear, like a pin, a pendant, or a bracelet. Or, you could create some kind of art piece that you would display in the Helpful People area of your home to symbolize an enduring friendship.

Q: What's the Feng Shui opinion about giving my best friend a cutting board as a housewarming gift for her new home? I'm thinking it's gotta be negative because it's related to cutting.

A: Since a cutting board is used for cutting and chopping, it could represent cutting a friendship. Instead of buying it, give your friend a gift certificate and a photo of a cutting board, so she can buy it herself.

CHAPTER 6: OBJECTS OF DESIRE FROM A-Z

Fast 5

Avoid Negative Gifts

Even the most well-meaning gift can have hidden negative messages. Here are five gifts to avoid giving, and suggestions for turning around any negative message if you happen to receive them:

1. **Sharp Objects.** Never give knives, scissors, letter openers, or can openers as gifts since they represent cutting a relationship. If you're the recipient of any of these as a gift, hand over a coin to the giver to symbolize that you bought the object, and restore the bond between you.

2. **Empty Wallet.** Avoid giving an empty wallet, purse, or backpack because it represents a lack of prosperity. Instead, give a new red wallet filled with a money—as little or as much as you want—to send the message that your gift will always be overflowing with wealth for the recipient.

3. **Thorny Flowers and Plants.** Never give cactus or other spiky plants, and avoid giving roses with the thorns still on the stems because these can pierce a relationship. If you receive roses with thorns, remove them before displaying to symbolize a smooth romance or relationship.

4. **Stunted Trees.** Bonsai trees or other miniature plants make poor choices as gifts since they represent stunted growth. Instead, choose full, healthy plants with rounded leaves to symbolize prosperity and long life.

5. **Clocks and Timepieces.** Gifts that show time symbolize a limited life span or stealing time from others. Instead, give a gift certificate with a picture of a watch so recipients can choose their own timepiece.

House Plants

Q: I read somewhere that real plants should be avoided in the bedroom. Is this true? And what are your thoughts about fresh cut flowers in the bedroom. I know to get rid of them once they're dying.

A: Living plants in the bedroom represent positive Feng Shui as long as they're not spiky or have sharp pointed leaves. Fresh flowers are great in a bedroom as long as they don't have thorns. You're right that you need to get rid of them as soon as they start to fade or drop their blossoms.

Q: I am wondering about my bonsai plant. I have read that bonsai plants are not good Feng Shui because they represent stunted growth. I have had my bonsai for more than 30 years, and it was 35 years old when I got it. I hate to throw it out as it is beautiful and surviving well. Any suggestions?

A: Bonsai plants aren't considered positive in Feng Shui because they symbolize limited growth potential. However, I agree that it seems wrong to get rid of a healthy plant. The first consideration would be whether the "limited potential" symbolism applies to your life in any way. If it does, you're better off removing the tree. If you don't feel that your life and work are being limited, display the bonsai surrounded by bushy plants with rounded leaves to counterbalance any negative energy. It would be especially auspicious if one of the surrounding plants was flowering. There's no ideal location for a bonsai, but I would recommend keeping any stunted plant out of the Wealth, Love, or Health areas.

Q: I recently purchased a small jade plant and put it next to my desk. I was wondering if this kind of low-maintenance plant is also good for my bedroom because it doesn't get a lot of natural light?

A: A jade plant is ideal near your desk because its round leaves symbolize coins, and therefore, wealth. The best choice for a bedroom is a plant with bushy leaves. Avoid plants that have sharp or spiky edges (no cactus, please!) since they send harsh energy that could disturb your sleep. While living plants are always the first choice, if you can't grow them because of limited lighting in your bedroom or a chronic case of brown thumb, use high-quality silk plants, photos of plants or trees, or fabrics with leafy patterns.

CHAPTER 6: OBJECTS OF DESIRE FROM A-Z

Q: Most bamboo plants are sold in containers of stones rather than dirt in order to slow their growth. Doesn't that send a message of slow wealth growth? Wouldn't it be better to have an artificial bamboo in the wealth area, or just a picture of bamboo?

A: People seem to have different reactions to lucky bamboo, some thinking it is the Feng Shui wealth plant, and others don't like it at all. Personally, something in my water turns it yellow so I avoid it. It sounds like your reaction to lucky bamboo is negative. If you look at lucky bamboo as stunted, then avoid displaying it. Silk plants are an acceptable alternative to natural plants as long as they are kept clean and replaced if they fade. A picture of growing bamboo is also acceptable.

Q: When choosing a plant to put in the Wealth/Prosperity area, is the shape of the leaves important, and is there any particular plant that works best?

A: Round leaves are considered good for a Wealth area, because the shape represents coins and therefore, wealth. However, any healthy plant will work fine, or you could use a silk plant if there's not enough light in the space for a natural plant.

Q: Is it OK to place a fake ficus tree in the Wealth area instead of real green plant or tree?

A: The rule of thumb is to first choose healthy, living plants and trees. If you can't grow plants because of light conditions or you travel frequently, choose silk. The faux ficus is a good choice if it's a high-quality silk. Keep the leaves well dusted, and replace the tree if it fades.

Q: I know that living plants improve the chi in a home. I have tried, but they keep dying! I don't know whether it is lack of light or my brown thumb, but I cannot grow plants.

A: As with so many other things in life, I've found that with plants, it's location, location, location. Stop beating yourself up over your dying plants—that's pulling down your positive chi. Skip the living plants and instead go straight to silk plants. If you don't like faux plants, display art with images of plants, flowers, and nature to symbolize growth.

Q: HELP!! I have gone through my Feng Shui books, searched the internet and cannot find an answer to my problem. My son bought me a terrarium with small rocks, bark, a green moss-like plant, three cactus plants (a red one in the center with spiky ones on either side) and four sponge-like cactus plants with bark separating each. The terrarium has three mirrors in the back and three glass panels in the front. I have always read cactus plants were not a good thing. My son is really excited he bought it for me and seemed very hurt at my suggestion we get rid of it. What can I do, and where should it be placed to turn it into a **GOOD THING?** He's a very sensitive 10-year-old and I do not want to hurt his feelings. It is currently sitting behind my computer monitor—I thought it might absorb emissions!

A: This is a complicated question because this gift came from your son, and he is so excited about giving it to you. Feng Shui does recommend against spiky plants like cactus because they can symbolically pierce a relationship. Maybe over time, you and your son can select new plants without sharp spikes to replace the cactus. There are some succulent plants without thorns that can grow in a terrarium. Or, you could replace the cactus with a collection of rocks that you go out and find together. Plants placed near your computer do absorb some of the electromagnetic energy, but I would rather you have a plant there that's more pleasing to you.

Letters

Q: In going through a trunk in my attic, I found a box of old letters from friends. I've been reading the letters and realized that I have let wonderful friendships fall by the wayside. Though the letters don't say anything important, it made me realize how much I have changed, for the better and for the worse in some cases. Should I throw away the letters or keep them?

A: Get rid of the letters because they represent old, stale energy. Then, instead of pulling down your positive chi by obsessing about ways you think you have changed for the worse, learn from the wisdom that finding the letters has provided you. Call, write, or e-mail your friends and restart your friendships.

CHAPTER 6: OBJECTS OF DESIRE FROM A-Z

Q: I just moved and found old letters from a recent ex-relationship. I thought about having a burning ceremony or maybe sautéing them on the stove. How do I dispose of these things? Off to the landfill? Throw them over a cliff? I hope I don't sound nuts.

A: I've had clients burn letters before, but no one has ever considered sautéing them! Whichever way you choose to discard them, what's most important is getting rid of any items that have negative associations for you. The less fuss you make about getting rid of the letters, the more you lessen their power. Nothing new flows into your life until you make room for it. Out they go!

Mirrors

(Also see Chapter 3, "Bedroom Mirrors")

Q: How am I supposed to use a mirror to improve my life? I've read lots of things that are conflicting. Are there places I shouldn't hang a mirror?

A: Mirrors do a lot of different things in Feng Shui, and in fact, they are often called the aspirin of Feng Shui. But like aspirin, mirrors should be used sparingly and only as needed. It all depends on where you place them and your intention. Mirrors are used to either attract, move, or redirect energy and light. I recommend against using a mirror across from a door or at the end of a long hallway, because it will redirect the energy right back out the door or back up the hall. I also recommend against using a mirror at the foot of the bed where it will keep you awake at night. You should also avoid using a mirror wherever it reflects something negative or unattractive.

Q: I recently moved into a new end unit townhouse that I love, and the energy feels really good inside. However, the trash and recycling for the building is near my back deck, just outside the Wealth corner of my unit. I was wondering if this is a good place to use a Feng Shui mirror? And if so, would I use the convex or concave type? Thanks again for all your great teachings!

A: Hanging a bagua-shaped mirror on an outside wall is a good way to push away the negative energy from the trash/recycling center. Choose a convex mirror to push it away, rather than a concave mirror that would draw it toward you. Hang the mirror on the building, facing the trash area. Also, if possible, place evergreen shrubs in containers on your porch to further block the negative energy generated by the trash

SUCCESS STORY

Leslie Reloads the Laundry

Mirrors can be used to bring in an attractive view, but when they reflect something that isn't so appealing, they can symbolically double it. One of the issues my client Leslie needed help with was feeling overwhelmed by all the household chores that were distracting her from spending time on her home-based business. One of the things I suggested was that she take note of where all her mirrors were hung, and what they were reflecting.

Here's what Leslie wrote:

❝ I was walking around the house thinking about the Feng Shui fixes you recommended and not concentrating on any one area. I noticed that when the bathroom door was closed, the mirror on the front of it reflected my laundry hamper and ironing board. Well, no wonder I felt like I always had piles of laundry to wash and iron. I immediately moved the mirror, because, who needs double the amount of laundry? I have to tell you that it worked. I still have laundry, of course, but I no longer feel "buried" under piles. And I no longer feel compelled to take care of laundry during the day when I should be working in my home office. And magically, now my family helps me fold it when I bring it into the TV room after dinner. ❞

Q: I would like to put a mirror in a black frame over our couch in the living room to bring in more light. The walls are gray and the room is in the Fame and Reputation area of the bagua. We already bought the mirror, but I haven't put it up due to my understanding that mirrors represent water and this bagua area is fire. Water quenches fire. Is there a way to use the mirror without harming the energy in the Fame and Reputation area?

A: Mirrors do represent the Water Element. You're right, the general Feng Shui recommendation is to avoid hanging a mirror in the Fame/Reputation area, because this would symbolically drown the Fire Element that should predominate here. Plus, the black color of the frame adds more of the Water Element. Hang the mirror in a Water area near the front of your home rather than in a Fire area. To bring in more light, paint the walls in this room a more neutral, earthy color instead of gray, and choose a light-reflecting paint specially designed to help disburse light throughout a room.

Q: I need clarification on the difference between concave and convex bagua mirrors. Also, should these mirrors be used both outside and inside the house? I want to hang a convex mirror and was told that it should be hung inside the house and facing inside only.

A: Concave mirrors bulge inward, while convex mirrors bulge outward. Use a concave mirror when you want to draw the energy from an object toward your home. In contrast, use a convex mirror when you want to deflect away the negative energy from an object pointed at your home. You only use the traditional bagua mirror—octagon-shaped in a yellow wood frame with Chinese writing—on the outside of your home because of its strong energy. It is never used inside. Other concave and convex mirrors can be used inside or outside.

Q: Why is it considered good Feng Shui to hang a mirror behind the stove, and is it really necessary? I like mirrors, but not in my kitchen.

A: Classical Feng Shui believes that cooking is related to wealth, and the more burners you have, the more people you can feed, and consequently, the wealthier you'll be. A mirror symbolically doubles the number of burners. If your stove is located where you stand with your back to the door, a mirror will assure that you can see behind you and won't be caught off guard by anyone entering the room. However, a reflective backsplash, stainless appliance, or a shiny tea kettle on the stove top will achieve the same purpose.

Q: I have a large antique mirror in a beautiful frame on the wall across from my front door. I love the mirror and don't want to move it, but I read in your book that this is negative Feng Shui placement. Are there any options other than removing the mirror?

A: A mirror across from the front door repels the good chi that enters your home, rather than reflecting it around your space. If you can't remove the mirror, one option is to place something in front of it. For example, you could use a bushy plant with rounded leaves, a piece of furniture, or a sculpture. That way, you'll still get to see the frame and get some reflected light. Mirrors double what they reflect, so before you cover up this one, first see if you can find another location where it reflects something beautiful.

Fast 5

Take a Look at Your Mirrors

Mirrors, often called the "aspirin" of Feng Shui, are used to attract, move, or re-direct chi to correct a problem. Different shapes of mirrors achieve different things. Here are five places to hang a mirror:

1. **Walls.** On a wall, a mirror will symbolically push out the wall and correct a missing bagua area.

2. **Windowless Room.** In a dark or windowless room, a mirror will reflect and disburse the available light.

3. **Columns.** A mirror can make an unattractive column or pillar symbolically disappear.

4. **Stove.** Hang a mirror behind a stove to symbolically double the number of burners and symbolize wealth to feed many people.

5. **Foyer.** Hang a mirror in the foyer, but not directly across from the door, to attract opportunities into your home.

CHAPTER 6: OBJECTS OF DESIRE FROM A-Z

Photos

Q: I read in your book that I should remove family pictures from my bedroom. Where do you recommend hanging them instead to encourage family harmony?

A: The recommendation is to avoid displaying photos of your family and friends in your bedroom, so this space can be reserved for rest and romance for the two of you only. The ideal locations for family photos are in the Family, Creativity, and Helpful People areas of your home.

Q: Where is the best place to display family photos in my home, especially of my wedding and of the kids? And where do I store the photos of me and ex-boyfriends? My husband and I don't agree on a place for them.

A: Display photos of your parents in the Family area to help connect with the power of your ancestors, place photos of your children in the Creativity area to add lively energy, and display your wedding photo in the Love area or in your bedroom. Avoid placing photos of your family, friends, and children in your bedroom since this room should be reserved for you and your husband. It's time to get rid of photos of your ex-boyfriends. As long as they're stored in your home, the energy from past relationships is negatively affecting your marriage.

Q: I was advised that it was not a good idea to have photos of deceased persons mixed in with photos of the living. So, I took down the photo of my Dad that I had in every room. Now Mom is gone, and I wonder where is the best place to hang their photos together, based on the bagua map.

Q: What is the appropriate place to display photos and objects that remind me of my mother? She died last year, and I want to create a sort of shrine with photos, a framed letter from her, and other things.

A: Combining photos of your ancestors with photos of your living relatives sends a wonderful message of family history and harmony. The difficulty arises if you have such an overwhelming number of pictures of a deceased person that it keeps you living in the past. The best place to display family photos, including photos of your parents, is in the Family or the Helpful People areas of your home. Avoid hanging photos of deceased relatives in your bedroom, kitchen, or dining room.

Q: I am starting the process of deep cleaning and organizing my house. We have several beautifully framed, overly-large pictures of the four of us in our family that are 20-25 years old, taken by a professional photographer. I don't want to just throw them away. I was thinking of taking them out of the frames and rolling them up, then keeping the frames. How would the Feng Shui maven respond to this?

A: Scan the images so you'll always have a digital record of them. If they're too big for your scanner, take them to a professional reprographics service that has the equipment to scan large-size images. If you think it's not worth spending that much money on preserving, you have your answer about whether the scanning is worth it. Then, dispose of both the photos and the frames (yes, I know, the Maven's advice can sometimes be tough love). You could throw them out with some kind of ceremony, wishing your family continued growth and harmony.

Q: Why am I supposed to have a current photo of my husband and me in our bedroom? We don't have one. The only photos we have in frames right now are our wedding photos, which are nine years old, but obviously, we are very happy in them.

A: It's good to display your wedding photos in your bedroom, but it's equally important to balance them by adding recent photos to emphasize your current life together. Just as you grow your relationship throughout the years, I recommend you also update your photo display. Symbolically, your relationship would be stuck in the past if you're surrounded by only 9-year-old photos. This is the perfect reason to take a new, professional photo of the two of you, and display it in your bedroom.

Q: I love your newsletters. Several years ago, we bought a photograph at a flea market that has an image of the ghost of a Civil War soldier superimposed over a view of a battlefield. We thought it was different. It was in our family room in our last house but that was before my interest in Feng Shui. Now, I'm not sure where to put it. I'm not sure if it should be in a prominent area. I'm not sure about that ghost. What do you think?

A: Ghosts have several meanings in Feng Shui, so I would have to know more about the room where you're considering placing this print, and its location on the bagua, before I could give you any specific advice. In general, the Feng Shui

CHAPTER 6: OBJECTS OF DESIRE FROM A-Z

recommendation is that you should love all the art you hang on your walls. When you repeatedly wrote that you're "not sure" about this photograph, you're sending a strong message that this art no longer feels good to you. It might be time to put the ghost print to rest, at least for a while.

Purses and Wallets

Q: I like to carry a pocket diary in my purse. Is there a color that the outside cover should be to attract more good days?

A: There are several options for calendar colors, depending on which of the Feng Shui Elements you want to activate in your life. If you want things to flow smoothly, choose a blue calendar; if you want to attract wealth, use a red calendar; if you want your daily activities to expand and grow, choose a green calendar; if you want to feel more stable, select a brown calendar.

Fast 5

Check What's in Your Wallet

"What's in your wallet?" is more than an advertising slogan; it says a lot about how you respect yourself and your money. Try these tips if you're having a hard time getting a grip on your finances:

1. **Bills.** Straighten out the bills and put them in order by domination.
2. **Clubs.** Get rid of expired membership cards for clubs, the gym, or services.
3. **Photos.** Replace old family photos (do you even need to carry these if you have a smartphone?).
4. **Receipts.** Throw away ancient receipts.
5. **Credit cards.** Take out credit cards you don't use, especially if you use mobile apps to pay.

Q: I wonder every year as I buy my new red wallet if another color in the red family will do the same trick, so this year, I broke from the usual and I ordered a HOT pink wallet. I'm not sure how Feng Shui it is. What are your thoughts?

A: It sounds like you're setting the intention to bring in even more abundance this year. All shades of red are Fire Element colors, including pink. The fact that you used all caps tells me that your shade of pink is a fiery one. There are colors that are considered more fortuitous in certain years of the Chinese calendar, but buying a new wallet every year shows you're ready for new wealth, regardless of the color.

Q: I won a wallet from a website I do business with, but it will arrive empty of money, of course. I know you say never give a wallet empty, but what about winning an empty one? What can I do to ensure I keep my wealth?

A: Winning a wallet sounds like terrific, positive chi to me. Take a $50 dollar bill (or the highest denomination you can afford), fold it up, and tuck it into your wallet. Then, never plan to use it. This will symbolize that you always have money in your life and that you'll never need to dip into this hidden "stash."

Q: I know you recommend a red wallet, but are other wallet colors considered bad Feng Shui? I saw this gorgeous green wallet online that I want to buy, but don't want to risk it if that color will repel wealth.

A: Yes, I like to carry a red wallet, but if that color doesn't make you happy, it's not a good choice for you no matter what Feng Shui energy it carries. Green is the color of the Feng Shui Wood Element, which represents growth and expansion. That makes green an acceptable choice for a wallet. Generally, the deeper the color, the stronger its energy. So, if you buy a green wallet, make sure it's a deep green or teal rather than a pastel.

CHAPTER 6: OBJECTS OF DESIRE FROM A-Z

SUCCESS STORY

*Ruby Buys a New
Red Wallet*

For years, I've been collecting "red wallet success stories" from people who've followed this tip: *If you want to attract wealth, buy yourself a new red wallet.* The color red represents wealth and abundance, and a new, uncluttered wallet makes room for that wealth to flow into your life.

Here's what Ruby wrote:

❝ This is long overdue, but I just had to get this to you since the red wallet advice is still working! I just landed ANOTHER client who wrote a check to secure my services right away. At the beginning of the year, I was a bit worried about my business and my finances. You suggested that I carry a red wallet with a $50 bill stashed away in it. That immediately made a difference, and I received two job offers and got two new clients in that same month! I just finished a project for one of those clients and they recommended me to someone else. I met with them yesterday and they hired me immediately. Since I got my new red wallet, I've felt more confident regarding my finances. I feel I have plenty of money to be able to buy exactly what I need. What a difference the red wallet made! And duh, it never occurred to me before that a ruby-red wallet was obviously the right choice for me considering my name. ❞

Vision Boards

Q: I always create a new vision board at the end of each year and hang it up on New Year's Day. Can hanging it be considered a type of Feng Shui cure or remedy, and if so, where do you recommend locating it?

A: A vision board, also called a dream board or treasure map, is a powerful way of using images to create the intention to attract something into your life, and that's what Feng Shui is all about. I frequently remind my clients that *you are what you see*, so yes, you can use your vision board as part of a Feng Shui adjustment. The ideal place to display your creation is in the Fame/Future area of your home or office. Another Feng Shui take on this is to arrange the images on your board according to the Feng Shui bagua. For example, place the images that relate to wealth in the upper left-hand corner of the board, those that relate to love in the upper right-hand corner, etc.

Workout Equipment

Q: Can we put our elliptical machine in the room that is in the wealth area of our home? Would that be detrimental to wealth, or would it serve as a good purpose for that room?

A: Where to place your workout equipment can be a complicated issue, especially an elliptical or treadmill, because there's some concern that when you're using the equipment, you're "walking to nowhere." In a perfect world, the ideal location for your elliptical would be in your Health or Grounding areas. If that's not possible, yes, you can place it in your Wealth area. Just be sure to add something to the room that represents moving forward toward wealth and prosperity, like art or objects that make you feel prosperous. The exception would be to avoid locating any equipment in your bedroom. Wherever you locate the equipment, make sure you use it frequently. When workout equipment and gear is ignored, it represents negative energy, because every time you look at it, you might blame yourself for letting it just sit there.

CHAPTER 6: OBJECTS OF DESIRE FROM A-Z

Q: I need lots of motivation to use my treadmill. It's located where I face into a corner. Should I hang mirrors on both walls of the corner? What about colors for decoration?

A: It's OK to hang a mirror in a workout area so you can check your form, but only one mirror. Multiple mirrors facing each other are disorienting, because they bounce the chi chaotically back and forth. For colors, try using a Metal Element color like gray to help you focus, or a Water Element color like deep blue to represent movement. You can add accents of the Earth Element color yellow to help you settle down into a routine. I recommend avoiding too much of the Fire Element (red, hot orange), which can make you aggressive when working out.

Zen

Q: I don't know much about Feng Shui, but I heard you have to get rid of most of your stuff. I need to bring more good things into my life, that's for sure, but I'm not willing to turn my home into a Zen-like shrine. I like my stuff, so I'm resisting all of this. Any tips?

A: I like my stuff, too! But sometimes, we surround ourselves with stuff that has lost its meaning, and it becomes a negative reinforcement rather than a positive symbol. There's no reason you have to give away all your things and live in bland surroundings. On the contrary, contemporary Feng Shui principles tell us to keep the things that we love and that support us. Schedule a clutter-clearing session for 20 minutes a day so you can start to separate the keepers from the clutter. That will help you open up your space and make room for good things to naturally flow into your home and your life.

Q: I am constantly re-arranging the furniture and moving around the objects in my home, but somehow it never brings me the Zen-like harmony I think my home should have. Did I just buy the wrong furniture and "things?" What am I doing wrong?

A: You might not be doing anything wrong. It may be a simple question of what energy you are bringing to the items around you. One of the underlying beliefs of Feng Shui is that you make changes so your home is the outward expression of the balanced energy inside you. The goal is to create an interior environment that aligns who you are and what you want to attract. The best way to get started is to think about how all of your objects have their own energy. If you don't really like something, it doesn't have a place in your home. Then, the decisions you make about where to place objects will allow the positive energy (chi) to flow throughout every room in your home. This will ultimately bring the balance you are seeking.

Q: Is there a difference between decorating a room to make it feel Zen and making it feel like it meets Feng Shui guidelines?

A: In Feng Shui design, the goal is to create an environment where the energy is balanced, and it flows throughout the room in a gentle "wind-water" way. On the other hand, Zen décor is typically minimal and basic. Zen design uses straight lines and simple accessories, while Feng Shui features curves and movement. Feng Shui is known as the "art of placement," so it focuses primarily on locating furniture and objects so nothing blocks the movement of energy. Five Element Feng Shui also adds the principle of using color and shape to move the energy around the room.

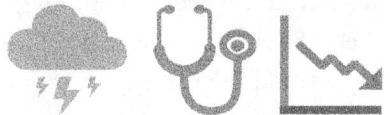

CHAPTER 7
TROUBLE, CHAOS, CLUTTER

What's stressing you today? It could be natural disaster, terrorism, violence, credit card hacking, politics, or illness. You could be recovering from divorce, dealing with the challenges of a blended family, or mourning the death of a loved one. Sometimes, it feels like every day we find something new to worry about. The world around us is in constant change, challenging our stability and making it harder to stay centered.

Many people who contact me these days say they feel angry and powerless. My *Modern Coping Skills* series of workshops sell out. In this time of great uncertainty, we're all seeking feelings of safety, security, and comfort. Many of us are re-evaluating our life and career priorities in light of the changing national and international political landscape.

How can Feng Shui help? When a client contacts me because they are looking for ways to create harmony at home, I ask these three questions, and many times they can't answer:

Q: Does it feel relaxing when you open your door and enter your home?

Q: Do you have at least one clutter-free room or space at home?

Q: Where do you go at home to rest, restore, and de-stress after a hard day?

Many of us spend the bulk of our time away from our home at a workplace or in a home office, which makes it important to create a special place to relax when the workday is done. I call this your home sanctuary. Feng Shui home sanctuary doesn't mean a religious space. Rather, it is a special safe haven at home where you can renew, restore, slow down, and just let go. Your

CHAPTER 7: TROUBLE, CHAOS, CLUTTER

sanctuary could be a special room or area in your home, or it could be a comfortable reading chair near a sunny window where the cat can't go (or where the cat *can* go with you). Any area that feels nourishing, comforting, and inspiring can be your home sanctuary. It's the place where you surround yourself with your favorite things.

I wish I could give you one Feng Shui solution for all of the world's problems, but I can't. What I can do is share answers to the questions I get from people like you who need help handling troubled times and stressful situations. These tips help keep your home as peaceful and harmonious as possible, so it can be an oasis of calm in a sometimes crazy world.

> *The best criterion for choosing what to keep and what to discard*
> *is whether keeping it will spark joy.*
> — Marie Kondo

Q & A

TROUBLE, CLUTTER, CHAOS

Breakups

Q: I had a failed relationship two years ago. I kept the mattress but bought a new metal bed. Since then I met a new friend last year, but we separated in December. I know that I should replace the mattress, but do I also have to replace the bed I brought two years ago? I hate to spend the money.

A: The Feng Shui advice would be to replace the mattress, because when you continue to sleep on bedding from a failed relationship, you continue to sleep with all the problems from that relationship. If your unfortunate luck with relationships continues, you might want to think about a completely new bed. Choose a wood headboard to represent growth in your relationship.

Q: My boyfriend broke things off, and while I'm not ready to date again just yet, I want to make sure I arrange my apartment so I'm ready for what the universe brings me next. For a single person, what things can I do to eventually attract a new relationship?

A: The Feng Shui recommendation for moving forward after a breakup is to remove everything from your apartment that reminds you of your former relationship. That includes photos, gifts, your former partner's clothes, and other objects you acquired during the relationship. The goal is to clear out old energy to make room for a new relationship to find you. Be sure to arrange things in pairs in your bedroom, and avoid artwork or objects that feel single, solitary, and lonely, especially in this room. Good luck!

Q. I broke up with my long-time boyfriend a few months ago, and I am ready to attract someone special. Do you have any suggestions for quick things I can do?

CHAPTER 7: TROUBLE, CHAOS, CLUTTER

A. Here are three fast-fix Feng Shui suggestions to make room for a new love to come into your life: First, remove past relationships by getting rid of photos and other shared objects from your boyfriend. Next, buy new sheets. These are notorious collectors of past energy, so donate yours to a local nonprofit and start with a fresh set. Finally, arrange your bedroom like you already have a relationship by getting two night tables, placing pairs of objects in the bedroom to represent togetherness, and decorating with romantic artwork.

Q: I'm staying in an apartment hotel and when I'm in bed, I can see myself in the mirrored closet doors across from the bed. I recently broke up with my boyfriend and wonder if it could be because of the mirrors. Is there anything that I could do to repel the negative effect of the mirrors so I won't be "reflecting away" my next relationship?

A: The Feng Shui recommendation is to avoid having mirrors in your bedroom, especially across from the foot of your bed. Mirrors expand and enlarge a space, which is why they can be disruptive to a good night's sleep. This, in turn, can affect health and relationships. When you can't move the bed, one option is to place a floor screen in front of the mirrors at night. Or, you can hang curtains in front of the mirrors, which you can keep closed at night and tie back during the day. If that isn't possible because you're in a hotel, drape the mirrors with a scarf or lightweight fabric at night as a symbolic gesture that you're separating yourself from the mirrors.

Q: It's Valentine's Day again and I'm alone again since I just broke up with my boyfriend last month. Are there some simple Feng Shui changes I can make so I can fall in love so next year, I won't have to ask this question again?

A: Valentine's Day puts so much pressure on us to have a perfect relationship. I can't reduce that societal pressure, but I can give you three simple changes for your bedroom to help make room for love to find you. First, remove art with single images and replace it with images that are paired, coupled, and romantic. Next, remove stuffed animals and extra pillows from the bed so there's room for a lover to join you. Finally, remove clutter from your closet as a symbol you have room for your new lover's clothes.

Q: How do I get my "ex" out of my life? I am trying to move forward, but I feel like I am still surrounded by memories of my ex-husband, especially in the bedroom.

A: If you're still sleeping in the same bed and on the same sheets as you did before your divorce, you run the risk of sleeping with any negative energy from that previous marriage. It's time to replace your bed and buy yourself new bed linens. If you can afford it, replace any bedroom furniture that you acquired during the marriage. If you still have photos of the two of you, move them out of the bedroom, along with any objects you acquired during your marriage and gifts your ex-husband gave you. When you keep these objects in your bedroom, you continue to sleep with all their memories. If these items are valuable, sell them; if they have family history value, give them to a family member who might not have so much emotional energy invested in them. Redecorate your room with artwork that shows images of the positive way you want your future romantic relationship to feel.

Q: Besides Feng Shui-ing my bedroom and romance corners, what can I do to help let my husband's ex-girlfriend cut loose from him romantically? They have a 9-year-old child together, and she invites herself to our home and on our vacations. She subscribes to magazines that come to our house, and she sends books to us. There are tons of pictures of her in boxes in our attic and in my husband's home office. My husband thinks throwing away photos is like throwing the person away, so he's resistant.

A: I've worked with clients in a similar situation, where an ex simply won't let go, so I know how it can drain away your energy. It's especially complicated when there's a child involved. Your sentence about the photos your husband keeps in his office sent up lots of red flags. Symbolically, this woman continues to occupy a place in your lives when you have so many images of her around. Get rid of anything around your home and his office that previously or currently belongs to this woman, or that reminds you or your husband of her. The photos in the attic symbolically "weigh down" on you, and keeping additional photos of her in your husband's office could negatively affect his work. If your husband doesn't want to get rid of the photos, rent an off-site storage unit for them. Donate the books, magazines, and other things she sends to a charity. Make sure she knows that you've removed the photos and donated her gifts, and that you won't keep any new ones in your home. Don't give her the specifics of your vacation plans until you're already on your way.

Broken Things

Q: I read in your newsletter about the problem with holding on to things that are broken. What does Feng Shui say about repairing broken things? I chipped a favorite plate I picked up in Greece. I hate to get rid of it. Can I repair the plate and continue using it without negative consequences?

Q: I read that it's not good to hold on to broken things. I found a chip in a favorite serving platter that I always use for Thanksgiving dinner. I hate to get rid of it because it was Mom's. What should I do?

A: Yes, of course it's fine to repair an object, especially when it has pleasant memories associated with it. The Japanese have a name for this kind of repair, *Kintsugi*, which is the century-old art of fixing broken pottery with a special lacquer dusted with powdered gold, silver, or platinum. You don't have to use precious metals to repair broken objects. What matters most are the feelings you bring to the object after the repair is made. If you look at the object and feel that a treasured object has been restored, you should keep it. If you look at the plate and see only the damage, then you're better off getting rid of it.

Q: I am avoiding doing some needed household repairs because I don't have time and don't want to spend the money. I have heard that in Feng Shui, everything should be in good working order. Why?

A: In Feng Shui, things that don't work in your home are equivalent to things that don't work right in your life. Leaking plumbing represents the loss of abundance, creaking doors represent the lack of smooth progress in your life, burned-out light bulbs represent blockage in your life. If you don't have time to do the repairs yourself, then find a good repair service. It may help to consider this expense an investment in a balanced life rather than just a cost.

Fast 5

Learn to Just Say Throw

Is your utensil drawer so full you can't close it? Are you ever going to use that Bundt pan? Here are five things you can donate, give away, or trash, and end up with a tidy, clutter-free, peaceful home:

1. **Kitchen utensils and mugs**. Do you really need all those duplicate spatulas and servers? Do you drink enough coffee or tea to justify all the mugs you're keeping? Offer some to your friends, then donate the remaining good ones and throw away the rest.

2. **Plastic Containers.** Do you have more tops than bottoms, or vice versa? Match up what you have, then toss the singletons.

3. **Unread Books**. Do you have a stack of books you should read but never get around to opening? Donate them to the local library, or trade and sell them online.

4. **Electronics**. Do you have a jungle of power cords and electronic paraphernalia in your desk drawer that may not work with your current equipment? Match up the cord with the device, then let go of the rest.

5. **Linens**. Do the sheets in your linen closet fit the current size of your beds? Keep two sets of sheets per bed, then donate the rest to a local animal shelter.

Q: What does Feng Shui say about failing to repair my broken gutter? I hate to spend money replacing it, but it's right in front of the house. I'd rather buy something for inside the house.

A: Broken things are part of the clutter cycle. When you ignore things that need to be repaired, replaced, or removed, you set an intention of neglect. But, when you fix broken things, you remove whatever is blocking prosperity from entering your life, and instead set an intention of abundance. The money you spend on repairing the gutter (and other needed household repairs) will come back to you multiplied.

Q: I'm embarrassed to admit, but there's lots of stuff around me that I've been meaning to fix but it never gets done. Like the broken stuff I can never get rid of, the wallpaper that's peeling in the bathroom (I hate that pattern), and the leaky kitchen. I never seem to have the money or time to take care of all this. Am I asking for trouble here?

A: Conditions like cracks, holes, chipped paint, peeling wallpaper, dead plants, etc., represent negative forces in your life since they block the flow of positive energy around you. Water represents abundance in Feng Shui, so leaks represent a drain on your finances. The good news is that when you fix what's broken or not working in your home, you can fix your life. I recommend you go through every room in your house to identify things that are leaking, clogged, burned out, broken, or stuck. Repair what you can immediately, then schedule dates to hire others to fix everything else.

Clutter

Q: Is there any time of the year when it's better to do a big clutter clearing? I know I sound like I'm putting it off (well, I guess I am), but if I'm going to have to go through all the things I have stuffed into my spare room, I want to make it especially auspicious. Thanks!

A: June is the perfect time for a mid-year clutter clearing. Try calling it your mid-year home tune-up, to reduce some of the pressure and to help motivate you. Start slowly. For example, never leave a room without picking up something that belongs in another location, and actually taking it there. Or, place one piece of old clothing, one unneeded book, and other items in a bag in the trunk of your car each morning. At the end of the month, you'll have 30 items to take to your favorite charity. If you don't use it, lose it. Go through your closet, and if you find something from last season that you didn't wear, put it in a bag marked "donate." Pull out an old photo album, scan the photos, and then get rid of the originals. Follow the rule of *one in, one out* so that nothing new comes in until you make room for it by getting rid of something.

Q: I was leafing through your book a week or two ago, and ran across your great idea of clearing out unfinished projects. I mentioned this to a friend, and she gave me a horrified look and said, "Surely, that doesn't mean I should throw out all the photos and albums I've been meaning to put together all these years!" Were we taking your idea too literally?

A: Your friend doesn't have to clear out all unfinished projects, just those she knows she's never going to finish. But the bigger question is, why has your friend been putting off doing something with all those photos? Since this was the first unfinished project that popped into her mind, she might set aside a block of time and just do it. She can go through the photos, pick the best, and throw out the duplicates and similar shots. Next, she can scan in the good ones, or upload to an online service for creating albums. Then, she can get rid of all the printed photos without fear that the images will be lost forever.

Q: I read a *New York Times* article that said clutter and messiness are good. What do you think?

A: According to the article, *Say Yes to Mess*, an anti-clutter clearing movement is urging people to embrace disorder. The article cites studies showing that people with messy desks earn higher salaries than those with neat offices, and that people with messy closets may be better parents than their tidier counterparts. In Feng Shui, clutter represents postponed decisions and the inability to move forward. Clutter is the number one problem for the thousands of clients, students, and readers who write to me. When they clear their clutter, amazing things flow into the open spaces in their lives. You be the judge: clear the clutter and see what flows in to take its place.

SUCCESS STORY

*Kim Takes the
Big Purge Challenge*

How much stuff do your need to achieve happiness and joy? That's the question I asked my newsletter readers when I invited them to join my Big Purge challenge. Every September, I clear out my filing cabinet in order to make room for new clients to find me. That always leads to purging and tidying up in other areas of my office. Last year, I challenged readers to join me.

Here's what Kim wrote:

❝ I totally relate to your purging adventure. We move a lot. I don't shop much so the majority of my clutter is from gifts, both small and large. We also have become the family that gets items from family members who have passed away, and we end up with all sorts of things including furniture. I am thankful to receive some of these items, but it has become overwhelming. Each time we move, we have three tag sales and then make 6-10 trips to donation centers as well as giving things away for free. It never seems to be enough. With the last move, we did the usual donations and tag sales, and we still packed nine pods! We took our time purchasing a new home and took up temporary living for a year and a half. We only took with us what we absolutely needed and only stayed at furnished dwellings. By doing this, it helped me to finally let go of more items. Being separated from them by choice released some of the fear of not having "enough," and it let me release the need to keep deceased family members' possessions simply because they loved those things. This time as I am unpacking, instead of finding a closet or drawer for most of

(continued)

> those items, they are going directly into donation boxes. I am keeping the items I love and releasing the other things for someone else to enjoy. I have already donated 10 large boxes of household items and can't wait for our next tag sale! When the next move happens, I will still have plenty to release, but it will be much easier to choose what to keep. I am by no means a minimalist, but I enjoy the feeling of space and openness with less furniture and no small decorations. Not everyone can use this method of purging but perhaps something in my story can be helpful to someone else. 🙢

Q: What's your take on Marie Kondo's Japanese method of decluttering and tidying up? Is it really the "life-changing magic" she calls it, and is there any Feng Shui parallel?

A: I support the strong decluttering message in Marie Kondo's tidying up process, so I tried her folding methods. She wants us to talk to our clothes as we gently smooth them before folding in a distinct method, and tell them how much we appreciate them. In Feng Shui, clutter represents postponed decisions and the inability to move forward, so when you organize your stuff—by whatever method—you feel better. I'm in agreement with Marie's philosophy that you should own things that spark joy. That's why I've added her book *The Life-Changing Magic of Tidying Up: The Japanese Art of Decluttering and Organizing* to my Mindfulness Bookstore at FengShuiForRealLife.com.

Q: Clutter is an endless issue in my house. My husband is skeptical about Feng Shui. Any advice to help my husband understand how Feng Shui clutter clearing is practical rather than far-out New Age thinking?

A: Feng Shui is a design system for unblocking whatever is keeping positive energy from coming into your home. While some approaches to Feng Shui use Chinese symbols and objects to attract good things into your life, this isn't necessary for everyone. You can start your Feng Shui clutter-clearing by getting rid of things you don't like, don't use, or don't need, to make room for new things to flow into your life. There's nothing New Age about that. When your home is blocked with clutter, there's no room for good energy to enter. But, if you open up space by removing clutter, good things will naturally find you. Suggest to your husband that he clear out one closet, drawer, or cabinet and then step back and watch what good things flow into his life to fill the extra space.

Q: I keep everything and I worry it's bringing me bad Feng Shui. Maybe that's why I feel that nothing is going my way right now. Is there something to remove that's more important in Feng Shui terms? I'll take any help I can get here.

A: Clearing out your closets will give you needed space to symbolically let new opportunities find you. There isn't necessarily one type of item that's better than the other to get rid of, but here are categories of things that people typically keep, but don't really need: old costumes; duplicate free tote bags; bridesmaid dresses; expensive things you never wear; gift you never liked; stretched-out clothing; items in the fix-it pile that never get fixed; shoes that leave you limping; tangled or discolored costume jewelry; duplicate sets of clothes for painting or gardening.

Q: I still have things like school papers, art projects, and birthday cards from my twin boys. Yes, that means I have double everything. I'm embarrassed to say they are about to graduate from college. Does holding on to them represent negative energy?

A: It's not negative to collect memorabilia, until it turns into clutter for you. And, it's different holding on to artwork and memorabilia while your young children are living at home, in contrast to when they're adults living on their own. When you hold on to so much memorabilia that you don't have enough room for new things, it symbolizes restricting your life. An option is to take photos and keep digital copies of all your children's artwork and the cards they sent you. Then, choose one or two representative items to save in a keepsake box, and get rid of the others.

Q: I need to do a major, house-wide clutter cleaning but I don't know where to start. Can you help me?

A: The best way to jumpstart a major clutter clearing is to do the "Feng Shui Fling." Grab a big plastic bag and move quickly through you home and fling 27 things into it. Open drawers and cabinets. Dig down under the sink. Don't think, don't analyze, don't hesitate…just fling. Good candidates for flinging include "orphan" socks, address labels for your old address, a bent emery board, old phone books (when's the last time you used a printed phone book?), a frying pan with a loose handle that can't be tightened, the dog's chewed-up toys. As you go through your house and fling things into your bag, you'll figure out quickly which rooms deserve more clutter-clearing attention than others.

Q: I am overwhelmed with the amount of stuff I have stored all over my house. Sometimes, I think it's all important and I need to keep it, but other times, I get so frustrated with it I think it's all junk and I should get rid of everything. How do I decide what I can get rid of?

Q: Help! I'm drowning in clutter. I work long hours and have an equally long commute, so when I get home, I get overwhelmed and don't where to start to get my life in order. Are there some simple steps I can follow to just get started?

A: I feel your pain! We're all busy, and some days you only have a few minutes to spare. When your time is limited, try these quick organizing tricks that can be completed in 10 minutes or less:

Find it. If you have books all over your home, collect them and return them to their proper space. Or maybe it's coffee cups, drinking glasses, or shoes. Pick just one category of items and quickly get it in order.

Enter it. Are there phone numbers on business cards, on scraps of paper, or in emails that need to be entered into your address book? Give yourself ten minutes and scan or enter as many contacts as you can into your permanent system. Get rid of the cards and paper.

Empty it. Collect and store your out-of-season coats, hats, and gloves, snow shovels, beach towels, window scrapers, etc. Go through the pockets of your things before you send them to the cleaners or pack them away.

CHAPTER 7: TROUBLE, CHAOS, CLUTTER

SUCCESS STORY

Brianna Attracts
Mr. Right

The first thing Briana talked about when I arrived for her home consultation was how she couldn't meet the right guy, but the first thing I noticed was that her closets were so overloaded, there was no room for anyone else's clothes or personal things. When I asked what she was holding on to, she admitted she had trouble getting rid of things from past boyfriends. When we went to her bedroom, she pulled down a box of costume jewelry from the top shelf of her closet that included a bracelet from a high school boyfriend. I explained to Briana that in order to make room for a new relationship, she needed to get rid of the clutter she was holding on to from all her Mr. Wrongs, to make room for the one and only Mr. Right to enter her life.

Here's what Brianna wrote:

66 Your message came through loud and clear. I started with the dreaded master bedroom closet. I couldn't believe what I found there, like a t-shirt some guy had given me when we played on the same softball team, photos of guys whose names I don't even remember, and some more pieces of jewelry that had sentimental meaning at one time, but that sentiment was long gone. So much clutter! I took no prisoners...the jewelry all went to my little niece for dress up and the rest of the stuff went out. You guessed it—not long after I finished the bedroom closet, I met this really great guy at a party in my apartment complex.

Not sure why I hadn't noticed him before, but maybe everything was just too cluttered for him to find me. How's that for my new Feng Shui speak? 99

Cobwebs and Bugs

Q: I keep finding cobwebs and dead bugs all over my deck. I hate to look at them so I just leave them and avoid the deck. Is there any Feng Shui symbolism?

A: Bugs are creepy and they do die, and cobwebs accumulate around everyone's outdoor living space. That's all natural. But, too many dead bugs can represent negative energy—we call this *sha chi*—in the bagua area where they accumulate. Too many cobwebs left untouched symbolize you're so wrapped up and stuck that you can't move forward. Accumulated dust can represent lack of respect for what's going on in your life. Get a new broom or duster and sweep out all this negative chi from around the outside of your home. Sweep away from your house, rather than toward it. Don't forget places like in the window screen tracks, under furniture and grill legs, and around outdoor ceiling fan blades.

Death and Bereavement

Q: My sister has our mother's ashes in an urn that she keeps in her home office, and it creeps me out. What room should she keep them in?

A: In Feng Shui, ashes are considered extremely yin (low) energy, and it's inauspicious to keep them anywhere in a house along with the living. It's especially inauspicious to keep ashes in an office where you are trying to grow your business or career. Some cemeteries and memorial gardens have places where ashes can be stored, and the family can visit. Another suggestion is to return them to nature. Perhaps you and your sister could scatter or bury them with permission in a place where your mother liked to visit.

Q: I am a home stager. The owner of a house I staged died unexpectedly, and the family is getting rid of everything and asked if I would like some of the furniture and other objects. I worry how much bad energy would items from this home carry, considering the home owner died in an unhealthy way. People buy from yard sales and flea markets all the time, but is there a special concern getting things and not knowing about their past life?

CHAPTER 7: TROUBLE, CHAOS, CLUTTER

A: Trust your gut on this one. If you have uncomfortable feelings about any of the items, don't bring them into your own home. There's nothing inherently bad about acquiring items from someone who has passed away, whether from yard sales, auctions, consignment stores, and antique stores, or as gifts. But, if something feels unhealthy to you because of where it came from, that object will continue to carry negative energy into your home.

Q: I read a news article with a photo of a woman who has a lovely urn with her mother's ashes in her living room bay window. She also has several lovely boxes containing the remains of pets long gone. I was aghast! Even with my limited knowledge of Feng Shui, years ago I eliminated the dried flowers from the house because they no longer had life energy. Dead plant, dead flowers, something dead in the house? Goodness, I loved my mother and my dog but would not want to have the sunshine filtered through their urns and boxes. What does Feng Shui say about all this?

A: I agree with you that it wasn't a wise decision to glorify the practice of keeping ashes in a home. Feng Shui principles believe that remains of dead relatives and pets don't belong in the house because they represent dead energy. A better way to honor and think of parents and pets in a positive light is to bury or scatter their ashes, and instead keep a tangible memento of them in a place of honor in your home.

Q: My mom died many years ago, but I still feel blue around Mother's Day. I've decided to create a collection of photos and objects that remind me of her and wanted to know the appropriate place to display it.

Q: I have been putting off going through the boxes of things I brought back after we closed down my mom's apartment after she died. Can you offer Feng Shui advice on what to do with all this stuff? I'm overwhelmed.

A: I understand the difficulty of dealing with sentimental clutter, whether your relative died recently or years ago. The Family/Community area of the home is the perfect location to display objects from a deceased family member. Make sure you also display current family photos and objects near your mom's memorabilia, to symbolize a positive future for your family, in addition to the tribute to a deceased relative.

Fast 5

Clear Sentimental Clutter

Feeling overwhelmed by going through the boxes of things you brought back after clearing out a deceased relative's home? Try these five Feng Shui steps:

1. **Intervals.** Limit your clearing sessions to several hours rather than one day-long blitz. A fresh, rested mind will help you make smart decisions and avoid purger's regret.

2. **Photos.** Take digital images of sentimental things, both to save space and because of the risk of fading or loss of the original. You can create keepsake books at online sites to preserve memories.

3. **Save/Toss.** Save the best and toss the rest. If your loved one had a bulk collection—like every greeting card received, or every one of your child's art projects that you shared—pick some favorites and toss the rest.

4. **Relocate.** Give things a new home. It's easier to part with beloved objects if you can visualize others using them. Ask your relatives and friends if they want your family heirloom items before you distribute them. Often, one person's junk is, well, another one's junk as well.

5. **Box It.** If you're grieving because of a death, downsizing, or in an empty nest, put things you can't decide about in boxes labeled Future, hide them away somewhere, then wait at least six months before sorting through them. Then, when you have perspective, open the box and toss unwanted items and donate the rest.

CHAPTER 7: TROUBLE, CHAOS, CLUTTER

Divorce and Blended Families

Q: Hi, Carol, I am a newsletter reader in Finland. I have a large photo of my late husband who died five years ago displayed in the living room with a candle in front of it. For the last three years, my young children and I have had a wonderful new man living with us. I am wondering whether the photo of my first husband acts like a guardian angel over our home, or if the photo is holding us in the past. The children love both of their fathers, the current one and the angel one. We are happy together, but I have started to wonder if the picture has a hidden, wrong type of energy towards our home.

A: It sounds like you and your children are fortunate to have a new, loving man in your lives. The fact that you asked the question of whether the large photo of your late husband is anchoring you in the past makes me think that perhaps it is. I recommend you remove the photo from your living room and place it in an album, or scan and keep it digitally. To help your children connect to both of the fathers in their lives, place two, smaller photos in wood frames in each of their rooms: one with them with their natural father and another with all of you and their new father. That way, both fathers can watch over them, but your late husband won't be quite such a prominent figure in the public part of your home.

Q: My husband's ex-wife is a constant presence in our life, and she even shows up at family events where she is not invited and ends up in the photos. There are boxes of photos of her in our attic. Could that be part of why she still has a hold on him? I am working with him on this, but I need Feng Shui help.

A: Storing any of the ex's things could be a big part of the problem. Get rid of anything around you that belonged to, or reminds you of, this woman. It's especially important to remove the photos from your attic because anything that's above you symbolically weighs down on you. Symbolically, when you have so many images of this woman stored around, she is occupying a place in your home. Destroy the photos or send them back to her without making a big deal out of it.

Q: I'm divorced, and my children want a photo of their father, my ex-husband, in the house. Is this a good idea?

A: While it's not a good idea for your ex-spouse's photo to occupy a prominent position in the public areas of your home, his photos can certainly be displayed in your children's room. Try to make sure it's a current photo of your ex where he's doing something happy with each child, or with the children together.

Q: I'm separated from my husband. He's a good father to our teenage children, but the marriage is over. I've already cleared out a ton of marriage clutter, bought new bedding, and removed our wedding photo from my nightstand. I placed my wedding memorabilia in a keepsake box for the kids, but I still have my wedding rings. We had a large family portrait hanging on the dining room wall and it's still there because I don't know what to do with it. How do I balance my need to get rid of past memories with my children's need to have their father in their lives?

A: Your use of the word "ton" of marriage clutter is revealing, since clutter could represent the accumulated weight of what was wrong in the relationship. All the things you removed from the bedroom were positive steps in moving forward. Move the box with the wedding items out of the house. You could rent a storage unit or store it at a relative's home. The rings could go in a safe deposit box for the children, or they could be sold or traded-in for a piece of jewelry you buy for yourself as a symbol of your self-worth. Take the family portrait off the wall and put it in storage, then replace it with new artwork that you and your children select, such as a painting or photograph of your favorite place to visit. When your children help select what you display in their home, they become part of the process of moving forward.

CHAPTER 7: TROUBLE, CHAOS, CLUTTER

SUCCESS STORY

Kate and Jeremy
Fix the Damage

Kate and Jeremy moved into their new home in the fall. After being together for 10 years, their relationship was undergoing a transition, they were arguing a lot, and considering a separation. The first thing I noticed about their home was that it was missing the Love area of the bagua. To anchor that missing area and symbolically anchor their relationship, I recommended they make a correction. Kate placed two matching terracotta pots in the backyard at the point where the walls would come together if the house were a complete rectangle. She reported that their communications improved immediately. Then, after the long winter, I received a follow-up message.

Here's what Kate wrote:

❝ Things in our life continued to improve after I placed the two pots to complete the missing bagua area, but then in January, we began arguing more frequently. I have to admit I was furious at Feng Shui for not working. Once the weather finally started to get warmer and the snow melted, I went out into the backyard to do some cleanup and noticed that both pots were badly cracked from being filled with snow and ice. Wow, was that message ever clear to me! I got rid of those broken pots and we replaced them with a pair of beautiful stone carvings to more permanently ground our relationship. We're a happy couple again, and I'll never doubt the power of Feng Shui to help keep us that way.❞

Electronics

Q: Is there anything I can do to reduce the impact of the electromagnetic field from an electrical transformer box in our backyard? Unfortunately, it is only 20 feet behind our bedroom.

A: Dealing with a transformer near your bedroom is a complicated issue because the electromagnetic energy (EMFs) can negatively affect health and relationships. Hang a rug or fiber art on the bedroom wall that backs up to the transformer to shield you. Search online for special paints and fabrics for that room that help shield and deflect electromagnetic energy. If you can, plant soft bushes around the transformer, and/or plant trees between the transformer and the house—either in the ground or in big pots. Another option is to hang a convex bagua mirror outside on the house facing the transformer to reflect the negative energy away from your bedroom. This octagon-shaped mirror should only be used outside.

Q: Reading last month's Q&A in your newsletter about an electrical box in the front yard made me realize something similar could be happening to me. The fuse box for my house is located on the northern outer wall. Could that contribute towards financial imbalance? If so, can I place something between the box and house, or will I have to place something on the interior wall?

A: Yes, the electrical box on the outside of your home could be creating an electrical imbalance. And when things are imbalanced, your prosperity, health, and well-being can suffer. One thing you can do is hang fabric, like a rug or fiber artwork, on the interior wall that backs up to the box to block some of the electromagnetic energy from entering. You could also keep healthy house plants in that room near that same wall.

Q: We just moved, but in our rush to find a new home, we never noticed the electrical utility box on the corner of our property. Now I can't stop thinking about it, and I'm concerned it is sending bad energy our way. Is there anything I should do?

A: The first thing you can do is plant flowering shrubs all around the utility box to absorb any negative energy. Additionally, you could also place a wind chime on your house, between the electrical box and your home, to symbolically move the negative chi away from you. [See previous question for additional options.]

Financial Woes

Q: I am about to buy a home that was a foreclosure. Is there anything that I should do to make sure the previous owner's negative financial situation doesn't affect me?

A: Hire a professional cleaning service to clean everything, inside and out, as thoroughly as possible before you move in any of your furniture. Wash all the windows, clean the front door, scrub wood cabinets and floors, and paint all the walls with new colors so you don't inherit any negative *predecessor chi*, which is the energy from the previous owners. Next, conduct a space clearing before you move in any of your furniture. Also, pay special attention to the furniture, art, and decoration you add to the Wealth area of the home and make sure this area feels prosperous. You could write an affirmation to release the former owners of the home and wish them a better and more prosperous future in another location. Place this message in a silver-colored box in your Helpful People area.

Q: This is the second year I have been called in for an IRS tax audit, and both times, I ended up being assessed a penalty. Any Feng Shui changes I can make?

A: Look for water issues in your home, especially slow leaks in the faucets and drains in your bathrooms and in the basement. Water represents wealth in Feng Shui, so if you've been leaking water, you've also been losing your wealth. Also, take care of any maintenance issues you've been ignoring. Control your tax record clutter, because clutter represents the inability to move forward. In your situation, that means moving forward past a tax audit. Keep only the paperwork and records you need and organize them neatly in boxes for each year.

Fast 5

Keep Stuff Out of Your Home

What you keep out of your home can be as important as what you invite into it. Try keeping these five things out of your home:

1. **Violent Images.** Avoid displaying images that show destruction, chaos, or violence. It's better to fill your walls with upbeat images and your shelves with objects that make you feel happy.

2. **Ashes.** When you're grieving, it's tempting to hold on to ashes from your loved one or pet for comfort, but keeping them in your home represents trapped energy. Instead, chose a symbolic place to bury or scatter the ashes. Then, surround yourself with a few cherished mementos and photos of your loved one.

3. **Gifts from Negative People.** If you receive a gift from someone who is angry, hostile, or negative, you'll feel that anger every time you use it. This is especially the case if their gift was given out of obligation rather than love. Sell, donate, or discard all gifts that come from negative people, no matter how expensive the items.

4. **Broken Objects.** If something is broken, ripped, or stained, either repair it, clean it, or move it out of your home.

5. **People You Don't Like.** If you don't get along with someone, don't invite that person into your home. If you must entertain business associates you don't like, or if there's hostility whenever your family gets together, meet these people at a restaurant or another neutral place.

Q: My business is not doing well, so I'm trying to be frugal. But, in the back of my head, I am hearing a voice that says that if I cut back, then the universe will say, "OK, your wish is my command," and it will send me less. I have lowered my rate for some clients because I don't want to lose their business, and I'm holding on to things instead of replacing them. How do you balance spending less and holding on to more?

A: Try practicing a type of "frugal Feng Shui" to tap into the positive energy of change, harmony, and hope. That is, make a list of what needs to be repaired, then come up with a timeline to fix it as quickly as your budget allows. Also, take a look at what you're hanging on to and make sure these things aren't holding you back. For example, are you keeping objects that you associate with unhappy memories from past clients or customers? If so, replace these items with other objects that remind you of more prosperous times.

Floods and Leaks

Q: Why is the slow leak in my guest bathroom faucet such a problem? We hardly ever use the room, and I don't have money for a plumber right now.

A: Moving water represents prosperity, abundance, and cash flow in Feng Shui. However, when you have plumbing problems, that water is being lost, which equates to money problems. That means when your faucets are dripping—even in infrequently-used rooms—your money is slowly running down the drain. When your faucets leak, you could find it hard to stay ahead of your expenses, even if plenty of money is coming into your life. I recommend fixing that drip as soon as possible.

Q: What does a flood symbolize in Feng Shui? Our basement was drenched during the recent rainstorm and we had to get rid of a lot of stuff. There were some sentimental things, but mostly it was junk we hadn't looked at in decades, and some of it had unpleasant memories. Was the flood actually a positive Feng Shui event?

A: I've received many questions about flooded basements, especially when one area of the country experiences torrential rains. Sadly, some people lose useful and sentimental items, but many people end up seeing the flood as the perfect opportunity to get rid of all of the stuff they'd been storing in basements just because they had the space. Slow leaks and drips are considered negative in Feng Shui because they represent a constant drain of your wealth, but there's also some belief that a flood represents an immediate clearing of stuck energy. What you keep in a basement supports what goes on in the rest of the home above it. Most people tell me that although it was tough work mopping up and clearing out after the flood damage, their homes—and consequently their lives—felt lighter after the flood forced them to clear out their basements. Of course, you want to first fix any outdoor drainage or indoor sump pump issues to prevent future problems. Hang in there!

Q: The weather has been extreme this winter. Our basement is cold to begin with, and we forgot to shut off the outside faucet and it froze while we were out of town. What is the Feng Shui message in all the water that flooded our house?

A: While water represents abundance in Feng Shui, conditions that make you lose water, like a leaking roof or a flooded basement, create negative energy that symbolizes a loss of wealth. Don't delay in fixing storm damage. Even the action of scheduling a contractor to make the repairs begins to redirect your chi on a positive path. Sometimes things just happen, and other times, they have symbolic meaning. Were you having communication problems in your home or office? A flood could be a response to the lack of flow of words. Check that all your interior and exterior doors are well oiled and working properly. Just as this allows your doors to move properly, it will allow for the easy flow of words.

CHAPTER 7: TROUBLE, CHAOS, CLUTTER

Health and Medical Issues

Q: Our young son has been diagnosed with ADHD, and I want to do everything I can to help. Are there Feng Shui suggestions for how to arrange his bedroom?

A: Avoid using bright or hot colors, and instead choose soothing, earthy colors and soft neutral tones that represent the Earth Element to help your son feel grounded. Remove as many electronic devices as you can. Clutter creates chaos, which is especially difficult for children with ADHD, who are easily distracted. Avoid artwork with images that are flying and falling. Try to remove as many active and stimulating toys as possible, and limit the amount of stuff he displays on the shelves. Keep the walls, window treatments, and artwork simple, use solid colors, and avoid busy prints, stripes, and dots.

Q: My husband has been diagnosed with clinical depression. Is there a particular bagua area where I need to make some Feng Shui adjustments? He says the house feels like it's weighing him down. What do I do to help him?

A: Take a look at the Family, Creativity, and Grounding areas of your home and remove all the clutter, then makes sure that all the furniture in those areas is in good condition and the artwork is pleasant and uplifting. If the house feels heavy, look for things like a low or slanted ceiling, heavy exposed beams, or textured ceilings. You want to symbolically raise these by aiming lights at them, painting beams and low ceilings the same color as the walls, or by hanging artwork with images that are vertical rather than horizontal. You can also place tall plants, floor lamps, or tall furniture in the corners of the room to symbolically lift the chi in a room.

Q: We have a couple of pairs of crutches and canes that have served us at various times when we've had torn ligaments and the like. I realized that I might be storing them in the health/well-being sections of the bagua in my house. Short of getting rid of them, is there a cure for keeping old medical equipment in your home? My husband doesn't want to get rid of them because of the replacement cost if we ever need them again.

A: The Feng Shui symbolism of keeping these mobility aids in the house is that you expect to need them in the future. Therefore, the recommendation is to move these out of your home, because keeping them sends a negative message. Donate them to a nonprofit, sending them on the way with the affirmation that you'll continue to be healthy, won't need them anymore, and that you'll be taken care of in the future. If all else fails and your husband won't let them out of the house, wrap them in red cloth or red paper and store them out of sight in a closet.

Q: Is it possible to Feng Shui a hospital room? I'm scheduled for surgery and want to know if there is anything I can do to make the environment conducive to healing?

A: First, use the bagua map to locate the Health and Grounding areas of your home. Then, remove clutter, dead or sickly plants, and anything that doesn't look healthy or whole from that area. Display lots of bushy plants with rounded leaves, and other green and wooden objects, along with images of healthy growing things, like meadows or forests, in this area. For the Grounding area, add some rocks or ceramic objects and images of mountains to give you a solid base. In your hospital room, surround yourself with sweet-smelling flowers and plants, and avoid sharp plants like cactus or stunted plants like bonsai. Display photos of your family and friends who support you. Bring upbeat reading material—no murder mysteries or horror stories, please. Play soft, pleasant music on your mobile device so you don't have to deal with unpleasant hospital noises and conversations. If you can, bring your own nightgowns or PJs rather than wearing those institutional ones. I'm sending positive chi your way for a speedy return to good health.

Q: I am re-reading your book and one sentence is sticking out to me this time. You said that if you are not meant to do something, the Universe will place obstacles in your way. I'm only 30 years old and have been in chronic pain for the past 3 years and have had to take two leaves of absence from work. When I think about obstacles in my life, the only one I can see is my health. I can't imagine that the Universe does not want me to work, but it's certainly making it difficult for me to do. How can I make changes

CHAPTER 7: TROUBLE, CHAOS, CLUTTER

if I don't know the reason for why the obstacles are being placed in my path? Thank you for any help you can provide and just for listening.

A: Thanks for your thoughtful question. I'm sorry to hear that you're dealing with so much pain, and I can't begin to imagine how frustrating it is for you. The context of that statement in my book is related to something like a career change. In your situation, it sounds like your health issues are preventing you from even exploring what passions you can pursue. The Feng Shui adjustment would be to do a thorough analysis of your surroundings to determine if there's anything contributing to your health issues. For example, do you sleep with your head near a wall with a toilet on the other side, are there electromagnetic issues in the house, is there a bathroom in the Health area, is there geopathic stress in the land, etc.? There are many other issues to first consider before you can make Feng Shui changes to remedy these situations and assure that your home is supporting your good health. Different areas of the home relate to different areas of the body, so that would also be something to investigate. The book that's considered the ultimate source for this is *Feng Shui and Health* by Nancy Santo Pietro.

Q: My question concerns a friend who is getting injured a lot and can't do her regular exercising. The injuries don't happen while she's working out, but when she's just walking or doing normal things during the day. When I asked what she has in her Health area, she said that her apartment was pretty bare and needed help figuring out where to make changes. My first thought is to put a couple of living plants there, but I defer to your awesome knowledge!

A: Of course, the first thing your friend can do is consult a medical practitioner. Then, from a Feng Shui perspective, you can help her use the bagua to locate the Health area, plus pay attention to the Helpful People and Grounding areas as well. Next, help her clear the clutter and remove anything that's broken, malfunctioning, or cracked. She should avoid storing in these areas the crutches or other medical devices that she needed when she was injured. She can add plants or images of lush, growing plants with rounded leaves in these areas, and obviously no cactus, other spiky plants, or bonsai with their stunted growth. She can add Earth to the Grounding area in the form of images of mountains or earthy things, like pottery, clay, and terra cotta objects.

Military Deployment

Q: My husband has just been deployed overseas with the Air Force. Are there Feng Shui changes I should make to keep our life balanced at home while he's gone, and to keep him safe while he's away?

A: Place two current photographs of your husband in the Family area of your home: one in civilian clothes and the other in his uniform to symbolize a safe tour and a speedy return home in perfect health. Put the photos in vertical, dark brown wood frames. The composition of the frame is the Wood Element that encourages growth and health, while the brown color represents the Earth Element that promotes grounding. Keep fresh flowers or a healthy plant in the same area, especially a philodendron that has shiny, heart-shaped leaves. If you can't grow live plants, use silk, but avoid dried flowers since they don't contain living energy. Also, go through your home and give all your plants a good pruning, and remove dead branches to encourage the new growth that represents good health. If you have silk plants, give them a good dusting on a regular basis to keep the positive chi moving.

Negative Chi

Q: I have heard about Mercury retrograde being the time when I shouldn't make any decisions. Is this part of Feng Shui, and how much should I worry about it?

A: Several times during the year, the planet Mercury turns in an apparent backward motion, which some people believe has a negative affect on our communications and electronics. This can range from airline schedule delays, to bad haircut days, to computer problems. While this is more astrology than Feng Shui, a few simple, practical Feng Shui suggestions can help during these Mercury retrogrades. For example, things can get lost at this time, so be extra vigilant about computer back-ups. Leave extra time when traveling, and make sure your suitcases have visible tags. Slow down and rethink things, especially relationships. Since a retrograde isn't a good time to start new projects, it can be a great time to finish existing projects. Bring your resume or portfolio up to date, clean out your closets, or repaint the family room.

CHAPTER 7: TROUBLE, CHAOS, CLUTTER

SUCCESS STORY

*Barbara Renovates
the Basement*

Barbara's home was in a state of neglect when she called me for a consultation. She and her husband were having communication difficulties and the house was obviously both the cause and the effect of their issues. A serious clutter-clearing and redecorating was in order. The couple didn't have funds to make all the needed changes, so they had to postpone the basement renovation.

Here's what Barbara wrote:

❛❛ After your visit, we decided we had to shift the budget around so we could start the remodel. Both the old carpeting (sad, as you described it) and wallpaper are gone. The whole inside of the house, except for the basement, has been painted. Our bedroom is now in a skin-tone color and our daughter's is a youthful lavender. The outside of the house has been power-washed and is being painted tomorrow. Our bedroom was cleared of the computer, desk, and nasty old carpet, and we are already sleeping better. The floor on the entry level was ripped up today and the new flooring should be finished in the next couple of days. There have been many trips to the dump and Goodwill, and many more to be made. So right now, we're in the thick of it. Our pictures, wall stuff, and remaining junk are in the basement, waiting to be sorted. We realize we are in the necessary chaos that must happen in order for us to get to the other side. But the good news is that my husband and I are on

(continued)

the same page with our communication and desire to make this happen. He's been cool about letting go of stuff that's not connected to who he is anymore, and he is more in tune with how we want to express ourselves. The house has been so symbolic of our personal and marital stuck-ness. There's already a more positive, cheerful energy that has opened, even from just removing all the negative stuff we have. Our sense of creativity is open now that we have cleared so much space.

And then, an unexpected thing happened to the couple. One of the painters left the hose on near the house, and the couple woke up to a flooded basement one Sunday morning. Here's Barbara's progress report:

We had to bring EVERYTHING upstairs and called one of those emergency flood services. The whole carpet down there had to go. But painters owned up to doing it and are making it right. So now the basement will also have new carpet and fresh paint. At first, it felt like a huge step backwards and we were very stressed and bummed. But it forced us to deal with our STUFF, like books, music, papers, and pictures. Since it's all in our face in the living room, we can't procrastinate dealing with it like we did when it was downstairs. It also fascinated me that the damage was from the Water element. Maybe it is a washing away the past sort of thing, or something profound like that. Progress continues! ✿✿

CHAPTER 7: TROUBLE, CHAOS, CLUTTER

Q: Negative chi or good luck? I was sitting on the bathroom floor sorting some things as I cleaned out the bathroom vanity, when out of the blue the mirror over the sink fell off the wall. I was surrounded by sharp, shattered glass. I remembered my grandmother saying something about broken mirrors being bad luck, but I came through without a scratch! What do you think? Negative or positive?

A: Sometimes, things just happen; objects do fall off the wall because of vibrations or other causes, and there's no Feng Shui symbolism. But, keeping a mirror that's broken or cracked is definitely considered negative energy, because mirror fragments will make you feel like you're "broken up." Also, the spider web-like cracks in a mirror represent being held back and unable to move forward. The important thing is that you weren't hurt. That's definitely good Feng Shui!

Q: We have a beach house, and this summer when we opened it up for the season, it just felt, well, I don't know how else to describe it, but the house just feels sad. Is there anything I should do?

A: Sometimes, the energy in a home you only use occasionally becomes stagnant because there's no life chi flowing through it. Start with a thorough clearing and airing out of your house. Then, check outside to see if any vines or weeds are covering the house and symbolically strangling it. Vacation homes sometimes have second-hand or second-best furniture that can carry negative chi, or overly-yin energy that pulls down the chi. Make sure all your furnishings are clean and fresh and replace anything that's feels stale and outdated. Repaint the walls in a bright color if they feel faded, and make sure the artwork shows happy, upbeat images. When you're in the house, play music and/or add a fountain so there's movement in the house. Finally, make sure you have lamps and a radio on timers in the house so there's always a light on and sound playing during the times when you don't occupy the house.

Fast 5

Feel Grounded at Home

*When you come home at the end of a long day,
do you have a place to rest, relax, and let go? If not,
try these five tips for assuring a harmonious home:*

1. **Colors.** Switch out red and hot orange color accessories and furniture, and instead surround yourself with the color blue for relaxation and green for renewal.

2. **Scents.** Add the scent of lavender to your environment for its calming effect.

3. **Flowers.** Treat yourself to fresh flowers or artwork that shows flowers and images of natural settings.

4. **Photos.** Display photos of special people, or art that shows your favorite places.

5. **Objects.** Remove anything you don't love, don't use, or don't need.

CHAPTER

8

WORKPLACE, CAREER, BUSINESS

When I give a Feng Shui workshop and talk about the *wind-water* feeling of gentle flow that characterizes Feng Shui, I ask how many people feel that way about their homes. Then, I ask how many walk through their front door and take a deep sigh of relief. Usually, several hands go up. They talk about things like comforting colors and soothing art. Then, I ask how many feel that way when they enter their home through their garage. Usually, several hands stay up. Finally, I ask how many people feel the same way when they enter their offices and workplaces. Most hands go down.

Why is it that no matter how much care we take with our homes, we tend to neglect our workspaces? The space where you work should nurture and grow your career just like you're nourished at home. But all too often, the typical office is filled with hard objects, noise, bright computer screens, harsh overhead florescent lighting, metal filing cabinets and desks, hard work stations, cubicle walls, ringing phones, and a whole lot of clutter. All this creates strain, tension, irritability, and feelings of isolation, instead of support and comfort.

It used to be that "going to the office" meant you worked at the same desk every day. It was your spot where you could place the photos of your family and your pets. Then came cube farms, where you sat alone in a nondescript cubicle. You were isolated, yet you had no privacy. Now, along comes the workplace hoteling trend, where there's no assigned seating and employees must reserve a work space every week or every day. Whether you sit at a workstation, share an office, or hang out in a pod or huddle room, you

CHAPTER 8: WORKPLACE, CAREER, BUSINESS

still don't even have a place to call your own. This adds to the isolation and aloneness of our modern workplaces.

If you telecommute, or run a home-based business, it's especially hard to separate your professional life from your personal relationships. The first Feng Shui consideration is which room or area of your home to use. Then, you have to consider how your work time at home harmonizes with your family time. All this raises questions about how to use Feng Shui to grow your career.

The good news is that you can take Feng Shui to work with you. Whether you work in a corner suite, in a spare room, a studio, a store, or you operate out of your car, a Feng Shui workplace makeover can help you move forward in your profession and career.

The brain is a wonderful organ; it starts working the moment you get up in the morning and does not stop until you get into the office.
— Robert Frost

Q & A

WORKPLACE

Q: Our home is a lovely, calm, neat and tidy, beautiful abode where we are very happy. But as organized as we keep our home, I am negligent at my workplace office. I love my job and the people I work with, but try as I might, I cannot keep the clutter down. I know I am more productive with fewer things on my desk, but the stacks of paper just grow and grow. From now until February is our busy season, and I need to get a grip on this, especially since the busy season in itself generates a lot of paper and supplies.

A: Without actually seeing the space and without knowing what kind of work you do, it's hard to give specific advice. But in general, office clutter problems typically relate to either having too much stuff or having too little storage space (or both for many of my clients). What kind of storage options do you have in the office, like shelves, cabinets, etc.? If they are filled to capacity, clear out old stuff and make room to store some of the things that are on your desk but you don't use all the time. Can you scan files and store them electronically? Or, is there an option to store some files and supplies out of your office in a central location? Another issue is the size of your desk. Is it adequate for the work to be done? If your desk is too small for the work you do, it can make you feel overwhelmed and can lead to an accumulation of things.

Q: There is a job posted at my company as a supervisor. I am totally qualified, but they are dragging their feet about promoting me. What changes can I make to get promoted to the position? One thing I've done already is to hang my diploma on my back wall behind the desk. My desk is in the power position like you recommend. My office is in the wisdom area of the office suite. Another thing I've been doing is actively looking for clutter to get rid of. As always, I thank you for your advice and wisdom.

CHAPTER 8: WORKPLACE, CAREER, BUSINESS

A: One thing that popped out in the photo you sent is that the art on the wall behind you is hung almost in a straight line, which represents lateral growth. It looks like the diploma is hung slightly higher, but it's from your past, not your future. It will help to choose something more current, larger, and specific to the new job you want, and hang it distinctively higher than the rest of the images. This symbolizes upward growth toward the promotion and the job you want. Good luck!

Q: There is a tremendous amount of tension in my office these days, and many people are being let go. What Feng Shui cures for my workspace can I try to make me feel more secure?

A: Make sure your desk faces the door to your office, so you're in a power—or command—position and can't be caught off guard. If you can't turn around your desk, position a small mirror so you can see what's going on behind you. Place a healthy plant and a piece of turquoise on your desk. Turquoise is the stone associated with security in your surroundings.

Fast 5

Declutter Your Office Junk Drawer

Everybody has at least one drawer that's always a mess. If you want to bring wealth and harmony into your career, remove these five categories of things to make room for those good things to find you:

1. Old **cell phones** and cases
2. Out-of-date **receipts** and expired gift cards
3. Dried-up **pens** and markers
4. Bent and twisted **paper clips**
5. Reading **glasses** with scratched lenses

Q: Is there anything I can do to stop all the gossiping in my office?

A: In Feng Shui as in many cultures, roosters are symbols of fame, recognition, and success, and they keep the evil spirits away. That's because the rooster wakes up early. announces the new day, and disperses the nighttime darkness and any bad spirits. Roosters are also a great symbol for curbing destructive office politics, so consider placing a small statue of one on your desk if you're troubled by gossip and backstabbing. A statue of a rooster is especially useful if you share an office with others or work in tight space, so you don't get caught up in their personal office politics.

Q: Where is the best place to sit at a conference table during a meeting?

A: Whenever you can, choose the power or command position. This isn't always the head of the table. Rather, it's the seat farthest from the door, facing it on a diagonal rather than in a direct line with the door. Try to avoid sitting with your back to the door, which is considered the most vulnerable position. When you're not in command position, things happen behind your back actually and symbolically because you can't see the door.

Q: I work in a cubicle. I am lucky that I face the door, but I have a half wall behind me to accommodate a shared printer with the person in the next cube. Unfortunately, that guy is impatient, angry, and aggressive. Is there any way to deflect his negative energy, especially since I feel exposed by the half wall?

A: Try to create a friendly barrier between you and your colleague by placing living plants with soft, bushy leaves, or fresh flowers. Orange is the color that encourages conversation, so choose soft orange or peach-colored flowers and container. Stay away from hot orange or red because these colors could make an already-aggressive person more hostile. If there's no place for actual living plants, try displaying artwork showing orange flowers. Place a small rooster statue or art with a rooster image where you both can see it. Images of roosters deflect negative talk and promote your fame and reputation. Place a piece of turquoise on your desk, because when used in an office where there are a lot of arguments, this stone helps achieve connectedness and security. If your back is to the person in the next cubicle, you can be ambushed by his aggressive personality. Place a small mirror on your desk so you can see behind you. You'll feel more grounded against his anger, and you'll feel more secure when you can see what's going on behind you. There will be no more negative surprises.

Q: I am trying to build teamwork among the members of the small work group I manage within a large company. Several of the team members telecommute from different states, and we only meet in person as a group a few times a year. How can I use Feng Shui to keep my team connected?

A: When a work group is separated, whether geographically or by corridors or floors in an office building, the Feng Shui solution is to connect them by using symbols. First, make sure each team member has items imprinted with the company logo or brand in the company colors—like a company mug, golf shirt, backpack, etc.—to tie them into the organization. Then, gift each member with an object that's a symbol of your team goals, such as a small statue of an eagle to represent soaring toward success. Suggest they display the object on their work area where they will see it each day, and especially when you teleconference.

Q: We are relocating our offices. Where is the best place to located the boss's office?

A: The location of the head of the office is important to the success of the business. Ideally, the boss would be located in the Wealth area, which is the left rear section when you're standing at the main entrance to the suite of offices. Also, the boss's desk within that individual office should be located in the power or command position, which is facing the door but not in a direct line with it.

Q: I work in an office that has no windows and overhead fluorescent lighting. How do I make my office feel more comfortable?

A: First, turn off the fluorescent lights and use desk and floor lamps instead. If your company won't buy them, invest in your career and health by bringing in your own lighting. Choose artwork with an image that's looking out through a window, or images of trees, water, and anything you find in the natural world. Hang a mirror to the side of your desk to give the illusion of expanding the space. Add a few living plants to your office.

SUCCESS STORY

Marissa Pictures Success

Marissa was having difficulty moving ahead in her career when she contacted me for an office consultation. She felt stuck in a rut in her job, couldn't understand why she was continually overlooked for a promotion, and had lost the ability to visualize herself succeeding in her career. There were several things I noticed immediately in her office: she was sitting with her back to the door, which is considered an inauspicious and vulnerable position; she was staring at a blank wall; and the few pieces of art she had were uninspiring and were hanging in a straight line, symbolizing lateral rather than upward growth. I recommended a few strategic changes, and a few months later, I received this email from Marissa.

Here's what Marissa wrote:

❝ The first thing I did was move my desk so that I could see out the doorway, and I couldn't believe how much more noticed I felt when colleagues would walk down the hallway and smile or acknowledge me. Then, I found a picture of a mountain to hang behind me to represent feeling supported as you suggested, and I replaced the horizontal line of bland prints that had been hanging in the office when I moved in. I now have a photo of a beautiful sunrise and a print of a landscape with lush trees. This is what I thought represented career growth for me, as you recommended. Out of the blue, I was selected to be part of an ad hoc task force, which has given me greater visibility and respect in the company. Finally, I can picture my prospects for moving up in my career. ❞

CHAPTER 8: WORKPLACE, CAREER, BUSINESS

Q: How can I Feng Shui the junk from my computer to help bring career success?

A: Feng Shui clutter clearing isn't just for your physical house; it's for where your house your data as well. Just like you remove the trash from your house on a regular basis, you need to do the same for your computer. The act of simply moving a file into the trash doesn't get rid of it; you also need to empty your virtual trashcan. Individual photo and email applications may also have separate trashcans. Don't forget to empty your spam and junk mail folders. Another way to declutter your computer is to arrange your desktop folders according to the bagua. For example, on my own desktop, I keep the Feng Shui folder in the upper left-hand corner, which is the Wealth area. I keep the folder for my books in progress in the lower middle, which is the Career area. My upcoming workshops folder is in the upper middle, which is the Future area.

Q: I just started a new job and my office is so close to the restrooms that I can hear the flushing toilets. I knew this was going to be a problem but took the job anyway with the promise that I would be relocated to another space as soon as possible. Anything I can do in the short run to protect my career?

A: This is obviously not the best Feng Shui location, because the negative energy from the toilets can affect your health as well as your job performance. First, make sure your desk is located as far as possible from the wall adjacent to the restroom. Next, get a white noise machine to block out the flushing noise, or play music on your mobile device using headphones if allowed. Also, hang a rug or textile art on that wall adjacent to the toilet to help block the negative energy, as well as to muffle the sound.

Q: I share an office and my colleague wants to hang a world map on the wall behind me. I don't mind the idea of the map, but I want to know if that's the place for it.

A: The ideal place to locate a map or globe is in the Knowledge/Wisdom area of the room. To find that area, stand outside the entrance to your office looking in. The Knowledge/Wisdom area is in the lower left corner.

FENG SHUI TO THE RESCUE

Q: I don't have a permanent office space, but instead, I work in a hoteling setup where I have to reserve a workstation in advance or find impromptu work spaces. Sometimes, I just work at Starbucks and similar places. Are there simple things I can do to make my temporary space Feng Shui-friendly? I'm looking to move to another company where I can have my own space.

A: When you do get to reserve a workstation in advance, choose one in a command position, which is located where you can see the main door to the space, but not directly in front of it. Put together a backpack or tote that not only includes the office supplies you need, but also a few items that will activate good Feng Shui wherever you land. One of these items can be a red sweater or burgundy jacket that you can drape over the back of your chair for protection. Carry sanitizing wipes so you can actually and symbolically clean your space to remove the *predecessor chi*, or energy, from the former occupant. Choose a screensaver for your laptop that's upbeat and inspiring because it's the one thing that will always be with you at your workspace. Use headphones when you working in a public location. Dress for the position you aspire to achieve, rather than the position you have now. Keep your backpack or tote clutter free as you move around, because it's your travelling office. The same goes for your car.

Q: There is a corner of a wall behind me when I sit at my desk in my office. There is no other place for the desk in the space. I do get backaches and wonder if the two are related.

A: The protruding wall pointing at you is called a *poison arrow*, and yes, it could be causing your backaches, and eventually it could cause job problems. If you can't move your desk, try hanging a plant with a long, trailing vine to cover the sharp edge of the wall that's aimed at you. Philodendron and peace lily are two plants that grow well under artificial office lighting. If there's enough room, place a piece of furniture, like a small table or bookshelf, between you and the edge.

Q: I'm having a problem with my staff coming into my office to ask a question, and then overstaying their welcome. How do I get them to stay for shorter periods of time so that I can get my own work done?

A: Make sure you're seated in the power, or command, position, which is facing the door, preferably on a diagonal. If you move around the chairs when people visit your office, remain in command position rather than giving it up to your visitors. Also, consider hanging a clock with a second hand or a picture of moving water. These will create and encourage movement in your office.

Q: I finally moved into an office with windows! I arranged the furniture, so I can look at the view. The problem is my back is to the door when I am working at my computer. A colleague told me this position is not good Feng Shui. What do you think is the best desk position for me?

A: When you sit with your back to the door, you're in the most vulnerable position. Things go on behind your back, actually and symbolically. Similarly, sitting with your back to a window represents turning your back on the outside world. (Think about the obvious implications at the White House, where the President sits in the Oval Office in front of a window.) Turn around your desk so you can see what's coming in the door. If that's not possible, position a mirror where you can easily glance at it to see what's going on behind you.

Q: Where's the best place for a plant in my office? I don't have a window and there are harsh overhead fluorescent lights. Can any plant survive in this environment?

A: Plants help diffuse harmful electro-magnetic fields created by the large number of electronic devices in our environment. They can also help neutralize the harsh fumes that are released by some types of furniture, carpeting and building materials. Try placing a plant placed within three feet of your computer. Good plants for offices with artificial lighting include jade, lucky bamboo, peace lilies, and philodendron. You can find a description of more beneficial plants in my article *Feng Shui-Friendly House Plants*. [See *Resources* section at end of this book.]

Q: My job feels pretty secure right now, but there are major layoffs in my field. Can you recommend some Feng Shui changes to make in my office to help increase my job security?

A: Make sure you're sitting with your back against a solid wall, facing the door so you can see who is coming into the room. Having your back protected relates to job security. If you can't move your desk into this position, consider switching to a chair with a tall back, even if you have to buy it yourself, or placing a mirror where you can use it to see the door. Also, add some tall plants, natural or silk, to your office, which represent growth in your career. This will not only give you some protection, but it will also encourage respect.

Q: The energy in my office feels stagnant. Is there anything I can do?

A: First, give your office a good cleaning: clear out drawers, files, bookshelves; dust and vacuum; clean the windows; trim back or replace any dead plants. Next, move 27 things, a classic Feng Shui tip for changing around the energy. Even if it is a simple as moving a photo from one side of your desk to another, the act of changing things forces you to look at them differently, and that gets things moving. Finally, replace some of your artwork to be sure you're looking at images that have specific, positive associations with your career goals.

Q: The corner of an adjacent building is pointing right at me when I work at my desk. I'm uncomfortable in the office, and my mom said it could be because of this point aimed at me, and that I need to put something on the windowsill. You did a consultation at her home and since then, she looks at everything from a Feng Shui point of view.

A: Yes, this is called a *poison arrow*, and yes, your mom is right (I trained her well!). This sharp point is making you uncomfortable in your space. To remedy this negative situation, you need to put something on the windowsill to block the harsh energy it generates. I recommend placing a bushy plant with rounded leaves on the windowsill to also help block your view of the building edge. A plant like philodendron grows well in an office and needs little care. If you need more protection, you can add a mirror aimed out at the edge of the building. You can either place it on a stand on the windowsill or hang it in the window.

CHAPTER 8: WORKPLACE, CAREER, BUSINESS

Q & A

Career

Q: What color should I wear for a job interview? I am applying for a new position that will essentially be a promotion. I have been using your Feng Shui principles in my home with fruitful results. I'd like to know if I should wear a specific color when I go on interviews.

A: The classic Feng Shui recommendation is to wear something red as an accent when interviewing for a job. Red is the powerful Fire Element that both radiates and attracts positive energy. It can be as little as a red or burgundy accessory. If you think wearing red clothes or accessories is too obvious, you might consider wearing something red that doesn't show (like underwear). You'll know where your new-found power is coming from even if your interviewer doesn't! Choose an outfit that fits with the style of dress for the company or industry where you want to work.

Q: I just made a change after a long period of being out of work. What can I do to sustain my new career?

A: Place biographies of people you admire, inspirational books, and self-help books in the Career area of your home to increase your work success. In your new workplace, hang art depicting mountains on the wall behind your desk, which will give you support in your new career.

Q: I wanted to update you: I got Employee of the Month just a few months after starting this job. It was a nice surprise. Now my question: my husband is job hunting and we'd love the opportunity to move back to New England. Are there cures and things to focus our energy toward to help steer the energy toward that goal? The only thing is, I'd have to transfer or find another job.

A: It's always good to hear from you, and congratulations on being named Employee of the Month! I know you always work hard and deserve it. My recommendation is to do the same kinds of things you have always done with finding your own new jobs in your local area. But this time, also place images of New England and/or the logos of companies your husband is considering in the Future and Helpful People areas of your home and where he sits when he's job hunting. As you do your own New England job hunting, make the same adjustments in your home office. Good luck with the job hunting and the move!

Fast 5

Clear Your Computer Chaos

Feng Shui clutter clearing isn't only for your actual house; it's also for where your store your data. Do these five tasks regularly to remove trash for your computer like you remove it from your home:

1. **Trash.** Empty the trash. The act of simply moving a file into the trash doesn't get rid of it; you also need to empty the virtual trashcan. Individual applications, like photo and email programs, may also have separate trashcans. Don't forget to empty your junk mail folder.

2. **Apps.** Delete apps, software, and files you don't use. If you tried out an app and you decided not to use it, it's probably still somewhere in there and needs to be removed.

3. **Cache.** Clear your browser cache. Most web browsers will cache sites, and these files tend to grow over time. You'll find an option to clear your cache in your browser's preferences.

4. **Files.** Eliminate nonessential files. Run apps that are designed to find and eliminate unnecessary files or that defragment your drive.

5. **Desktop.** Clean up and organize your computer desktop. Arrange desktop folders according to the bagua.

CHAPTER 8: WORKPLACE, CAREER, BUSINESS

Q: My husband was fired without warning and had to quickly move out his personal items and artwork. We are storing all of it in the shed right now. Can we bring these things into our house and display them or is that a bad idea?

A: Right now, your husband's personal items from his former office are associated with negative energy. Keep them out of your house, at least until he finds a new job. Hang artwork with upbeat, positive images in the area where he sits when he sends resumes and makes calls about a new job. When he finds a new position and settles into a new office, he can decide about the old artwork. If anything reminds him of the unfortunate end to his former job, I recommend he doesn't bring it to his new surroundings.

Q: Is there such a thing as Feng Shui for a resume? My friend was unexpectedly laid off and sent me her resume to review.

A: Your friend should pay as much attention to the area where she works when she sends out cover letters and resumes as she does to the resume itself. I recommend setting up a special work area, so the action of finding a new job becomes her full-time occupation right now. She can decorate that space with artwork that sends a positive message about her job search, such as a picture of a rising sun to suggest a new beginning for her career, birds flying, or a hot air balloon rising to give flight to her career, and a healthy live plant with rounded leaves to represent wealth. She can decorate the space with artwork and objects that specifically relate to her career field or to a specific company.

Q: Do you have any recommendations for quick action in attracting a desired job? I recently began graduate school. I plan to purchase your book from the local store tomorrow.

A: Take a look at what images, furniture, and objects you have in the rooms that occupy the Future, Knowledge, and Helpful People areas of your home. Make sure everything is future-oriented and represents where you want to be going with your career. Remove anything that's broken, dirty, damaged, negative, or relates to the past. If there's a specific company or industry you want to work for, display images that specifically relate to it in your Future area. Good luck with your studies and job hunt.

Q: I am a new to the real estate business. What's the most effective way to use Feng Shui, especially during the holiday season when sales are typically slower? And I have heard different opinions of where I should place my signs to assure a quick and profitable sale.

A: Feng Shui improvements can help make a home more appealing to prospective buyers. But even Feng Shui can't overcome the problem of listing the house at too high a price. My primary recommendation is to fairly price the homes you list. As for the sign, place it to the right of the front door as you're facing the home, because that's the side most people naturally look to when they approach a home. Also, place your marketing materials just inside the front door on the right-hand side if possible. And make sure you display them upright in a rack rather than flat on a table, since you don't want them "lying down" on the job.

Q: I'm a blogger trying to turn my posts into a novel, but I'm suffering from an extreme case of writer's block. I have this quote by Somerset Maugham above my desk and wonder if maybe it's sending a negative message about my writing: "There are three rules for writing the novel. Unfortunately, no one knows what they are." What Feng Shui changes can I make in the area around where I write?

A: The rules for writing a novel may be a mystery, but the Feng Shui "rules" for setting up the space where you write are well known. Whether you're a professional writer, a would-be author, or just someone who needs a creative boost to get your writing juices flowing, writing in a balanced and harmonious setting can help make all your writing efforts successful. Whether it is a separate room or only a corner of the kitchen, designate an area where you write, then try to use the space at the same time every day. Sit in the power position, diagonally across from the door, so you're *in command* of your writing. Hang artwork directly in front of you that shows gently moving water, which symbolizes flow and creativity for your writing projects. Surround yourself with plants and flowers to represent the Wood Element, which encourages growth of your writing skills. Display copies of your published works, complimentary letters, and awards you've won in the Fame/Future area of your writing space to encourage you to move forward. And finally, place copies of books or

CHAPTER 8: WORKPLACE, CAREER, BUSINESS

articles from writers you admire in your Helpful People area to act as mentors for your writing projects. If you have second thoughts about displaying the Maugham quote, take it down.

SUCCESS STORY

Rose Remedies Her Writer's Block

My client Rose was suffering from a case of writer's block when she contacted me for a consultation that centered around her home office. She had a lovely office space on the first floor of her home, but there was a bit too much sha chi (negative energy) that was keeping her from moving forward with her writing projects.

Here's what Rose wrote:

❝ I have made about 60% of the changes you recommended. I painted designs on both places on the sidewalk to fill in the missing areas of the bagua, fixed the problems with the fireplace, trimmed the overgrown shrubs in front of the office window, moved my desk so I was facing the door, and added an "L" to give me even more room to spread out. I loved your explanation of how my too-small desk was limiting my growth. I plan to have everything finished by the end of the year. Remember my prayer, "I want to touch the minds and hearts of millions of people"? Well, an interesting shift is happening: I have been invited to co-author a book with a woman who has published about 15 books on corporate issues! The writing has begun. Long live Feng Shui! ❞

Q & A

BUSINESS

Q: I have been trying to promote my business, and specifically my upcoming lecture series. I'm primarily using my website and printed materials, but with limited success. How can I use Feng Shui to get more exposure for my business brand?

A: First, make sure the room where you design your materials is supporting you. For example, what have you placed in your Wealth and Clients/Helpful People areas? You should be working in a space where everything surrounding you is positive, upbeat, prosperous, and supportive. Next, take a look at your website and marketing materials to make sure they conform to good Feng Shui guidelines and placement according to the bagua. Choose colors for your marketing materials and online presence that reflect what message you want to send through your communications, such as red for passion, yellow for cheerfulness, etc. Use the bagua to decide where to place these colors and images. As an example, I designed the home page of my website, FengShuiForRealLife.com, according to Feng Shui power principles. At the top of the home page, I placed mountains for strength (Fire Element in the Future area of the bagua), and at the bottom, I placed wavy lines for creativity (Water Element in the Career area). I placed everything on the home page according to the bagua.

Q: I wait to deposit checks from clients until I have enough to make it worth a trip to the bank. Is it better to deposit them immediately?

A: It depends on how long you wait. Checks sitting on your desk represent static chi, so if they sit around for weeks or months, you're not taking advantage of your wealth. I recommend depositing them as often as possible, at least within a week of receiving them. A check doesn't represent wealth until you deposit it in your account and it begins to go to work for you. Consider using a mobile banking app so you can get the money deposited immediately.

CHAPTER 8: WORKPLACE, CAREER, BUSINESS

SUCCESS STORY

Diana Rescues the Family Business

Diana and her two sisters had run an office cleaning business for more than a decade, but lately, they were losing customers. When I arrived at their office condo for the consultation, it was obvious that the space was overwhelmed by clutter, especially boxes of cleaning products blocking the main entrance. In addition, the front door was warped, difficult to open, and badly in need of repainting. I explained how the front door is the *mouth of chi* where all the positive energy and wealth enters a space, and that a door that was blocked and hard to open represented missed opportunities for their business. All this was symbolically blocking new clients from entering. We moved around a lot of furniture, and I gave them a plan to clear their space.

Here's what Diana wrote:

❝ I can't fully express what an impact your session had on me, my sisters, and everyone else in our office. Thanks so much for getting us started on this path. After you left, we immediately called our handyman, who came the next day to sand and repaint the door. We decided on a red door, since you explained how this represents power and wealth. We have cleared out the entry area, and now we are working through your long-term plan to get rid of all our unnecessary supplies, files, and assorted junk. By the way, business has exploded since your visit, and I'm sure the Feng Shui process helped to clear the way for new clients to arrive at our now easy-to-find and shiny front door. ❞

Q: I run my own business recruiting employees and need more people to call me about jobs to fill existing openings. Where should I place my cell phone stand to get more calls from people applying for jobs?

A: Keep your phone in the upper left corner of your desk (the Wealth area), because more calls would equal more wealth for you. Also, take a good look to see if there's anything around the phone that's negative or that's symbolically holding it down and keeping it from ringing. For example, a heavy rock or paperweight near the phone could be symbolically weighing it down. Keep fresh flowers or a healthy plant near the phone to symbolize growth and a *blooming* of the number and quality of people who call you looking for job placement.

Q: I'm an acupuncturist. When a patient drops out of care, should I remove the chart from the folder where I have active client charts? My gut says yes, but I just wanted to check with you on this. And, what should I do with the files I remove?

A: First, make sure you're aware of all the legal requirements for your profession to retain patient files. If there's no legal impediment, then it's okay to remove former clients' charts from the active files. If the patient's treatment has been a success, you certainly want to retain the folder in your main filing cabinet. If possible, that cabinet should be placed in the Knowledge/Wisdom area. If for any reason your interaction with the patient was negative, you might want to get rid of the folder. Another option is to scan files and store them electronically.

Q: My business has been losing a lot of clients lately. Any ideas that will quickly stop the losses?

A: Based on the photos that you provided, I recommend these quick fixes: Replace the weak-looking plants at the reception desk with healthy flowers, since a sick-looking plant will create a poor first impression with prospective clients. Make sure that your logo in the lobby is well-lit, so that it makes a shiny first impression. Assure that each office in the suite has an object with your logo or brand prominently displayed, to connect everyone to the company. The offices for the CEO and CFO should be at the back of the space in the Power/Wealth position, while your PR staff can be closer to the front of the space.

Fast 5

Take a Vacation from Clutter

Whether your vacation was a grand tour of Europe, a long holiday weekend, or anything in between, returning to your workplace can be difficult. Try these five tips before you leave for your next trip:

1. **Return.** Find all the things in your office that don't belong to you and return them to your coworkers. If you work from home, return things to the appropriate rooms in your house.

2. **Collect.** Collect all the sticky notes off your monitor and enter their data into a more appropriate and permanent storage location. Check bulletin boards for outdated calendars, memos, takeout menus, and phone directories. Remove, recycle, or shred what's not up to date.

3. **Dust.** Dust your desk, chair, and electronics. Work from the top of your office downward so you're not brushing dust onto something you have already cleaned.

4. **Do.** Complete any task on your to-do list that could take fewer than three minutes to finish. Set a timer for 15 minutes and get five of these tasks done right now.

5. **File.** If you're still feeling unmotivated after completing these tasks, you can always tackle your stack of filing.

Q: We are looking for a new location for our small store. Are there Feng Shui things we should look for to help bring in more customers and ultimately, more money?

A: Make sure the access from the sidewalk or the street to the store location is clear, so customers can easily see the door and know where to enter. It's also important to have obvious signage and a visible address number. When searching for a new location, look for a large front door, ideally facing the south or east. Also, look for a building that's level with the street or higher, rather than below street level. Avoid locating adjacent to major power lines or electrical transformers because of their potentially negative affect on the health of people who work in your space.

Q: I am an artist who shares working studio space in a small arts center in a suburban town center. The artists create and sell their work in the space. The studio used to be a gallery with doors at both ends. Should we keep both doors open or only one?

A: The concern about having multiple doors in any space where you sell merchandise is two-fold. First, it's difficult for potential customers to know which door to enter. Second, customers have a tendency to walk in one door and then right out the other door without seeing everything the space has to offer. Also in your case, they may avoid entering because they don't want to interrupt an artist at work. I recommend you keep only one door open, and clearly mark it as the entrance to the studio. This will encourage buyers to enter the space and assure they look at all of your creations

Q: Our business is located in a strip mall, and there is a large trash can right in front of the door. I'm thinking this is not a good Feng Shui symbol. What's your opinion?

A: I agree that having a trash can across from your front door isn't conducive to attracting positive chi into your business. Ask the landlord if the trash can be relocated to another area. If that's not possible, make sure you're vigilant about assuring that management empties the trash can frequently. You could also consider hanging a bagua mirror outside, above your entrance door facing the trash, to reflect any negative chi away from your business.

CHAPTER 8: WORKPLACE, CAREER, BUSINESS

SUCCESS STORY

*Eileen and Steve
Advance Their Careers*

When I showed up for my appointment at Eileen and Steve's house, the first thing I noticed was that the home had no real foyer, so when I stepped into the home, I was standing right in the middle of where the couple had located Steve's office. No wonder he was struggling to finish writing his first screenplay—he was too distracted by everyone and everything coming and going around him. Eileen, an artist, had set up her studio in the basement, which she shared with the washer and dryer, old paint cans, and lots of clutter. They both talked about feeling stuck in their careers, and it was obvious that neither one was working in a space conducive to career success. I recommended a few strategic changes that paid off in big results for the couple.

Here's what Eileen wrote:

❝ I have to admit that I was more skeptical than Steve about whether the changes you recommended would really help our businesses, but I figured why not. First, we bought the three standing floor plants, area rug, and small table that you recommended to simulate a wall and to create a foyer. Boy, I didn't realize how much of a difference that would make. Everyone has commented that the house feels more welcoming. Next, we used more plants as a living screen to create a space in the living room where Steve could work. He feels like he finally has privacy now. Downstairs in my space, I screened off the laundry area with a pretty bamboo floor screen. You were so right,

(continued)

> that's much more attractive then watching the laundry go round and round. We painted the area a sunny yellow, and as you suggested, I hung a few of my favorite creations on the wall for motivation. We both feel more positive and more creative. And can you believe, now Steve has an option on his screenplay and I was offered the opportunity to exhibit at a local gallery that previously didn't have any interest. More clutter clearing this weekend! 🙶

Q: We are a farm-school program. I have a rack of boots that the students use daily when they go out in the mornings and afternoons to feed animals and work on the farm. They had been stored on the front porch of the school. We have been frustrated over the years because it seemed like we can never keep staff members—even the ones where there was a mutual good job/good fit have now left us. Then, I realized that the boot rack was in our Helpful People area. So, now I'm thinking this could be why the staff were walking away. What would you recommend? Any storage does need to have some roof or shelter over it. We have four new staff members and I sure would like to keep them, along with growing our enrollment.

A: You're right that symbolically, this location for boots could be contributing to your staff turnover. Storing shoes near an entrance is related to *walking away* from something. In your case, this was compounded by the placement of the boots in the Helpful People area. The typical remedy when you can't relocate shoe storage to a closet is to keep them in a closed storage container. Build a storage box to keep on the porch (your students can help!). This would keep the shoes covered, and symbolically be the same as putting them behind closed doors and out of sight in a closet.

CHAPTER 8: WORKPLACE, CAREER, BUSINESS

Q: I am a consultant and executive coach. When I walk into a client's site for a workshop or a meeting, what can I do to bring some Feng Shui balance to a space I know nothing about? I won't be able to rearrange the furniture.

A: You might be able to do more rearranging than you think. For example, if you have a choice of where to sit, pick the seat that faces the door and puts you in control of the meeting. If you're facing the window and there's a glare, ask your client to close the blinds or ask to move to another location in the office. You can also think about the colors you wear based on what you know about the client. For example, wear red if you need to exert power over the situation, blue if you want to help things move smoothly, brown or earthy colors if you think your client needs some grounding.

Q: I am working on a fundraiser for a community group. It is a dinner and live and silent auction. Any do's and don'ts in relation to flow, color, and stuff like that, that would help or inhibit a successful evening?

A: The colors red and orange encourage conversation and excitement, which would be especially good at a fundraiser. Flow is important for the tables displaying the silent auction items, so avoid setting up the tables in long lines. This configuration would act like arrows that direct people down a straight line and keep them from stopping and looking at the items. If possible, arrange items on round tables, which direct people to take more time to look each item as they go around each table. Round shapes are the Metal Element and the shape of gold coins. Scatter chocolate wrapped in gold foil on the tables. These remind people of money and encourage them to bid higher at the auction. In general, when you're setting up the space, think of the analogy of an art gallery or a museum where people are gradually drawn into the space, rather than directed straight through it by long corridors.

Q: My small, family-friendly restaurant has been losing customers over the past few months, so I've hired a designer to update the interior. Are there a few Feng Shui ideas you can give me to suggest to the designer to make things flow smoother and bring in more business?

A: The first thing I would look for doesn't have anything to do with your designer: clutter. In Feng Shui, clutter represents postponed decisions and the inability to move forward. Is your restaurant being held back by too much "stuff?" This is especially important around the area where your customers pay, or where you servers run credit card charges. Keep this area clean to allow room for new wealth to flow into your business. If possible, locate a lush green plant near the cash register or payment station. If you have an office in the restaurant, try to locate your desk is the Wealth corner of the room, and keep your desk and your office cutter free. I'm glad to hear you're working with a designer, because it's important to keep your décor fresh, clean, and updated. Don't forget to update your menus, business cards, shopping bags, and everything that has your logo and brand colors and theme. Play upbeat, current music throughout the space. And, don't forget to update the bathrooms and keep them clean. Pay some attention to the outside of your restaurant. Is your signage clear and visible from the street? This will help you attract walk-in customers. If possible, place attractive ceramic or terracotta planters on both sides of the front door and keep red flowers in them in the growing season. Clean your windows, both inside and outside, on a regular basis.

CHAPTER
9
QUESTIONS FOR ALL SEASONS

Picture a beautiful May day. The sun is brilliant in a cloudless blue sky. There's a light breeze tickling your skin as you relax by a meandering clear stream. You feel wonderful. You're creative, you can solve any problem, you can figure out any troubling issues. If you're with your spouse or partner, you're feeling romantic. If you're with your children or family members, everyone is happy. This is the feeling we call good Feng Shui.

Why shouldn't your indoor environment make you feel the same way?

The goal of Feng Shui adjustments is to bring your interior surroundings into balance with the natural world around you. You do this by tuning in to the changing seasons, and making adjustments inside to reflect what's going on outside at different times of the year. You already do some of this automatically, for example, when you bring out your warmer clothes in the fall. And, there are additional Feng Shui ways to make changes to match the seasons.

At the beginning of the year, you could clear old energy out of your home and office by removing clutter and entering the year with a clean slate. As winter days approach with their limited daylight, you can bring in more light by switching to full-spectrum light bulbs that simulate natural daylight. When spring arrives, your focus can be on changes that mirror the growth around you, like buying new houseplants. As you enter the hot, yang energy of the summer months, work on cooling down your home by using cool blue sheets and a lighter-weight comforter on your bed. As autumn approaches and you find yourself spending more time indoors, it's time to work on projects that you've put off and prepare for the upcoming family holidays.

CHAPTER 9: QUESTIONS FOR ALL SEASONS

Like it or not, the clothes you wear affect your emotions and influence how others judge and respond to you. When you're looking for new clothes each season, select the color, pattern, fabric, and shape of your clothes based on Five Element theory. Each Element has specific attributes, so when you wear the colors and shapes that represent that Element, you project its attributes. That way, you stay tuned-in to the seasonal changes around you.

When you connect to nature by making seasonal Feng Shui changes, you take advantage of natural rhythms. That's how you attract love, wealth, harmony and so much more into your life.

When you tug at a single thing in nature,
you find it attached to the rest of the world.
— John Muir

Q & A

QUESTIONS FOR ALL SEASONS

JANUARY: Resolve to Start with Good Feng Shui

Q: Is there something I can do at the start of the year, Feng Shui wise, to make sure it's a good one? I don't do Near Year's resolutions anymore, but I want to start doing something special to set my intentions. I made lots of changes during the past year.

A: I recommend beginning each year by conducting a Feng Shui audit to make sure the changes you have made are still in place and working for you. In the course of everyday activities and changes in lifestyle, you may have unknowingly changed furniture, objects, art, or colors in a way that subtly affected the energy in your home or created obstacles. An annual walk-through and re-adjustment where necessary will help recharge your space to assure a better year ahead. Follow-up on your audit by doing things like clearing clutter, pruning plants and removing dead leaves, and repairing all those things you've been putting off. It's especially good to fix leaky faucets, because leaking water represents wasted wealth. Negative chi accumulates after an illness, so if anyone in your household just got over an end-of-the winter cold or flu, leave your windows open for an hour after thoroughly cleaning your home. Whether or not you make actual resolutions, here are five areas where people resolve to make a change at the beginning of the year, and the related Feng Shui adjustments:

Wealth and Prosperity. Make sure you place an object that feels wealthy, abundant, and prosperous in the Wealth area of your home, which is the room in the upper left-hand corner. For example, buy a healthy plant in a red ceramic planter, and place a new $100 bill in a red envelope under the pot as an additional symbol of prosperity.

Love, Relationships, Marriage. Make sure your bedroom is reserved for R&R (rest and romance) only. Remove all work-related objects from the room, hide the hamper, remove the kids' toys, and display artwork that feels romantic, coupled, and paired.

Weight Loss. Holding on to unneeded things symbolizes holding onto weight in Feng Shui. Remove the clutter, especially in the kitchen, and you'll see your way clearly to stay on your eating plan. Also, remove unneeded things from your closet, because holding on to old clothes that don't fit symbolizes holding on to old behavior patterns.

Job Change or Job Security. The entrance to a home represents the Career area, so make sure it feels clean and welcoming. Outside of the front door, clear away any dead leaves or cobwebs, which represent being caught up and stuck. Inside, add a healthy plant, water fountain, or artwork that shows water flowing into your home.

Travel. Place pictures of places you want to visit in the Helpful People/Travel area of your home. You can also include guide books, maps, a globe, and travel magazines in this area. This is an alternative place where you can tuck away a $100 bill as a symbol that you'll have enough money to take your dream trip.

FEBRUARY: Rev-Up Your Romance

Q: Valentine's Day is coming up. This year I am finally in a relationship and have someone to celebrate with, and I want to make it special without going over the top since we haven't been dating very long. What does Feng Shui suggest I do?

A: Whether you want to rev up the love you already have or invite a new relationship into your life, here are some of my favorite Feng Shui tips for romance that can help:

Do you want to get closer to your Valentine? Plan a romantic dinner at a table with only two chairs. If you have a large table, move out the extra chairs and set two places at one end, at right angles to each other rather than directly across from each other, which can be confrontational. Use the rest of the table to display flowers and candles.

Does your sweetheart need to relax and de-stress? Use the Water Element to encourage relaxation. Set the table with a vase of blue flowers, and use decorations that are flowing and curvy.

Is your Valentine shy? Use the Metal Element to help keep the conversation focused by floating white flowers in a round glass bowl. Round shapes and white colors represent this Element.

Does your sweetheart need help making a commitment? Use the Wood Element to grow the relationship. Choose a tall, rectangular vase and a pair of orange flowers to stimulate change.

Are you spending Valentine's Day alone this year? Invite a new love into your life, and you won't be alone for long. Clear out some space in your bedroom closet, medicine cabinet, and fridge to make room for a lover's possessions. Be sure to leave room for extra towels in your bathroom.

Do you need to rev-up your love life? The bedroom should be a place reserved for rest and romance and nothing else. Remove the family photographs—your love life will improve if your children, parents, or pets aren't staring at you in bed!

MARCH: Spring Clear Easy-to-Forget Places

Q: It feels silly to say this, but as soon as the weather gets mild, I really do get the urge to start spring cleaning. Is there some extra special Feng Shui magic I can add to my cleaning obsession?

A: This year, try clearing out stale chi instead of just cleaning house by remembering those easy-to-forget places that you might otherwise ignore. When you clear your clutter on a seasonal basis, you take advantage of the natural changes around you to make room for new energy to flow in to take its place:

Sweep your **deck, patio, balcony, or porch** to get rid of dead leaves and dust. Be sure to sweep the dirt away from your home, rather than toward it.

Uncover the **chairs and barbeque grill** and clear the way to start using the space again. Make sure you get rid of cobwebs because they represent being so stuck and caught up, you can't move forward.

Your **front door** is where all the positive energy enters your home, so clean, re-paint, or re-stain it. Use some lubricant like WD-40 on the hinges, and clean the glass.

Windows are the "eyes" of your home, so **clean your windows** and you can see the world with clarity. It's especially important to clean the windows in your home office or you'll be looking at your career through a dirty lens.

Clear out **behind or under furniture** that you haven't moved in years, like the living room sofa, the master bed, and the china closet.

When it's time to change out your **winter clothes**, dust the shelves before you bring in your spring clothes. Replace those misshapen wire hangers with more substantial versions. There's a reason the dry cleaner gives them out free, and they don't belong in your closet.

Prune your living plants, and dust or wash your **silk plants**, or replace any that are faded or dull looking.

APRIL: Invite Feng Shui to Your Holiday Dinner

Q: We're an interfaith family, Christian and Jewish, and for the most part, we all get along. But that all falls apart when the family gets together for the spring religious holidays. How can I get everyone to respect our differences and celebrate our similarities?

A: Start with the two spring family holidays, Passover and Easter, and focus on new beginnings and making your home ready for that Easter dinner or Seder. There are many parallels between these two holidays and Feng Shui, including freeing yourself from clutter, arranging your home to promote a fresh start, and creating a fresh flow of energy in your home. The Feng Shui parallel to the Passover tradition of searching the house for crumbs of bread (called *chametz*) is to search for dust, remove old dried flowers, replace air filters, wash windows, and make other seasonal adjustments. Try these tips:

A **round or oval table** is the best to encourage the easy flow of conversation. If you have a rectangular table, soften the hard edges with a white tablecloth.

Avoid **seating** spouses or partners directly across from each other because this confrontational arrangement could cause arguments.

Decorate the table with a Feng Shui color scheme that includes blue for harmony and new beginnings, white for clarity, and gold for power.

Place **fresh flowers** in the room to symbolize growth and rebirth, preferably in front of a mirror to symbolically double their positive energy.

Buy **new clothes**, but avoid wearing red at your dinner. This color represents the hot Fire Element, and adding more heat and fire could lead to family disagreements, especially mixed with the heat of all that cooking.

MAY: Eliminate Tax Filing Clutter

Q: Simple question: how do I keep more money and give the government less at tax time? I leave everything to the last minute (drives my wife crazy), and then I leave everything in stacks on the dining room table for too long because I hate thinking about what I should keep and what I can pitch (drives her even crazier). Any advice?

A: Keeping too much paper clutter represents postponed decisions and the inability to move forward. Everyone has to deal with some amount of record-keeping clutter at tax time, but in Feng Shui terms, extreme paper clutter holds you back and keeps you from making progress. When you open up space by limiting paper clutter and shred unneeded files and records, you not only *go* green but you can *attract* green as well. If you still have tax files cluttering up your space after you filed your taxes last month, answer these three questions to help decide whether a piece of paper is clutter or a keeper:

1. If I throw this away, will I get arrested? If the answer is no, then toss it out.
2. Did I need this during the last year? If the answer is no, out it goes.
3. Can I get it someplace else, especially online? If the answer is yes, you can trash it!

SUCCESS STORY

Pam Starts a Clearing Out Ritual for Lent

Pam's uplifting message taught me a lesson of humility. She started her clutter clearing to coincide with Lent, but you can choose any notable occasion or holiday to do the same thing.

Here's what Pam wrote:

❝ I was reading your monthly ezine this morning and thought I would share something new I've started just this year. I never really had a spring cleaning ritual; it just happened when it happened. This year, I decided I would start during Lent. Even after following your "move 27 things" advice earlier in the year, I realized that I still had cleaning to do. I decided that each day, I would take one item, like clothing, books, movies, jewelry, etc., and put it in a box. At the end of 40 days, I would take the box or boxes and donate them to a church or shelter. If I found more than one item a day, all the better. It's been enlightening to me to realize what I have and don't use or don't need, and how many people are just the opposite. I am in no way so well-off that these things don't matter, but I'm so much more blessed than some. I've always donated and helped where I can, but sometimes, it takes a change in circumstances to make you remember all those others. I normally don't do anything for Lent, but I felt this would be a good way for me to take a deeper look inward and help others out, and in the process, start my spring cleaning. ❞

(continues)

> *On a personal note, I read Pam's email the same day the plumber came to fix the slow leak in my bathroom sink that was driving me nuts (not to mention the negative Feng Shui), and I had to move everything out from the cabinet. What a sobering lesson in accumulating too much—unused lipstick in the wrong shade, mini-bottles of toiletries from hotels that I always planned to donate but never did, samples of dental floss from the hygienist that aren't the brand I like, and so much more. Sound familiar? I'm lucky to have these things, but reading Pam's story helped me realize that these items would serve a better purpose if I donated them. Nothing in Feng Shui happens by accident, does it?*

JUNE: Bring Feng Shui to Your Wedding Party

Q: I'm planning my own wedding. It's going to be medium size, and I do want to do it right so we start off life together in the best possible way. I'm not worried about the marriage, but I sure am about the party. Do you have Feng Shui tips for a nervous bride?

A: Whether the party you're planning is a grand celebration or an intimate dinner party for family and friends, incorporating Feng Shui can help assure harmony. From finding the right venue, to picking colors for the table linens, to finding the right clothes to wear, when you follow these simple Feng Shui guidelines, you'll take the stress out of party planning and party prep:

Choose the right colors. Certain color combinations for the bridal party, flowers, table linens, and cake decorations are considered auspicious, including yellow and red, green and blue, purple and green, red and pink, and metallics with yellow or blue. Avoid paring red with metallic because this is considered unlucky in Feng Shui. Choose table linen colors representing the Earth Element, like honey, olive, or cocoa to ground everyone and to reduce any stress.

Pick the right flowers. Select flowers for the bouquet or centerpieces according to their meaning: peonies represent longevity, chrysanthemums mean happiness, tulips bring sensuality, roses symbolize love, and orange flowers symbolize prosperity and encourage conversation. For wedding centerpieces, include a flowering branch to represent the Wood Element, and a symbol of growth of your union.

Select the right venue. If possible, choose a location where you can see beautiful gardens, flowing water, or rolling hills. Holding your wedding ceremony outside will attract positive chi, especially if the location is near gently moving water. If your reception is inside, make sure the venue has a high ceiling, and avoid a location where there are sharp edges of the walls pointed at guests, or that has heavy overhead beams that would symbolically weigh down on the occasion.

Round out your table shape. The best shape for a table is round or oval, which encourages harmony among the guests. This shape will make conversation flow easily and help your guests feel more relaxed. If you must use square or rectangular tables, cover them with quality tablecloths or drape the sharp edges with garlands.

Shine on. Make sure your venue is well lit, and decorate with crystal glasses and candlesticks to reflect even more light. The reflected light of crystal chandeliers will double the positive chi for the occasion. The bride and wedding party can add crystals to their dress, shoes, or wedding veil, and the extra sparkle will chase away any negative chi.

Remember something old, something new. Many Western brides follow the tradition of wearing *something old, something new, something borrowed, something blue*. If you follow this tradition, be sure you receive these items from a friend or relative who is happily married so they will transfer their positive energy of their relationship to you.

JULY: Take Feng Shui on Vacation

Q: Do you have any Feng Shui travel tips for hotel rooms, or can you only Feng Shui your own home?

A: If you're traveling this summer, or any time of the year, you can follow a few simple Feng Shui recommendations to protect your home while you're gone, bring along some of the comforts of home and assure harmony while you travel, plus plan for a pleasant return. These Feng Shui tips can help you retain the active yang energy in your home while you're away and keep it safe:

At Home

Put several lamps and a radio on **timers** and set them to come on and off during the evening to simulate your natural movements and sounds around the house during a typical evening at home.

Stop delivery of your **newspaper** a full day before your trip. That way, if it does get delivered before you leave, you'll have a second chance to stop delivery before papers accumulate around your home.

Clean your house before you leave and throw out all leftovers and food that could go bad while you're gone so you don't have to come home to bad smells.

Arrange with a **neighbor** or friend to take out the can on trash day so you won't come home to stagnant energy.

Change your **linens** before you leave, because whether you stay at a luxury hotel with 600-thread-count sheets or at a relative's house on the lumpy sleep sofa, you'll still appreciate the freshness of new sheets when you come home.

At Your Hotel

Check out your **room** carefully before you accept it, and request another room if it has any odors, stains, or unpleasant conditions.

Open the **windows** or the door to the patio or balcony if possible to let some fresh air and new positive chi into your room and to help remove any negative energy from a previous guest.

CHAPTER 9: QUESTIONS FOR ALL SEASONS

Unpack your **suitcase** as soon as you can to immediately settle in and bring your own positive energy into the room.

If you don't need the clock **alarm**, make sure it's set to *off* so you won't have an unpleasant surprise early in the morning. If you really need to relax, unplug the clock so you can't see the time.

Don't hesitate to rearrange the **furniture** if you think you'll risk walking into anything if you get up during the night. Return it to the original location before you leave.

AUGUST: Go Back to School with Feng Shui

Q: My youngest child is starting school this year, and I have two older children moving on to new schools. I want to make sure they get off to a good start. Is there anything I can do in their rooms?

A: August is *Get Ready for Kindergarten Month* for millions of American kids who will be entering, which brings up images of sweet little children with huge backpacks marching bravely each morning into the grownup world of school. But whether your children are just starting school, entering their last year of college, or anywhere in between, a creative use of Feng Shui in their rooms can help them effortlessly make the transition back to school:

Create a study area. Position the desk so your child can see the door to the room, and avoid locating the desk where your child must sit with his or her back to the door, which is considered a vulnerable and insecure position.

Position electronics correctly. Position the computer or tablet away from the bed and shut off all electronics at night to reduce any EMF or electromagnetic field, issues. If the room is too small to do this, place a living plant near the computer to absorb some of the EMFs.

Control clutter. Include storage options, like attractive boxes and baskets, to encourage your child to put things away when it's time to study. Some amount of clutter is normal for any child, but excessive clutter will distract from educational pursuits.

Decorate for success. Hang a cork or white board or create a display area near the desk to showcase achievements. This is the ideal place to hang your child's awards and citations, as well as artwork, report cards, and special papers to remind your child how he or she is succeeding and moving forward.

Encourage a good night's sleep. Avoid storing anything under your child's bed, especially shoes, because this represents walking away from peaceful sleep. Avoid art and objects that show images of flying, falling, driving, or running, and instead choose scenes that are tranquil and calm.

Clean the windows regularly. Dirty windows represent cloudy vision, an obvious deterrent to academic success. When you clean windows, you symbolically open up your child's vision of the world. Even dorm dwellers can occasionally give their windows a quick cleaning.

Place family photos in the study area. Photos of parents, grandparents, and happy family gatherings help communicate love and security to a child. With all that family support around the room, your child is sure to succeed.

SEPTEMBER: Transition into Cooler Weather

Q: Fall is my favorite time of the year, but I do suffer from seasonal affective disorder, so I'm challenged by the limited daylight that's coming. It's called SAD for a good reason, believe me. I've read your article about adjusting yin and yang as the seasons change, which was helpful. Are there other seasonal changes I can make starting now?

A: As you start spending more time inside your home, you can make a few Feng Shui adjustments to help transition into the cooler season. Fall is also a good time to check out your existing Feng Shui remedies to see if they need to be adjusted, because they can wear out over time: colors fade, furniture wears out or goes out of style, or your preferences in art change. Try these 10 simple ways to help you welcome the approaching season:

CHAPTER 9: QUESTIONS FOR ALL SEASONS

Replace your **doormat** to help attract fresh new opportunities to come in your door.

Make sure your **house number** is clearly visible from the street so positive chi can always find you, especially with the earlier darkness.

Pull up **dead flowers** in your garden, which represent stale chi, and replace them with colorful mums or hardy pansies that will give you active chi until the first frost.

Frequently **remove leaves** from your roof and gutters and trim back any overgrown limbs that overhang your house, which represent an added weight on your shoulders.

Remove any **vines** that are growing on your house. The image of an ivy-covered cottage may be romantic, but vines growing on your home symbolize something eating away at your life.

Display a bowl of **red apples** on your kitchen counter to symbolize that your home will always have food and you can always afford to feed your family.

Clear the **cobwebs** from the outdoor furniture before you cover it for the winter, because accumulated cobwebs symbolize being so wrapped up and stuck that you can't move forward.

Even if the weather turns chilly, **open your windows** daily during the cooler months, perhaps for a few minutes, to let in fresh air and circulate the chi.

Rearrange your furniture, even if you only move the sofa a few inches closer to the window or the lamp to a different side of the table, to bring new energy into your rooms.

Burn **scented candles** to change your perspective for a new season: vanilla to make a room feel comforting, peppermint to curb your appetite, strawberry to boost energy and make you want to exercise, a floral fragrance to enhance learning, pine to enhance well-being.

OCTOBER: Celebrate Halloween Colors

Q: I've made lots of Feng Shui changes around the house. Do I ruin everything when I put up creepy Halloween decorations? It's fun for our young kids and their friends, but I don't want to mess up the good things we have by un-shui-ing.

A: This is the time of the year when everything is decked out in orange and black, or covered with cobwebs and creepy creatures. But, there's no need to worry about ruining the positive Feng Shui of a home if you follow a few simple decorating guidelines for balancing the Five Elements:

Orange. It's natural to use lots of the orange color for Halloween decorations, but it's also good Feng Shui. Orange is called the social color because it promotes conversation and communication, which is especially important to assure a lively and festive Halloween for the whole family.

Black. The front entrance is the primary place to decorate for Halloween, and the best place for the color black, which is the Water Element color that represents the flow on energy. You can hang black wind chimes to attract good energy. Or, you can also hang an inexpensive round mirror in a black metal frame to the right of your front door, so your trick-or-treaters can see their reflection.

Lighting. Lighting is a major tool of Feng Shui, and for Halloween, this means displaying a lighted jack-o-lantern near your door or keeping the porch light on. You can also light the path to your home with lanterns or luminarias. For a Halloween party, use orange bulbs in some lamps and overhead fixtures, or black, orange, white, or metallic colored candles. Just be sure to avoid displaying these colors in your bedroom or in the Love/Relationship area of your home.

Cobwebs. Cobwebs around your front door or outdoor furniture represent being so stuck that you're unable to move forward. Halloween is the one time when cobwebs are considered positive energy because they are part of the fun of the night. Just remember to quickly remove all webs from around the outside and inside of your home after Halloween, and to also dust away the real cobwebs.

CHAPTER 9: QUESTIONS FOR ALL SEASONS

NOVEMBER: Give Thanks for Extra Space

Q: Are there Feng Shui changes I should make toward the end of the year?
A: In the month of Thanksgiving, you probably don't need more things to be thankful for, but you always need more room for thankfulness. It doesn't matter whether you donate, sell, trash, or recycle, or freecycle these objects; once they are out of your home, you make room for new, and better, things to flow in to take their place. Here are a few things you can get rid of this month and be thankful for the extra space in your life:

One **unfinished** project.

One object that needs **fixing**, but isn't worth the effort.

One **gift** you never liked, even though you love the gift giver.

One **souvenir** that no longer has meaning.

One item of clothing you've **outgrown**, physically or emotionally.

One stack of plastic **take-out** containers.

One small kitchen **appliance** you never use.

One **toy** your kids won't play with anymore.

One can of **paint** that doesn't match any of your walls.

DECEMBER: Relocate the Christmas Tree

Q: We always put the Christmas tree in the same place because my husband is more of a traditionalist than I am. This year, I want to try a new place for the tree and wondered if there's a perfect Feng Shui location for it?

A: An object can be more than one of the Feng Shui Elements. A Christmas tree connects you with the natural, living world, so it's considered a strong Wood Element symbol in Feng Shui. The triangular shape of the tree is also considered a Fire Element symbol, even more so when it is covered with twinkling lights. If you don't put up a Christmas tree but still want to celebrate the season, bring a bit of nature indoors by displaying evergreen boughs or poinsettias to counteract any winter gloom and encourage guests to enjoy the holiday. Here are some Feng Shui-friendly places to put your tree, and how to decorate it to balance the energy for that area:

Wealth, Fame, or Family area. These are the ideal locations for the tree. Decorate with lots of red ornaments and garland, and choose a red or green skirt.

Career area. Decorate with blue lights and decorations, icicle decorations, and blue/black patterned tree skirt to help bring water energy into balance.

Children or Helpful People area. Use metal ornaments, tinsel, white lights, and a silver or gold accented tree skirt.

Love or Knowledge area: Use lots of ceramic ornaments, yellow and red lights, and red skirt. Skip the tinsel and white lights here, since you don't need more metal.

Grounding area. Chose a yellow or gold tree skirt and a bright yellow star or angel with golden hair at the top of the tree.

CHAPTER 9: QUESTIONS FOR ALL SEASONS

SUCCESS STORY

*Martha Reboots
Her Feng Shui*

If you've been in one of my classes or workshops, you've heard me say, "A *purse on the floor means wealth out the door.*" Martha took that advice to heart. Since it had been a while since she did what she called "a Feng Shui reboot," Martha turned the spotlight on her purse and wallet in a symbolic effort to take better care of her money.

Here's an excerpt from Martha's post about the process on her blog, Damselwings.com:

❝ Opening my wallet to pay for something was simply embarrassing. The receipts seemed to come alive, trying to scurry out of their confinement as I was digging for cash or the credit card. Back! Back! Get back in there! Wait, had I said that out loud? Cashiers looked at me with concern. It took all of five minutes to clean out the wallet that had been sparking negative energy for months. As is so often the case, one small Feng Shui improvement in our lives often leads to another. I couldn't let my tidy wallet live in my pigsty purse. I could almost hear the wallet yelling Get me out of here! when I dropped it back into the fray. So, a couple of days later, I dumped the entire contents of the purse out on the counter. Though the task looked daunting at first, the process was liberating. First, I found a whole lot of money—crumpled bills and loose change that I didn't know I had. I smoothed out the bills with gratitude and provided clean housing (aka a tidy wallet) to the runaway money. And I found

(continued)

an un-deposited check from a photography client. Respecting my wealth seemed to make me wealthier on the spot! When the project was finished, I felt like I had taken a shower. As with all things Feng Shui, I only do what feels practical for me. I have no idea whether cleaning out my wallet and purse will actually make me wealthier. It doesn't matter. Feng Shui for me is more of a game to use to nudge me into action in my clutter-clearing and space-management efforts. But, I have experienced palpable benefits consistently after clearing pathways for positive energy to flow into my home, garden, and even in my head in that it dissolves my garbage thoughts. The feeling of spaciousness that comes after I remove clutter of any kind makes me feel calmer, more mindful, and happier.

Martha Brettschneider is author of "Blooming into Mindfulness: How the Universe Used a Garden, Cancer, and Carpools to Teach Me That Calm Is the New Happy." In Chapter 19, she chronicles my Feng Shui consultation for her home. The book is available in the Mindfulness Store at FengShuiForRealLife.com.

CONCLUSION
A FINAL QUESTION AND A STORY

Yes, I sometimes get questions about why Feng Shui *doesn't* seem to be working. No worries, I'm ready to answer them.

I do believe in the *practical magic* of Feng Shui, but the truth is moving the sofa or painting a wall won't fix all of your problems or save you from all the pitfalls of life. Feng Shui isn't a magic pill, but rather it's a serious and profound system and technique.

The practical approach to Feng Shui in this book is based on common sense, good design principles, regional geography, and a lot of my experience and intuition. Feng Shui works in any built environment. It's a simple matter of placing the right objects, colors, and shapes in the right locations to achieve harmony with nature and with yourself.

Although this book provides answers to key questions about improving your life, for Feng Shui adjustments to make you *feng shuiappy* (as one client described her mood after her Feng Shui changes), you need to be ready to make a change in your life.

Among the clients, students, and readers who contact me looking for answers, I find that people put up the most resistance to the changes they most need to make. Have they arranged their furniture and objects in a way that blocks positive improvements from occurring, or are they emotionally blocked and have arranged their furniture in a way that mirrors that blockage? Like the chicken-and-egg dilemma, it truly doesn't matter which came first, it only matters that you have the intention to change your life and take action to adjust your interior surroundings.

As Environmental Planner Ben Sussman reminds us in his forward to my previous book, our built environments do not occur by accident, but are instead the product of design and execution. At their best, our homes and workplaces are designed and built in a way that keeps us healthy, happy, and prosperous. Feng Shui deals with our most personal connections to the built

CONCLUSION: A FINAL QUESTION AND A STORY

environment—the homes, offices, and interior spaces where we spend most of our lives. Like good urban planning, Feng Shui blends existing elements with new components, brings life to the neglected places in our lives, and accentuates the places that contribute to our well-being.

In general, when making Feng Shui improvements, I recommend you focus clearly on what you *want* to change, then trust that the universe will bring you exactly what you *need*, even if that turns out to be something different from what you anticipated.

> *First we change our environment,*
> *then our environment changes us.*
> *— Winston Churchill*

Q & A

PULLING IT ALL TOGETHER

Q: I moved my bed, bought a plant, added a fountain, cleaned out my closet, but nothing is happening. Okay, that's not quite true. Good things are coming into my life, but I don't have the corner office, I haven't found the love of my life, and my bank account is still a little bleak. Why isn't Feng Shui working?

A: Feng Shui can come to our rescue, but you have to meet it halfway to benefit from all it has to offer. Almost 90 percent of the results from adjustments you make in your home or office come from the power of your intention to make a change. If you're blindly making Feng Shui changes because you think you *should*, you won't get the anticipated results because you lack strong intention. As the saying goes, it will be just another case of *shoulding* on yourself. Here are three of the major reasons why people resist making the everyday Feng Shui adjustments that, deep down, they know will make a difference:

People have a natural resistance to change. We like things to stay essentially the way they are, even though this is at odds with the natural rhythm of life, which is constantly in a state of change. Change is natural, and making Feng Shui adjustments can help you accept change as part of the cycle of life.

People see only what they want to see. We have selective vision, and tend to ignore what doesn't please us. Our dreams and desires sometimes blind us to what we have already accomplished. For example, even if business improves at a slow but steady pace, we might complain because we didn't land the multi-million-dollar contract yet. We tend to see failure where there's actually success.

People may not be ready to accept change. Sometimes we want something, but we actually aren't ready to accept it, or in the long run, it wouldn't benefit

CONCLUSION: A FINAL QUESTION AND A STORY

us. If you're supposed to do something, the universe will clear the way for it to happen. But, if you're not supposed to do something, the universe will place obstacles in your path to encourage you to find another route to achieve your goal. Everything happens in its own time.

Feng Shui works best when you focus on improving a specific aspect of your life, such as finding a new romantic partner, increasing the cash flow into your business, or locating the perfect new job. Targeting a specific goal allows you to focus on the areas of your home or office where Feng Shui improvements will be most effective. It's also helpful to remain flexible about the results of Feng Shui changes since there might be an even better possibility that you haven't imagined.

The ache for home lives in all of us,
the safe place where we can go as we are and not be questioned.
— Maya Angelou

SUCCESS STORY

Gale Cleans House

I received this wonderful note from my client Gale about her major clutter-clearing project. She released the dead energy from piles of stuff she had been saving, and as a result, she had what she called a "transformative" experience.

Here's what Gale wrote:

❝ I finished reading your book, then began the clutter-clearing process on my house. What a transformative experience! After two divorces and my mother's passing, my house had become a receptacle for dead energy and many past skeletons. I thought I had dealt with all these past events, but for some reason, I kept storing furniture, art, recipes, gifts, etc. from my past marriages. During the clutter-clearing process, I kept asking myself, Why are you keeping this? Throw it out and move forward with your life! I have huge piles of items to take to consignment, Goodwill, and the dump. I also did what you did—I turned my office desk around so my back is no longer facing the door. I love coming into my office now. I still have a fantastic view out my window, but now my desk looks so important the way it's positioned looking out into my office featuring my own photography and artwork! I've noticed an extra bounce in my step, I'm smiling more, and I'm full of energy! Thank you so much, Carol! ❞

ABOUT THE AUTHOR

Author **Carol M. Olmstead, FSIA,** is a Feng Shui practitioner, writer, and speaker who provides consulting and workshops through her company, Feng Shui For Real Life. Carol has taught thousands of clients, students, and readers the simple secrets of using Feng Shui to improve their lives. Her contemporary approach to Feng Shui focuses on the practical applications for our culture today. Carol first learned about Feng Shui more than 20 years ago when she was a marketing consultant. She re-arranged the furniture in her office, and two weeks later unexpectedly won a contract to consult for a week in Hawaii—that extended into a second week after she got there. After extensive study with the Feng Shui Institute of America, she became a Certified Feng Shui Practitioner, qualified to use the designation FSIA, and earned Red Ribbon distinction from the International Feng Shui Guild. Carol is frequently quoted in the media, ranging from *Cosmopolitan Magazine* and *The Washington Post*, to *The Scientist Magazine, Prevention Books*, and Law of Attraction Radio. She presents to diverse groups, including Marriott, IKEA, and NASA. Carol provided Feng Shui design for the curation of *Sacred Realm: Blessings and Good Fortune Across Asia*, an exhibition at the Museum of International Folk Art in Santa Fe, New Mexico. Carol's other books include the award-winning, *Feng Shui Quick Guide For Home and Office: Secrets for Attracting Wealth, Harmony, and Love*, and *365 Feng Shui Secrets*. These books are available from Amazon and at FengShuiForRealLife.com.

> *Have nothing in your house that you do not know to be useful,*
> *or believe to be beautiful.*
> *— William Morris*

ACKNOWLEDGEMENTS

This book is dedicated to my mother, Ruth. When she was 17, my mom entered her essay "What Democracy Means to Me" in a writing contest, where the prize was a trip to Washington, DC, to attend FDR's inauguration and to meet both Franklin and Eleanor. She won. My mom kept a diary of her journey from Brooklyn, complete with autographs from people she met. My dad, Sam, beamed with pride whenever my mom told this and her other stories throughout their 57-year marriage. I still have the essay and her journal. She was a prolific letter writer. I thank my mom for passing along the desire to share through writing. I wish she were here to read my books and poems.

I'm sending a big thanks to my loving husband, Tom, who is forever my patient reader and tireless supporter.

Yes, of course, Sam and Izzy, this book is for you. In my last book, I called you my "my most pleasant distractions from writing." You still distract, and you continue to amaze! Thanks to Ben and Jill for creating both of you.

Nothing happens
unless first a dream.
— Carl Sandburg

INDEX AND RESOURCES

Fast 5

Attract and Keep Wealth	25
Create Harmonious Holidays	30
Make Room for a Relationship	35
Set a Place for Love	40
Arrange Your Bedroom for Romance	51
Position Your Child's Room for Success	64
Dry Out Your Bathroom	75
Get Rid of Desk Clutter	89
Downsize, Even If You're Not Moving	100
See What's Lurking Behind Your Doors	113
Clear the Way for Weight Loss	121
Feng Shui for Your Pets	134
Decide Where to Hang It	154
Smooth Out Your Road Trip	159
Avoid Negative Gifts	170
Take a Look at Your Mirrors	177
Check What's in Your Wallet	180
Learn to Just Say Throw	193
Clear Sentimental Clutter	203
Keep Stuff Out of Your Home	209
Feel Grounded at Home	219
Declutter Your Office Junk Drawer	224
Clear Your Computer Chaos	233
Take a Vacation from Clutter	240

INDEX AND RESOURCES

Success Stories

Carol Makes Room for New Clients to Find Her 7
Jackie Uses the Power Principles 19
Jerry Receives Multiple Job Offers 27
Adele Does a Whole House Makeover 32
Natalia Replaces Single Girl Art 37
Michelle Finds a New Love 42
Nancy Recovers After Her Divorce 54
Lydia Fills Her Empty Nest 58
Karen Replaces Her Mirrored Bedroom Furniture 61
Melissa Helps Her Child Find Peaceful Sleep 67
Ana Opens Up Her Dining Room 79
Ted Decorates His Garage 83
Janis Triples Her Income 86
Alice and Jim Move Forward 92
Jo Witnesses an Apartment Miracle 102
Linda Turns a Negative into a Positive 136
Erica and Michael Finally Sell Their Home 140
Leslie Reloads the Laundry 175
Ruby Buys a New Red Wallet 182
Kim Takes the Big Purge Challenge 196
Briana Attracts Mr. Right 200
Kate and Jeremy Fix the Damage 206
Barbara Renovates the Basement 216
Marissa Pictures Success 227
Rose Remedies Her Writer's Block 236
Diana Rescues the Family Business 238
Eileen and Steve Advance Their Careers 242
Pam Starts a Clearing-Out Ritual for Lent 254
Martha Reboots Her Feng Shui 264
Gale Cleans House 271

Resources

Feng Shui to the Rescue Newsletter. Subscribe at bit.ly/FengShuiNews

Topics in Feng Shui

Bagua: bit.ly/BaguaArticle
Built Environment: bit.ly/BuiltEnvironment
Christmas Tree: bit.ly/FSChristmasTree
Clutter: bit.ly/FSClutter
Color Red: bit.ly/FSRed
Cul-de-sac: bit.ly/CuldeSacFS
Hotel Room: bit.ly/HotelFengShui
House Plants: bit.ly/FengShuiPlants
Lightbulbs: bit.ly/lightbulbarticle
Love: bit.ly/FSLoveTips
New Year's: bit.ly/NewYearTips
Numbers: bit.ly/FSLuckyNumbers
Office: bit.ly/OfficeArticles
Pregnancy: bit.ly/FSPregnancy
Prosperity Place: bit.ly/ProsperityPlace
Tools of Feng Shui: bit.ly/9ToolsFS
Weight Loss: bit.ly/FengShuiWeightLoss

*What the feng am I going to do
with all this shui?*
— Anonymous

www.ingramcontent.com/pod-product-compliance
Lightning Source LLC
Chambersburg PA
CBHW061633040426
42446CB00010B/1394